Richard Wiseman holds Britain's only professorship
in the Public Understanding of Psychology, at the
University of Hertfordshire. His research into a
range of topics – including luck, self-help, deception
and persuasion – has been published in the world's
leading academic journals, while his psychology-based
YouTube videos have been viewed over 150 million times.
He is the author of several books that have been
translated into over thirty languages, including
The Luck Factor, *Quirkology*, *Rip It Up* and
the international bestseller *59 Seconds*.

Richard Wiseman

59 SECONDS

Think a little, change a lot

PAN BOOKS

First published 2009 by Macmillan

First published in paperback 2010 by Pan Books

This edition published 2015 by Pan Books
an imprint of Pan Macmillan, a division of Macmillan Publishers Limited
Pan Macmillan, 20 New Wharf Road, London N1 9RR
Basingstoke and Oxford
Associated companies throughout the world
www.panmacmillan.com

ISBN 978-1-4472-7337-0

1 3 5 7 9 8 6 4 2

A CIP catalogue record for this book is available from the British Library.

Printed and bound by CPI Group (UK) Ltd, Croydon, CR0 4YY

Visit www.panmacmillan.com to read more about all our books
and to buy them. You will also find features, author interviews and
news of any author events, and you can sign up for e-newsletters
so that you're always first to hear about our new releases.

To a very good friend

in times of change

Acknowledgements

This book would not have been possible without the help and support of many people. First, thanks to the wonderful advice and guidance provided by my agent Patrick Walsh, editors Richard Milner and Jon Butler and press guru Dusty Miller. Thanks also to Clive Jeffries and Emma Greening for providing such insightful feedback at every stage, to Portia Smith for playing a key role in everything, to Jim Underdown and Spencer Marks for measuring the hands of so many famous people, to Roger Highfield for helping explore the psychology of surnames, to Rachael Armstrong for her insightful comments on romance and to Sam Murphy for her help in discovering the relationship between attraction and sport. Finally, as ever, special thanks also to the wonderful Caroline Watt for giving far beyond the call of duty. Thank you.

Contents

Introduction

Self-help exposed, Sophie's question and
the potential for rapid change.

Do you want to improve an important aspect of your life? Perhaps lose weight, find your perfect partner, obtain your dream job, or simply be happier? Try this simple exercise:

> Close your eyes and imagine the new you. Think how great you would look in those close-fitting designer jeans, dating Brad Pitt or Angelina Jolie, sitting in a luxurious leather chair at the top of the corporate ladder, or sipping a piña colada as the warm waves of the Caribbean gently lap at your feet.

The good news is that this type of exercise has been recommended by some in the self-help industry for years. The bad news is that a large body of research now shows that such exercises are at best ineffective and at worst, harmful.[1] Although asking you to imagine your perfect self may make you feel better, engaging in such mental escapism may also have the unfortunate side effect of leaving you unprepared for the difficulties that crop up on the rocky road to success, thus increasing the chances of you faltering at the first hurdle rather than persisting in the face of failure. Fantasizing about heaven on earth may put a smile on your face, but is unlikely to help transform your dreams into reality.

Other research suggests that the same goes for many popular self-help techniques that claim to improve your life. Attempting to 'think yourself happy' by suppressing negative thoughts can make people obsess on the very thing that makes them unhappy. Group brainstorming can produce fewer and less original ideas than individuals working alone. Punching a pillow and screaming out loud can increase, rather than decrease, your anger and stress levels.

Then there is the infamous 'Yale Goal Study'. According to some writers, in 1953 a team of researchers interviewed Yale's graduating seniors, asking them whether they had written down the specific goals that they wanted to achieve in life. Twenty years later the researchers tracked down the same cohort and found that the 3 per cent of people who had specific goals all those years before had accumulated more personal wealth than the other 97 per cent of their classmates combined. It is a great story, and frequently cited in self-help books and seminars to illustrate the power of goal-setting. There is just one small problem – as far as anyone can tell, the experiment never actually took place. In 2007, writer Lawrence Tabak from the magazine *Fast Company* attempted to track down the study, contacting several writers who had cited it, the secretary of the Yale Class of 1953, and other researchers who had attempted to discover whether the study had actually happened.[2] No one could produce any evidence that it had ever been conducted, causing Tabak to conclude that it was almost certainly nothing more than an urban myth. For years, self-help gurus had been happy to describe a study without checking their facts.

Both the public and business world have bought into modern-day mind myths for years and, in so doing, may have decreased the likelihood of achieving their aims and ambitions. Worse still, such failures often encourage people to believe that they cannot control their lives. This is especially unfortunate, as even the smallest loss of perceived control can have dramatic effects on people's confidence, happiness and lifespan. In one classic study conducted by Ellen Langer at Harvard University, half the residents in a nursing home were given a houseplant and asked to look after it, while the other half were given an identical plant but told that the staff would take responsibility for it.[3] Six months later, the residents who had been robbed of even this small amount of control over their lives were significantly less happy, healthy and active than the others. Even more distressingly, 30 per cent of residents who had not looked after their plant had died, compared to 15 per cent of those who had been allowed to exercise such control. Similar results have been found in many areas, including education, career, health, relationships, and dieting. The message is clear – those who do not feel in control of their lives are less successful, and less psychologically and physically healthy, than those who do feel in control.

A few years ago I was having lunch with a friend called Sophie. Sophie is a bright, successful, thirty-something who holds a senior position in a firm of management consultants. Over lunch, Sophie explained that she had recently bought a well-known book on increasing happiness, and asked me what I thought of the industry. I explained that I had serious reservations about the scientific backing for some of the techniques being promoted, and described how any failure to change could do considerable psychological harm. Sophie looked concerned, and then asked whether academic psychology had produced more scientifically-supported ways of improving people's lives. I started to describe some of the quite complex academic work into happiness, and after about fifteen minutes or so Sophie stopped me. She politely explained that, interesting though it was, she was a busy person and asked whether I could come up with some effective advice that didn't take up quite so much time to implement. I asked how long I had. Sophie glanced at her watch, smiled, and replied 'About a minute?'

Sophie's comment made me stop and think. Many people are attracted to self-development and improvement because it offers quick and easy solutions to various issues in their lives. Unfortunately, most academic psychology either fails to address these issues or presents far more time-consuming and complex answers (thus the scene in Woody Allen's film *Sleeper*, where Allen's character discovers that he has woken up 200 years in the future, sighs, and explains that had he been in therapy all this time he'd almost be cured). I wondered whether there were tips and techniques hidden away in academic journals that were empirically supported but quick to carry out.

Over the course of a few months I carefully searched through endless journals containing research papers from many different areas of psychology. As I examined the work, a promising pattern emerged, with researchers working in quite different fields developing techniques that help people achieve their aims and ambitions in minutes not months. I collected together hundreds of these studies drawn from many different areas of the behavioural sciences. From mood to memory, persuasion to procrastination, resilience to relationships, together they represent a new science of rapid change.

There is a very old story, often told to fill time during training courses, involving a man trying to fix his broken boiler. Despite his best efforts over many months, he simply can't mend it. Eventually he gives in and decides to call in an expert repairman. The engineer arrives, gives one gentle tap on the side of the boiler and stands back as it erupts into life. The engineer presents the man with a bill, and the man argues that he should only pay a small fee as the job only took the engineer a few moments. The engineer quietly explains that the man is not paying for the time he took to tap the boiler, but rather the years of experience involved in knowing exactly where to tap. Just like the expert engineer tapping the boiler, the techniques described in this book demonstrate that effective change does not have to be time-consuming. In fact, it can take less than a minute and is often simply a question of knowing exactly where to tap.

1. HAPPINESS

Why positive thinking often fails,
how the real route to happiness involves a pencil,
keeping the perfect diary, small acts of kindness
and developing the gratitude attitude.

Why is it important to be happy? Well, for one thing, by definition, you will feel better. However, there is more to it than that. Happiness does not just make you enjoy life more, it actually affects how successful you are in both your personal and professional life.

A few years ago, Sonja Lyubomirsky and her colleagues from the University of California set about the mammoth task of reviewing hundreds of studies in which experimenters cheered up selected people and then monitored the effects of their new-found joy.[1] All sorts of procedures were employed to make participants feel happy, including having them smell freshly cut flowers, read out positive affirmations ('I really am a good person'), eat chocolate cake, dance or watch a funny film. Sometimes the experimenters resorted to trickery, telling participants that they had performed especially well on an IQ test, or ensuring that they 'accidentally' found some money in the street. Regardless of the method used, the overall result was clear – happiness doesn't just flow from success, it actually causes it.

After trawling the data from over 250,000 participants, Lyubomirsky discovered impressive benefits to being happy. Happiness makes people more sociable and altruistic, it increases how much they like themselves and others, it improves their ability to resolve conflict and it strengthens their immune systems. The cumulative effect means that people have more satisfying and successful relationships, find especially fulfilling careers and live longer, healthier, lives.

Given the emotional and tangible benefits of happiness, it is not surprising that everyone wants a slice of the pie. But what is the most effective way of putting a permanent smile on your face? Ask most people the question, and you are likely to receive a two-word answer – more money. In survey after survey, the need for a fatter wallet consistently tops the 'must have' list for happiness.[2] But is it really possible to buy happiness, or do financial aspirations set you on the road to despair?

Part of the answer comes from a remarkable study conducted in the 1970s by Philip Brickman and his colleagues, from the Northwestern University.[3] Brickman wanted to discover what happens to people's happiness when their financial dreams come true. Does a huge windfall really create a long-term smile, or does the initial thrill quickly fade away as new-found fortune becomes commonplace? Brickman contacted a group of people who had won a major prize in the Illinois State Lottery, including several who had hit the million-dollar jackpot. As a control group, he randomly selected people from the Illinois telephone directory. Everyone was asked to rate how happy they were at that moment and how happy they expected to be in the future. In addition, they were asked to say how much pleasure they derived from everyday pleasures in life, such as chatting with friends, hearing a funny joke or receiving a compliment. The results provide a striking insight into the relationship between happiness and money.

Contrary to popular belief, those who had won the lottery were no more or less happy than those in the control group. There was also no significant difference between the groups when it came to how happy they expected to be in the future. In fact, there was only one difference – compared to those who had won the lottery, the people in the control group derived significantly more pleasure from the simple things in life.

As winning the lottery is a rather unusual way of obtaining financial security, psychologists have also examined the relationship between income and happiness among those who have worked for their wealth.

Some of this work has involved carrying out large-scale international surveys by having people rate how happy they are (usually using standard ten-point scales that run from 'very unhappy' to 'very happy') and then plotting countries' average happiness ratings against their Gross National Product (GNP).[4] The results suggest that while people in very poor nations are not as happy as those in wealthier countries, this relationship vanishes once a country has obtained a relatively modest GNP. Studies examining the possible link between salary and happiness found the same type of pattern. When people can afford the necessities in life, an increase in income does not result in a significantly happier life.

So why should this be the case? Part of the reason is that we all get used to what we have very quickly. Buying a new car or bigger house provides a short-term feel-good boost, but we quickly become accustomed to it and sink back to our pre-purchase level of joy. As psychologist David Myers once phrased it: 'Thanks to our capacity to adapt to ever greater fame and fortune, yesterday's luxuries can soon become today's necessities and tomorrow's relics.'[5] If money cannot buy happiness, what is the best way of putting a long-term smile on your face?

The bad news is that research shows that about 50 per cent of your overall sense of happiness is genetically determined, and so cannot be altered.[6] The better news is that another 10 per cent is due to general circumstances (educational level, income and whether you are married or single, etc.) that are difficult to change. However, the best news is that the remaining 40 per cent is derived from your day-to-day behaviour, and the way in which you think about yourself and others. With a little knowledge, this large chunk can be changed quickly, allowing you to become substantially happier in just a few seconds.

The problem is that much of the advice offered in some self-help books and courses is at odds with the results of scientific research. Take, for example, the power of positive thinking. Does the road to happiness really depend on people being able to simply push negative thoughts out of their mind? Actually, research suggests that such thought suppression is far more likely to increase, rather than decrease, misery.

In the mid-1980s, Harvard psychologist Daniel Wegner chanced across an obscure but intriguing quote from Dostoyevsky's *Winter Notes On Summer Impressions*: 'Try to pose for yourself this task: not to think of a polar bear, and you will see that the cursed thing will come to mind every minute.' Wegner decided to carry out a simple experiment to discover if this was true. Each person from a group of willing volunteers was made to sit alone in a room, and told to think about anything, but NOT to imagine Dostoyevsky's white bear. Everyone was then asked to ring a bell each time the banned bear sprang to mind. Within moments a cacophony of bells indicated that Dostoyevsky was right – attempting to suppress certain thoughts makes people obsess on the very topic that they are attempting to avoid.

Other work has shown how this effect operates in real life, with one study, conducted by Jennifer Borton and Elizabeth Casey from Hamilton College in New York, providing a dramatic demonstration of how it affects people's mood and self-esteem.[7] Borton and Casey told a group of people to describe their most upsetting thought about themselves, and then had half the group spend the next eleven days trying to push this thought out of their minds. The remaining participants were asked to carry on life as normal. At the end of each day, everyone indicated the degree to which they had dwelt upon their upsetting thought, and rated their mood, anxiety levels and self-esteem. The results were conceptually similar to those obtained by Wegner's 'white bear' experiment, with the group attempting to actively suppress their negative thoughts actually thinking about them more. Compared to those going about their business as usual, the suppression group also rated themselves as more anxious, more depressed and having lower self-esteem. More than twenty years of research has demonstrated that this paradoxical phenomenon occurs in many different aspects of everyday life, showing, for example, that asking dieters not to think about chocolate causes them to consume more of it, and asking the public not to elect fools into government encourages them to vote for George Bush.[8]

So, if thought suppression is not the answer, what can you do? One possibility is to distract yourself: spend time with your family, go to a party, get more involved in your work, take up a new hobby. Although this technique can often provide an effective short-term boost, it will probably not lead to a long-term sense of contentment. For that, research suggests that you need to know how to use a pencil, how to keep the perfect diary, how to carry out small acts of kindness, and how to develop the gratitude attitude.

Creating the Perfect Diary

All of us will experience unpleasant and traumatic events during our lives: perhaps the break-up of a long-term relationship, the death of a loved one, being made redundant, or, on a really bad day, all three. Both common sense and many types of psychotherapy suggest that the best way forward is to share your pain with others. Those adopting this 'a problem shared is a problem halved' approach believe that venting your emotions is cathartic and helps you release negative emotions and move forward. It is a nice idea and one that holds tremendous intuitive appeal. Indeed, surveys show that 90 per cent of the public believe that talking to someone else about a traumatic experience will help ease their pain.[9] But is that really the case?

To investigate, Emmanuelle Zech and Bernard Rime from the University of Louvain in Belgium carried out an intriguing, and important, study.[10] A group of participants were asked to select a negative experience from their past. To make the study as realistic as possible, participants were asked to avoid the trivial stuff, like missing a train or not being able to find a parking space, and think instead about 'the most negative upsetting emotional event in their life, one they still thought about and still needed to talk about'. From death to divorce and from illness to abuse, the issues were serious. One group of participants were then asked to have a long chat with a supportive experimenter about the event, while a second group were invited to chat about a far more mundane topic – a typical day. After one week, and then again after two months, everyone went back to the lab and completed various questionnaires that measured their emotional well-being.

Participants who had spent time talking about their traumatic event thought that the chat had been helpful. However, the various questionnaires told a very different story. In reality, the chat had had no significant impact at all. Participants thought that it was beneficial to share their negative emotional experiences, but in terms of the difference it made to how well they were coping, they might just as well have been chatting about a typical day.

So, if talking about negative experiences to a sympathetic but untrained individual is a waste of time, what can be done to help ease the pain of the past? As we saw at the start of this section, trying to suppress negative thoughts can be just as bad.[11] Instead, one option involves 'expressive writing'.

In several studies, participants who have experienced a traumatic event have been encouraged to spend just a few minutes each day writing a diary-type account of their deepest thoughts and feelings about it.[12] For example, in one study participants who had just been made redundant were asked to reflect upon their deepest thoughts and feelings about their job loss, including how it had affected both their personal and professional lives.[13] Although these types of exercises were both speedy and simple, the results revealed that participants experienced a remarkable boost in their psychological and physical well-being, including a reduction in health problems and an increase in self-esteem and happiness. The results left psychologists with something of a mystery. Why would talking about a traumatic experience have almost no effect, but writing about it yield such significant benefits?

From a psychological perspective, talking and writing are very different. Talking can often be somewhat unstructured, disorganized, even chaotic. In contrast, writing encourages the creation of a story line and structure that help people make sense of what has happened and work towards a solution. In short, talking can add to a sense of confusion while writing provides a more systematic, and solution-based, approach.

This is clearly helpful for those who have been unfortunate enough to experience real trauma in their lives, but can the same type of idea also be used to promote everyday happiness? Three different, but related, bodies of research suggest that this is indeed the case.

The Gratitude Attitude

First, take the research into the psychology of gratitude. Present an individual with a constant sound, image or smell and something very peculiar happens. They slowly get more and more used to it and eventually it vanishes from their awareness. For example, if you walk into a room that smells of freshly baked bread, you quickly detect the rather pleasant aroma. However, stay in the room for a few minutes and the smell will appear to disappear. In fact, the only way to re-awaken it is to walk out of the room and back in again. Exactly the same concept applies to many areas of our lives, including happiness. Everyone has something to be happy about. Perhaps they have a loving partner, good health, great kids, a satisfying job, close friends, interesting hobbies, caring parents, a roof over their heads, clean water to drink, a signed Billy Joel album, or enough food to eat. However, as time passes, they get used to what they have and, just like the smell of fresh bread, these wonderful assets vanish from their mind. As the old cliché goes, you don't know what you've got till it's gone.

Psychologists Robert Emmons and Michael McCullough wondered what would happen to people's happiness levels if they were asked to carry out the conceptual equivalent of leaving the bread-smelling room and coming back in again. The researchers wanted to discover the effect of reminding people of the good things that were constantly present in their lives.[14] Three groups of people were asked to spend a few moments each week writing. The first group listed five things for which they were grateful, the second noted down five things that annoyed them and the final group jotted down five events that had taken place during the previous week. Everyone scribbled away: the 'gratitude' group remarked on things from seeing the sunset on a summer's day to the generosity of their friends; the 'annoyed' group listed taxes and their children arguing; the 'events' group detailed making breakfast and driving to work. The results were startling. Compared to those in either the 'annoyed' or 'events' groups, those expressing gratitude ended up happier, much more optimistic about the future, physically healthier and even exercised significantly more.

Your Inner Perfect Self

When trying to write your way to a happier life, expressing gratitude is just the tip of the iceberg. There is also the notion of getting in touch with your inner perfect self. In the introduction I noted that a large body of research shows that visualizing a wonderful future is unlikely to increase the chances of achieving your goals. However, other work suggests that, when it comes to putting a smile on your face, such exercises are more likely to prove beneficial. In a classic study conducted by Laura King from the Southern Methodist University, participants were asked to spend a few minutes during four consecutive days describing their ideal future. They were asked to be realistic, but imagine that all had gone as well as it possibly could, and that they had achieved their goals. Another group were asked to imagine a traumatic event that had happened to them, and a third group simply wrote about their plans for the day. The results revealed that those who had described their best possible future ended up significantly happier than those in the other groups.[15] In a follow-up study, King and her colleague repeated the experiment, this time having people describe the most wonderful experience in their lives.[16] Three months later, assessments revealed that compared to a control group, those reliving an intensely happy moment were significantly happier.

Affectionate Writing

Finally, another body of research has examined the idea of 'affectionate writing'. It may come as no great surprise to learn that being in a loving relationship is good for your physical and psychological health. However, are these benefits the result of receiving love, expressing love or both? To find out, Kory Floyd and his colleagues from Arizona State University asked some volunteers to think about someone they loved and spend 20 minutes describing why this person meant so much to them. As a control, another group were asked to write about something that had happened to them during the past week. Each group repeated their writing exercise three times over the course of five weeks. Once again, this simple procedure had a dramatic effect, with those spending just a few minutes engaged in affectionate writing showing a marked increase in happiness, a reduction in stress and even a significant decrease in their cholesterol levels.[17]

In short, when it comes to an instant fix for everyday happiness, certain types of writing have a surprisingly quick and significant impact. Expressing gratitude, thinking about a perfect future and affectionate writing have been scientifically proven to work, and all they require is a pen, a piece of paper and a few moments of your time.

IN 59 SECONDS OR LESS

To help incorporate effective writing techniques into your life, I have put together a rather unusual diary. Instead of keeping a record of the past, this diary encourages you to write about topics that will help create a happier future. The diary should be completed on five days of the week, with each entry taking just a few moments. Maintain the diary for one week. Research suggests that you will quickly notice the difference in mood and happiness, and that these changes may persist for months.[18] If you feel the effects wearing off, simply repeat the exercise again.

Monday: Thanksgiving

There are many things in your life for which to be grateful. These might include having close friends, being in a loving relationship, being part of a supportive family, enjoying good health, having a roof over your head or enough food to eat. Alternatively, you might have a job that you love, have happy memories of the past, recently had a nice experience, such as an especially lovely cup of coffee, enjoyed the smile of a stranger, had your dog welcome you home, eaten a great meal or stopped to smell the flowers. Think back over the past week and list three of these things below.

1 ....

2 ....

3 ....

Tuesday: Terrific Times

Think about one of the most wonderful experiences in your life. Perhaps a moment when you felt suddenly contented, were in love, listened to an amazing piece of music, saw an incredible performance or had a great time with friends. Choose just one experience and imagine yourself back in that moment in time. Imagine how you felt and what was going on around you. Now spend a few moments writing down a description of that experience and how you felt. Do not worry about your spelling, punctuation or grammar. Instead, simply commit your thoughts to paper.

Wednesday: Future Fantastic

Spend a few moments writing about your life in the future. Imagine that everything has gone as well as it possibly could. Be realistic, but imagine that you have worked hard and achieved all your goals. Imagine you have become the person you really want to be, and your personal and professional life feels like a dream come true. All of this may not help you achieve your goals, but will help you feel good and put a smile on your face.

Thursday: Dear . . .

Think about someone in your life who is very important to you. It might be your partner, a close friend or family member. Imagine you only have one opportunity to tell this person how important they are to you. Now write a short letter to this person, describing how much you care for them and the impact they have had on your life.

Friday: Reviewing the Situation

Think back over the past seven days and make a note of three things that went really well for you. The events might be fairly trivial, such as finding a parking space, or more important, such as being offered a new job or opportunity.

The Power of Purchases

Out of the blue, two words suddenly pop into your mind – 'retail' and 'therapy'. Seconds later, you find yourself heading towards your nearest shoe shop or gadget emporium, convinced that your forthcoming purchases will lead to a more blissful existence. But is that really the case? Will you actually feel better after you have bought that new pair of shoes or latest hi-tech music player? And, if so, just how long will your new-found joy last? The results from recent research have yielded clear and consistent answers to these questions. Perhaps more importantly, they have also revealed the wisest way of spending your money in order to put a smile on your face.

Work conducted by psychologists Leaf Van Boven and Thomas Gilovich has examined whether, when attempting to buy happiness, you are better off spending your money on goods (that latest dress or impressive new smartphone) or an experience (going out for a meal, buying a ticket for a concert, booking a holiday). In one study, the duo conducted a national survey in which people were asked to think of an object or experience they had bought with the aim of increasing their happiness, and then asked to rate the degree to which the purchase had cheered them up. In another experiment, the researchers randomly divided people into two groups, asked one group to think about an object they had recently bought and the other to describe an experiential purchase (a holiday, for example), and then rate their current mood on two scales, with one ranging from −4 (bad) to +4 (good), and another ranging from −4 (sad) to +4 (happy). The results from both studies clearly indicated that in terms of short- and long-term happiness, buying experiences made people feel better than buying products.[19]

Why? Our memory of experiences easily becomes distorted over time (you edit out the terrible trip on the airplane and just remember those blissful moments relaxing on the beach). Our goods, however, tend to lose their appeal by becoming old, tatty and out of date. Also, experiences promote one of the most effective happiness-inducing behaviours – spending time with others. Sociability might be part of the experience itself, or it might happen when you tell people about the occasion afterwards. In contrast, buying the latest or most expensive new product can sometimes isolate you from friends and family, who may be jealous of the things that you have.

But choosing experiences over goods is only part of the story when trying to buy happiness. Time for a quick questionnaire.[20] Take a few moments to read the following ten statements, and assign each of them a rating to indicate the degree to which they describe you. Don't spend too long thinking about each statement, answer honestly, and no peeking at the answers.

		Rating
		1 = strongly disagree to 5 = strongly agree
1	I am impressed by people who own expensive cars and houses.	1 2 3 4 5
2	I tend to judge how well I am doing in life by the possessions I buy.	1 2 3 4 5

3 I like to buy things I don't really need.   1 2 3 4 5

4 I like to be surrounded by expensive   1 2 3 4 5
   items.

5 I think that my life would be better   1 2 3 4 5
   if I owned more luxury items.

6 I am sometimes bothered by the fact that   1 2 3 4 5
   I can't afford to buy certain luxury goods.

7 Buying expensive items makes me   1 2 3 4 5
   feel good about myself.

8 I seem to put more emphasis on material   1 2 3 4 5
   things than most of my friends and family.

9 I am prepared to pay significantly more   1 2 3 4 5
   money for branded items.

10 I enjoy owning items that others   1 2 3 4 5
   find impressive.

Now add up your ratings. Low scores are between 10 and 20, medium scores
between 21 and 39, and high scores between 40 and 50.

So what is this about? Well, it may come as no great surprise that this questionnaire is designed to measure your level of materialism. People who obtain high scores clearly tend to place a great deal of importance on the acquisition of possessions, frequently view such items as central to their happiness, and judge their own success and the success of others on the basis of what they have. In contrast, those people with low scores value experiences and relationships more than possessions. As is so often the case, those with middling scores are of little interest to anyone.

Researchers have spent a great deal of time looking at the link between people's scores on these types of questionnaires and happiness.[21] The findings are as consistent as they are worrying – high scores tend to be associated with feeling unhappy and unsatisfied with life. Of course, this is not the case with every single materialist and so, if you did get a high score, you might be one of the happy-go-lucky people who buck the trend. (However, before assuming this, do bear in mind that research also suggests that whenever we are confronted with negative results from tests, we are exceptionally good at convincing ourselves that we are an exception to the rule.)

So what explains this general trend? You might think that the answer lies in the financial consequences of continually having to have the latest thing. But in fact the problem is not due to the spending of money per se. It's about who benefits from the cash.

Materialists tend to be somewhat self-centred. Studies show that when presented with a hypothetical £20,000, materialists spend, on average, three times as much on things for themselves as on others. Also, ask them to rate statements about the degree to which they care for others ('I enjoy having guests stay in my house', 'I often lend things to my friends'), and they end up giving far more self-centred responses. As research conducted by Elizabeth Dunn from the University of British Columbia shows, this can have a detrimental effect on peoples' happiness.

Dunn and her colleagues have conducted several studies of the relationship between income, spending and happiness. In one national survey, participants were asked to rate their happiness, state their income and provide a detailed breakdown of the amount spent on gifts for themselves, gifts for others and donations to charity. In another study, Dunn measured the happiness and spending patterns of employees before and after they each received a profit-sharing bonus of between $3,000 and $8,000. Time and again, the same pattern of results emerged. Those who spent a higher percentage of their income on others were far happier than those who spent it on themselves.[22]

Of course, a sceptical materialist might argue that researchers have the direction of causality wrong, and that it is not the spending of money on others that makes you happy, but rather that happy people spend more on others. It is an interesting point and one tackled in a clever experiment conducted by Dunn and her team. In a simple but innovative study, participants were given an envelope containing either $5 or $20, and asked to spend the money by 5 p.m. that evening. They were randomly assigned to one of two groups. One group was instructed to spend the money on themselves (perhaps treating themselves to a self-indulgent present), while the second group was asked to spend their unexpected windfall on someone else (perhaps by purchasing a present for a friend or family member). The predictions made by the 'happy people spend more on others' brigade proved unfounded. In fact, participants who spent the money on their friends and family ended up feeling significantly happier than those who treated themselves to luxury gifts.

Why should this be the case? The answer, it seems, lies deep within our brains. Neuroeconomist William Harbaugh and his colleagues from the University of Oregon gave participants $100 in a virtual bank account and asked them to lie down in a brain scanner. Participants first saw some of their money being given to help those in need via mandatory taxation, and were then asked to decide whether to donate some of the remaining amount to charity or keep it for themselves. The scanning results revealed that two evolutionarily ancient regions deep in the brain – the caudate nucleus and the nucleus accumbens – became active when participants witnessed some of their money going to those in need, and were especially busy when they donated money voluntarily.[23] These two brain regions also spring into action when our most basic needs are met, such as when we eat tasty food or feel valued by others, suggesting a direct brain-based link between helping others and happiness. So, scientifically speaking, if you want some real retail therapy, help yourself by helping others. It has a direct effect on your brain that, in turn, makes you feel happier.

Of course, you might argue that you really don't have enough money to donate to others. However, once again, help is at hand. A few years ago, happiness researcher Sonja Lyubomirsky and her colleagues arranged for a group of participants to perform five non-financial acts of kindness each week for six weeks. These were simple things, such as writing a thank-you note, giving blood or helping out a friend. Some of the participants performed one of the acts each day, while others carried out all five on the same day. Those who performed their kind acts each day showed a small increase in happiness. However, those who carried out all their acts of kindness on just one day each week increased their happiness by an incredible 40 per cent.[24]

The Roots of Materialism

What makes people materialistic? Is a love of possessions the result of their personality, childhood experiences or due to events later in life? According to work carried out by psychologists Lan Nguyen Chaplin and Deborah Roedder John, materialism takes root in early childhood, and is mainly driven by low self-esteem.[25]

In a two-part study, the researchers first arranged for a group of children, aged between eight and eighteen, to complete a standard self-esteem questionnaire (rating statements such as 'I am happy with the way I look'). Next, they presented the children with display boards containing lots of images relating to five general topics: hobbies such as camping, skateboarding; sports – rugby, netball, etc.; material things like new shoes or my own computer; people – friends, teachers; achievements, for example getting good grades or learning to play an instrument. The children were asked to look at the boards and use any of the images to create a collage around the theme 'What Makes Me Happy'. This fun task allowed the researchers to calculate each child's level of materialism by counting the percentage of images each one took from the material things display board. The results revealed a strong link between self-esteem and materialism, with children low in self-esteem being far more materialistic than their friends.

But could the cause and effect be the other way

around? Could materialism cause low self-esteem? To test this possibility, the researchers arranged for a group of children to write nice things about one another on paper plates, and then presented each child with their very own plateful of praise and positivity. This simple 'nice things about me' plate significantly increased the children's self-esteem and, more importantly, subsequently caused them to halve the number of materialistic images they used when creating their 'What Makes Me Happy' collage. Together, this is compelling evidence that low self-esteem causes materialistic tendencies, and that such tendencies take root at a very young age. The work also demonstrates that, as with spending a small amount of money on others or carrying out a few acts of kindness, it only takes a few seconds and a paper plate to change the way in which people think and behave.

IN 59 SECONDS OR LESS

Buy Experiences Not Goods. Want to buy happiness? Then spend your hard-earned cash on experiences. Go out for a meal. Go to a concert, cinema or theatre. Go on holiday. Go and learn how to pole dance. Go paintballing. Go bungee jumping. In fact, get involved in anything that provides an opportunity to do things with others, and then tell even more people about it afterwards. When it comes to happiness, remember that it is experiences that represent really good value for money.

'Tis Better to Give Than Receive. Long-term happiness is not just about gyrating around a pole to raunchy music, or plummeting towards the ground screaming like a baby. Ask people whether they will be happier after spending money on themselves or others, and the vast majority will tick the 'me' box. The science shows that exactly the opposite is true – people become much happier after providing for others rather than themselves. The good news is that you really do not have to divert a huge amount of your income to charity, friends, family and colleagues. In fact, the smallest gifts can quickly result in surprisingly large and long-lasting changes in happiness. A few pounds spent on other people may be one of the best investments you ever make. And if you really can't afford to donate your hard-earned cash, remember that carrying out five non-financial acts of kindness on a single day also provides a significant boost to your happiness.

Happiness Is a Pencil

People behave in highly predictable ways when they experience certain emotions and thoughts. When they are sad, they cry. When they are happy, they smile. When they agree, they nod their heads. So far, no surprises, but, according to an area of research known as proprioceptive psychology, the same process also works in reverse. Get people to behave in a certain way and you cause them to feel certain emotions and have certain thoughts. The idea was initially controversial but was fortunately supported by a series of compelling experiments.[26]

In one now classic study, two groups of people were asked to add up a list of numbers. During the task, one group were asked to furrow their brows (or, as the researchers put it, 'contract their corrugator muscle') while the others were requested to adopt a slight grin ('extend their zygomaticus muscle'). This simple act of facial contortion had a surprising effect on participants' ratings of how hard they found the number-adding task, with the frowning participants convinced that they had expended far more effort than the grinning group.

In a different study, participants were asked to concentrate on various products moving across a large computer screen, and then indicate whether the items appealed to them. Some of the items moved vertically (causing the participants to nod their heads while watching) while others moved horizontally (resulting in a side-to-side head movement). Participants preferred vertically moving products without being aware that their 'yes' and 'no' head movements had played a key role in their decisions.[27]

Exactly the same idea applies to happiness. People smile when they are happy, but also feel happier because they are smiling. The effect even works whether people are aware of the smile or not. In the 1980s Fritz Strack and his colleagues asked two groups of people to judge how funny they found Gary Larson's *Far Side* cartoons, and rate how happy they felt under one of two rather bizarre circumstances. One group were asked to hold a pencil between their teeth, but to ensure that it did not touch their lips. The other group supported the end of the pencil with their lips but not their teeth. Without realizing it, those in the 'teeth only' condition had forced the lower part of their faces into a smile, while those in the 'lips only' condition had made themselves frown. The results revealed that the participants tended to experience the emotion associated with their expressions. Those who had their faces forced into a smile felt happier, and found the *Far Side* cartoons much funnier, than those who were forced to frown.[28] Other work has demonstrated that this increase in happiness does not drain away the moment people cease smiling. It lingers on, affecting many aspects of their behaviour, including interacting with others in a more positive way, and being more likely to remember happy life events.[29]

The message from this type of work is simple – if you want to cheer yourself up, behave like a happy person.

IN 59 SECONDS OR LESS

Smile. There is a host of happy behaviours that can be quickly incorporated into your everyday life. Most important of all, smile more. This shouldn't be a brief, unfelt smile that finishes in the blink of an eye. Instead, research suggests that you should try to maintain the expression for between 15 and 30 seconds. To make the grin as convincing as possible, try to imagine a situation that would elicit a genuine smile. Perhaps you have just met a good friend, heard a hilarious joke or found out that your mother-in-law isn't coming to visit after all. Consider creating a signal to remind you to smile regularly. Set your watch, computer or PDA to beep on the hour, or use a more random cue, such as your telephone ringing.

Sit Up. Your posture is equally important. In a study conducted by Tomi-Ann Roberts at Colorado College, participants were randomly split into two groups and asked to spend 3 minutes either sitting up straight or slumping down in their chair. Everyone was then given a maths test and asked to assess their mood. Those who had sat upright were much happier than those who had slouched down, and even obtained higher scores on the maths test. Interestingly, this result didn't apply for many of the female participants, causing Roberts to speculate that the act of sitting upright and pushing their chests forward may have made them feel self-conscious.[30]

Act Happy. Research by Peter Borkenau from Bielefeld University and others has revealed that happy people move in a very different way to unhappy people.[31] You can use this information to increase your sense of happiness by acting like a happy person. Try walking in a more relaxed way, swinging your arms slightly more, putting more of a spring in your step. Also, try making more expressive hand gestures during conversations, nod your head more when others are speaking, wear more colourful clothing, use a greater frequency of positively charged emotional words (especially 'love', 'like' and 'fond'), show a lower frequency of self-references ('me', 'myself' and 'I'), have a larger variation in the pitch of your voice, speak slightly faster and have a significantly firmer handshake. Incorporating these behaviours into your everyday actions will help enhance your happiness.

Putting in the Effort

According to researchers Kenneth Sheldon and Sonja Lyubomirsky, happiness does not come easily.[32] In several experiments, the duo recruited participants who had recently experienced one of two types of change in their life. The first type, labelled 'circumstantial change', involved relatively important alterations to their overall circumstances, including, for example, moving house, getting a pay rise or buying a new car. The second type, labelled 'intentional change', involved changes that required effort to pursue a goal or initiate an activity and included, for example, joining a new club, starting a new hobby, embarking on a different career. Both sets of participants were asked to rate their happiness levels for several weeks. The results consistently showed that although people in both groups experienced an immediate rise in happiness, those who had experienced a circumstantial change quickly reverted back to their initial levels, while those who had made an intentional change remained happier for a much longer period of time. Why?

According to Sheldon and Lyubomirsky, it is due to a phenomenon known as 'hedonistic habituation'. Unsurprisingly, humans derive a great deal of enjoyment from any new form of positive experience. However, give anyone the same wonderful experience time and again, and they quickly become familiar with their new source of joy and so cease to derive anywhere near as much pleasure from it. Unfortunately, circumstantial changes frequently produce hedonistic habituation. Although the initial thrill of a new house, pay rise or car is wonderful, the positive feelings caused by the change tend to be the same day in day out, and so this initial enjoyment quickly fades away. In contrast, intentional changes tend to avoid hedonistic habituation by creating a constantly changing psychological landscape. Whether it is starting a new hobby, joining an organization, initiating a project, meeting new people or learning a novel skill, the brain is fed with ever-changing positive experiences that prevent habituation and so prolong happiness.

So, to maximize happiness, choose intentional over circumstantial change. Make the effort to start a new hobby, begin a major project or try a form of sport that you have never tried before. Choose activities that fit your personality, values and abilities. It might help to think about what you already enjoy doing, identify the core elements that make this activity so pleasurable, and try other activities involving these elements. So if, for example, you enjoy oil painting, try taking up water colours. If you like playing tennis, consider taking up badminton or squash. If you are good at sudoku, try turning your hand to crossword puzzles. Whatever you decide to do, remember to avoid hedonistic habituation by making the effort to change what you do and when you do it. It may sound like hard work, but research suggests that when it comes to happiness, it is well worth the effort.

2. PERSUASION

Why rewards fail, how to give the perfect interview, improve your social life by making mistakes, never lose your wallet again, and convince anyone of anything by using your pet frog.

How do you persuade a child to complete a homework assignment, an employee to perform better in the workplace, or people to take more care of the environment? Many believe that the most effective way is to dangle the biggest possible carrot in front of their nose. But does research suggest this is really an incentive or is it just a myth?

In one classic study, Stanford psychologist Mark Lepper and his colleagues asked two groups of schoolchildren to have fun creating some drawings.[1] Before being allowed to play with the crayons and paper, one group was told that they would receive an elaborate 'good player' medal for drawing, while the other group were not given the promise of any reward. A few weeks later the researchers returned, handed out drawing paper and crayons, and measured how much the children played with them. Surprisingly, the children who had received the medals on the first occasion spent significantly less time drawing than their classmates.

Why did this happen? According to Lepper, the children who were offered the medals thought something along the lines of, 'Well, let me see here, adults usually offer me rewards when they want me to do something I don't like doing. An adult is offering me a gold medal for drawing, therefore I must not like drawing.' The effect has been replicated many times, and the conclusion is clear: if you set children an activity they enjoy and reward them for doing it, the reward

40

reduces the enjoyment and demotivates them. Within a few seconds, you transform play into work.

It could be argued that this only applies to activities people enjoy, and that rewards actually encourage people in relation to tasks they dislike. To test this theory, a few years ago I ran a study in which two groups of people were asked to take part in an experiment in which they spent an afternoon picking up litter in a London park.[2] Participants were told that they were taking part in an experiment examining how best to persuade people to look after their local parks. One group were paid handsomely for their time, while the others were only given a small amount of cash. After an hour or so of backbreaking and tedious work, everyone rated the degree to which they had enjoyed the afternoon. You might think that those clutching a large amount of well-earned cash would be more positive than those who had given their time for very little money.

In fact, the result was exactly the opposite. The average enjoyment rating of the handsomely paid group was a measly 2 out of 10, while the modestly paid group's average ratings were a whopping 8.5. It seemed that those who had been paid well had thought, 'Well, let me see, people usually pay me to do things I don't enjoy. I was paid a large amount, so I must dislike tidying the park.' In contrast, those who received less money thought, 'I don't need to be paid much to do something I enjoy. I did the tidying for very little, therefore I must have enjoyed cleaning the park.' According to the results of this study, it seems that excessive rewards may have a detrimental effect on the attitude of the people doing the tasks.

These findings have been replicated time and again in studies. Almost regardless of the nature of the rewards or tasks, those who are offered a carrot tend not to perform as well as those who don't expect to receive anything.[3] Some of the studies have shown short-term boosts in performance, but over the long haul rewards tend to destroy the very behaviour they are designed to encourage.

As we've seen, what does *not* work is to motivate people with the promise of a reward. So what form of incentive does work best? To encourage people to do more of something they enjoy, try presenting them with the occasional small *surprise* reward after they have completed the activity, or praise the fruits of their labour. When it is something that they don't enjoy, a realistic, but not excessive, reward is effective at the start, followed by feel-good comments that encourage them to pursue the activity ('if only everyone was a good park-tidying citizen like you').

However, there are alternatives to instant persuasion other than praise, modest rewards and cheesy comments. For quick and effective techniques, whether in negotiations, or help in an emergency, or getting the odd favour or two, think about putting your foot in the door, understanding groupthink and why it really is better to give than receive.

Giving the Perfect Interview

There is an old joke about a man being interviewed for a new job and being told, 'You know, in this job we really need someone who is responsible.' The man thinks for a moment, and then replies, 'I am perfect for you. In my last job, lots of things went badly wrong and they always said I was responsible.' Unfortunately, disastrous replies are common in genuine interviews, but help is at hand. Over the past thirty years, psychologists have investigated the key factors that impress interviewers. The work has resulted in several quick and effective techniques that can significantly increase your chances of being offered your dream job.

Ask any employer to explain why they choose one applicant in preference to another, and they will tell you that it is a matter of which candidate has the best qualifications and personal skills for the job. To help make the process as rational and fair as possible, many draw up a list of key skills required by the successful candidate, study each applicant's CV for evidence of those skills, and then use a face-to-face interview to discover a little more information. But research conducted by Chad Higgins from the University of Washington and Timothy Judge from the University of Florida suggests that interviewers are often deluding themselves about how they make up their minds, and that in reality they are unconsciously swayed by a mysterious and powerful force.[4]

Higgins and Judge followed the fortunes of more than a hundred students as they tried to obtain their first job after university. At the start of the study, the researchers examined the CVs of each student, measuring the two factors that interviewers consistently claim play a key role in separating successful and unsuccessful candidates – qualifications and work experience. After each job interview, students completed a standard questionnaire about how they had behaved, including whether, for example, they had made the most of their positive points, taken an interest in the company or asked the interviewers about the type of person they were looking for. The research team also contacted the interviewers and asked them to provide feedback on several factors, including the candidate's performance, how well they would fit in with the organization, whether they possessed the necessary skills for the job and, perhaps most important of all, whether the candidate would be offered the job.

After analysing their mass of data, the research team exploded some of the myths about why interviewers choose candidates for a job and discovered a surprising reality. Did the likelihood depend on qualifications? Or was it work experience? In fact, it was neither. It was just one important factor: did the candidate appear to be a pleasant person. Those candidates who had managed to ingratiate themselves were very likely to be offered a position; they had charmed their way to success in several ways. A few had spent time chatting about topics that were not related to the job, but that interested the candidate and interviewer. Some had made a special effort to smile and maintain eye contact. Others had praised the organization. This barrage of positivity had paid dividends and convinced the interviewers that such pleasant and socially skilled applicants would fit well in the work-place, and so should be offered a job.

Higgins and Judge's study clearly demonstrates that in order to get your dream job, going out of your way to be pleasant is more important than qualifications and past work experience. However, try explaining away twelve counts of murder and two convictions for major corporate fraud, and you will quickly discover that such ingratiation has its limitations. Given that is the case, what is the best way of dealing with the less impressive side of your CV? Should you mention weaknesses towards the start of the interview, or hope to make a good first impression and only introduce possible problems at the end?

This issue was investigated in a classic study conducted in the early 1970s by psychologists Edward Jones and Eric Gordon from Duke University.[5] In their experiment, participants were presented with a tape recording of a man (actually a stooge) talking about his life and asked to rate the degree to which he sounded likeable. During the interview, the man described how he had not completed a school semester because he had been caught cheating and had been expelled. The researchers edited the tape to ensure that half the participants heard this bombshell towards the start, while the others heard it towards the end. This manipulation had a large impact on how much the participants liked the man. When the cheating was mentioned towards the start of the tape, the man appeared far more likeable than when it was mentioned towards the end. Additional work has confirmed exactly the same effect in other contexts, with, for example, lawyers being judged to have a stronger case when presenting a weakness in their argument at the start of a trial.[6]

It seems that presenting weaknesses early is seen as a sign of openness. This is a lesson that many politicians, such as Bill Clinton, have yet to learn. Interviewers believe that they are dealing with someone who has the strength of character and integrity to relate potential difficulties first and who is not, therefore, attempting to mislead them.

Can the same be said of the more positive aspects of your CV? Actually, no. In another part of the same study, participants heard a positive reason for the skipped semester ('I was awarded a prestigious scholarship to travel round Europe'), but presented either early or late on the tape. Now the effect was reversed, with the man appearing far more likeable when he mentioned the award later. It seems that modesty, rather than honesty, is critical for positive aspects of your past. By delaying, it appears you would rather let your strengths emerge naturally, while playing your trump cards early is seen as boastful.

So, you have polished up on your ingratiating skills, are willing to declare your weaknesses early, and intend to leave the best till last. Does that mean you are guaranteed to be a success? Unfortunately, no. Despite the best of intentions and most extensive preparations, we all make mistakes. Perhaps you will knock a glass of water into your lap, inadvertently insult your interviewer or give an answer that is as bumbling as it is unconvincing. The fact is, you need to be able to cope with the odd unexpected disaster or two. To help, Thomas Gilovich from Cornell University and his colleagues undertook a series of studies in which they forced people to wear Barry Manilow T-shirts.[7]

In a typical study, Gilovich arranged for five participants to arrive at the same time at his laboratory. Everyone was led into a room, asked to sit along one side of a table, and each started to complete a questionnaire. The group began to tick various boxes, unaware that the researchers had arranged for another participant to arrive 5 minutes late. This latecomer was met before entering the room and told to wear a T-shirt bearing a large picture of Barry Manilow. Why Manilow? Well, the study was about the psychology of embarrassment, and carefully controlled pre-testing had revealed that the majority of Cornell students wouldn't be seen dead in a Barry Manilow T-shirt. Moments after putting on the T-shirt, the latecomer was then bundled into the room, and was confronted by a row of staring fellow students. After a few moments, the experimenter explained that it might be better to wait outside for a while, and promptly bundled the latecomer back out of the room.

Two things happened next. Everyone inside the room was asked if they had noticed the image on the latecomer's T-shirt, while the latecomer was asked to estimate the percentage of students who would have noticed the embarrassing image. The results from a series experiments revealed that, on average, about 20 per cent of the people in the room noticed Barry. However, the latecomers were convinced that they had been far more eye-catching, and estimated that, on average, about 50 per cent of the group would have noticed the T-shirt. In short, the latecomers significantly over-estimated the impact of their embarrassing encounter.

This bias, known as the 'spotlight effect', has been found in many different settings. From assessing the effects of a bad-hair day to performing badly in a group discussion, those who feel embarrassed are convinced that their mistakes are far more noticeable than they actually are. Why? It seems we focus on our own looks and behaviour more than others, and so are likely to overestimate their impact. So, if you make a mortifying mistake in an interview, think about the man in the Manilow T-shirt, and remember that it probably feels far worse than it is.

IN 59 SECONDS OR LESS

Increase your chances of giving a great interview in three easy steps.

First, likeability is more important than academic achievements and work experience, so . . .
- find something you genuinely like about the organization and let your opinion be known
- feel free to give a genuine compliment to the interviewer
- chat about a non-job-related topic that you and the interviewer find interesting
- be interested in them – ask what type of person they are looking for and how the position fits into the overall organization
- be enthusiastic about the position and the organization
- smile and maintain eye contact with the interviewers

Second, when you do have weaknesses, don't wait until late in the interview to reveal them. Instead, give your credibility a boost by getting them into the conversation towards the start of the interview. And remember, for positive aspects, modesty is vital, so retain something strong until the very last minute.

Finally, if you make what seems like a major mistake, don't over-react. The chances are that it is far more noticeable to you than others, and your excessive response or apologizing could just draw more attention to it. Instead, acknowledge it if appropriate, and continue as if nothing has happened.

4 Quick Tips for Persuasion

Choose the Middle Way. If you want to increase your chances of making a good impression in a meeting, sit towards the middle of the table. Psychologists Priya Raghubir and Ana Valenzuela analysed episodes of the television quiz show *The Weakest Link*.[8] In the show, contestants stand in a semi-circle, and each round one contestant is voted off by the other players. Contestants standing at the central positions in the semi-circle reached the final round on average 42 per cent of the time, and won the game 45 per cent of time. Those standing at the more extreme positions reached the final round just 17 per cent of the time, and won just 10 per cent. In another experiment, participants were shown a group photograph of five candidates for a business internship, and asked to choose which candidate should be awarded the position. Candidates in the centre of the group were chosen more frequently than those sitting at the edges. The researchers believe that when looking at a group, people use a basic rule of thumb – important people sit in the middle – and label the phenomenon the centre-stage effect.

K.I.S.S. When thinking about the name of a new project, campaign or product, keep it simple. Adam Alter and Daniel Oppenheimer from Princeton University tracked the fortunes of companies on the stock market, and found that those with simple and memorable names, such as

Flinks Inc., tended to outperform shares in companies with awkward names like Sagxter Inc.[9] Further research showed that the effect was not due to larger companies tending to have simpler names, but because of a natural tendency for people to be drawn to words that are easy to remember and straightforward to pronounce.

Mind Your Language. Who hasn't been tempted to slip the odd overly complicated word into a report or letter to make themselves sound especially intelligent and erudite? According to other research conducted by Daniel Oppenheimer, an unnecessary love of the thesaurus may have exactly the opposite effect.[10] In a series of five studies, Oppenheimer systematically examined the complexity of the vocabulary used in various passages (including job applications, academic essays and translations of Descartes). He then asked people to read the samples and rate the intelligence of the person who allegedly wrote them. The simpler language resulted in significantly higher ratings of intelligence, showing that the unnecessary use of complex language sent out a bad impression. Describing his findings in a paper entitled 'Consequences of Erudite Vernacular Utilized Irrespective of Necessity: Problems with Using Long Words Needlessly', Oppenheimer also found that passages written in a font that was difficult to read lowered people's evaluations of the author's intelligence, suggesting that you can increase how bright people think you are simply by improving your handwriting and simplifying your language.

Favours, Pratfalls and Gossip

Likeability matters. The Gallup organization has examined the public perception of American presidential candidates since 1960, focusing on the impact of issues, party affiliation and likeability.[11] From these factors, only likeability has consistently predicted the winning candidate. Similarly, research into relationships by Philip Noll at the University of Toronto shows that likeable people are around 50 per cent less likely to get divorced. Indeed, likeability might even save your life, as other studies indicate that doctors urge likeable patients to keep in contact and to return for more frequent checks.

But what is the best way to ensure that you top the likeability league? Self-help guru Dale Carnegie has rightly pointed out that one way of increasing your popularity is to express a genuine interest in others. In fact, Carnegie argues that people will win more friends in two months by developing a genuine interest in those around them than two years of trying to make others interested in them. Other writers have suggested alternative quick and easy routes, which include giving sincere compliments, matching people's body language and style of speech, appearing modest and being generous with your time, resources and skills. No doubt these types of common-sense techniques work. However, according to research, there are other, more subtle ideas that can also help you win friends and influence people. All it takes is a little advice from Benjamin Franklin, the ability to trip up once in a while and an understanding of the power of gossip.

Eighteenth-century American polymath and politician Benjamin Franklin was once eager to gain the cooperation of a difficult and apathetic member of the Pennsylvania state legislature. Rather than spend his time bowing and scraping to the man, Franklin decided on a completely different course of action. He knew this person had a copy of a rare and unusual book in his private library, and so Franklin asked whether he might borrow it for a couple of days. The man agreed and, according to Franklin, 'When we next met in the House, he spoke to me (which he had never done before), and with great civility; and he ever after manifested a readiness to serve me on all occasions.' Franklin attributed the success of his book-borrowing technique to a simple principle: 'He that has once done you a kindness will be more ready to do you another than he whom you yourself have obliged.' In other words, to increase the likelihood of someone liking you, get them to do you a favour. A century later, Russian novelist Leo Tolstoy appeared to agree: 'We do not love people so much for the good they have done us, as for the good we do them.'

In the 1960s psychologists Jon Jecker and David Landy set out to discover if this 200-year-old technique still worked in the twentieth century.[12] In an experiment, they arranged for participants to win some money. Then, soon after the participants had left the laboratory, a researcher caught up with some of them and asked a favour. He explained that he had used his own funds for the study, was running short of cash and wondered if the participants would mind returning the money. A second group of participants were accosted by a second researcher, the departmental secretary, who made the same request, but this time explained that it was the psychology department that had financed the experiment, not personal money and that it was the department that was now a bit low on cash. Afterwards, all the participants were asked to rate how much they liked each researcher. Just as predicted by Franklin and Tolstoy all those years before, the participants who helped the researcher on a personal basis liked him far more than the researcher who had been helped on behalf of the department.

Although it may sound strange, this curious phenomenon, referred to as the Franklin effect, is theoretically sound. Most of the time, people's behaviour follows from their thoughts and feelings. They feel happy and so they smile, they find someone attractive and so look longingly into their eyes. However, the reverse can also be true. Get people to smile and they feel happier, ask them to look into someone's eyes and they find that person more attractive. Exactly the same principle applies for favours. To encourage others to like you, ask for their help.

•

The Franklin effect is not the only counter-intuitive route to likeability. There is also the technique that once helped John F. Kennedy become one of the most popular presidents in American history.

In 1961, Kennedy ordered troops to invade Cuba at the Bay of Pigs. The operation was a fiasco, and historians still view the decision as a huge military blunder. However, a national survey taken after the failed invasion showed that the public actually liked Kennedy more despite his disastrous decision. Two factors could account for this seemingly strange finding. Kennedy didn't try to make excuses or pass the buck for the botched operation, but instead immediately took full responsibility. Also, until that point, Kennedy had been seen as a superhero – a charming, handsome, powerful man who could do no wrong. The Bay of Pigs disaster made him appear far more human and likeable.

Elliot Aronson and his colleagues from the University of California decided to take an experimental approach to the issue and discover if making a mistake or two really is good for your popularity.[13] In one part of their study, participants listened to one of two audiotapes. Both tapes related to a student and detailed his participation in a general-knowledge quiz, followed by him talking about his background. The student performed very well in the quiz, correctly answering more than 90 per cent of the questions, and then he modestly admitted to a lifetime of success. However, in one of the two editions, towards the end of the recording, the participants heard the student knock over a cup of coffee, ruining a new suit. All the participants were asked to rate how likeable they found the student. Despite the only difference being the fictitious knocking-over of coffee, as with Kennedy following the Bay of Pigs invasion, the student who had committed the blunder was considered far more likeable.

This strange phenomenon, often referred to as the 'pratfall effect', may work well for presidents and when listening to audiotapes, but does it also operate in other situations? To find out, I recently helped restage a version of Aronson's experiment, but this time in a shopping centre.[14]

The study was part of a television programme examining the psychology of everyday life. We gathered a crowd, and explained that they were going to see two trainees demonstrating how to make a fruit drink using a new type of liquidizer. First was Sara, who played the role of our 'perfect' person. Sara had spent the night before getting to grips with the device and learning a convincing script. In went the fruit, on went the lid, zoom went the liquidizer and out came a perfect drink. The crowd rewarded Sara with a well-deserved round of applause, and eagerly awaited our second demonstrator. Next was Emma, who was playing the part of our 'less than perfect' person. This time, in went the fruit, on went the lid, zoom went the liquidizer, off came the lid, and Emma ended up covered in fruit drink. Shaking the remains of the drink from the bottom of the liquidizer into a glass, she received a sympathetic round of applause from the crowd.

Having finished the first part of the experiment, it was time to explore the issue of likeability. We interviewed audience members about the two demonstrations. Which impressed them the most? Were they more likely to buy a liquidizer after seeing the first or second demonstration? Most important of all, who did they like most, Sara or Emma? Although the public tended to find Sara's demonstration more professional and convincing, it was Emma who topped the likeability league. When asked to explain their decision, people said they found it difficult to identify with Sara's flawless performance, but warmed to Emma's more human display. Although not the perfect experiment (for example, Emma and Sara were not identical twins, so maybe their looks influenced the crowd's judgement), it provides further support that the occasional trip-up can be good for your social life.

The third, and final, unusual route to likeability involves a very human trait – the desire to gossip. Most people like to pass on the odd juicy bit of information about friends and colleagues, but is such behaviour good for them? John Skowronski from Ohio University at Newark and his colleagues investigated the downside of spreading malicious gossip.[15] Participants watched videotapes of actors talking about a third party (a friend or acquaintance of the actor). Some of the actor's comments about his friend were very negative, such as, 'He hates animals. Today he was walking to the store and he saw this puppy. So he kicked it out of his way.' Afterwards, the participants were asked to rate the personality of the speaker. Remarkably, even though it was obvious that the person on the videotape was criticizing someone else, the participants consistently attributed the negative traits to the speaker. This effect, known as 'spontaneous trait transference', reveals the pluses and minuses of gossiping. When you gossip about another person, listeners unconsciously associate you with the characteristics you are describing, ultimately leading to those characteristics being 'transferred' to you. So, say positive and pleasant things about friends and colleagues and you are seen as a nice person. In contrast, constantly bitch about their failings and people will unconsciously apply the negative traits and incompetence to you.

IN 59 SECONDS OR LESS

Self-help gurus have argued that it is possible to increase your likeability by becoming more empathic, modest and generous. They are probably right. However, in addition, there are also three other surprising factors that can promote popularity.

The Franklin Effect. People like you more when they carry out a favour for you. However, the effect has its limitations and is more likely to work with small favours rather than more significant requests that either make people respond begrudgingly or, even worse, refuse.

The Pratfall Effect. The occasional slip-up can enhance your likeability. However, it is important to realize that the effect only really works when you are in danger of being seen as too perfect. In another part of the Aronson experiment, the researchers made two audiotapes of a more normal-sounding student who averaged just 30 per cent in the quiz, and then outlined a series of more mediocre achievements. Under these conditions, spilling the coffee in his lap sent him plummeting to the bottom of the likeability league because he was perceived to be a total loser.

Gossip. Know that whatever traits you assign to others are likely to come home to roost, and be seen as part of your own personality.

Quick Persuasion Tips

Make it Personal. In 1987, the public contributed £350,000 to assist a baby who had fallen into a well in Texas, and in 2002 £24,000 was raised to help a dog stranded on a ship in the Pacific Ocean. In contrast, organizations constantly struggle to raise funds to help prevent the 15 million or so deaths due to starvation each year, or the 10,000 annual child deaths in America due to car accidents. Why? In a recent study, researchers paid people for their involvement in an experiment, and then presented them with an opportunity to contribute some of the money to Save the Children. Prior to making any contribution, half the participants were shown statistics about the millions facing starvation in Zambia, while the other half saw a story about the plight of just one seven-year-old African girl.[16] Those shown the story of the girl contributed more than twice the amount given by those confronted by statistics. Irrational as it is, people are swayed far more by the individual than the masses.

'Yes, yes, yes.' In *How To Win Friends and Influence People*, Dale Carnegie argued that getting someone to answer 'yes' to a series of statements increased the likelihood of them agreeing with you in the future. Research conducted over fifty years after the publication of his seminal book has supported the importance of positive utterances. In the 1980s, psychologist Daniel Howard

from the Southern Methodist University arranged for researchers to telephone randomly selected people and ask whether a representative of the Hunger Relief Committee could visit their home and try to sell them some biscuits for charity.[17] Half the researchers started their conversations with a simple question designed to get a positive answer: 'How are you feeling this evening?' As expected, the vast majority of people responded favourably ('Great', 'Fine, thanks'). More importantly, this act had a dramatic influence on whether they would allow a biscuit seller into their house. Thirty-two per cent accepted the offer in the 'How are you feeling?' condition, compared to just 18 per cent in the control 'no question' condition. The message is that people are more likely to agree with you when they have already said something positive.

A Nickel Will Get You on the Subway, but Garlic Will Get You a Seat. In a series of studies during the 1930s, psychologist Gregory Razran discovered that people developed a special fondness for other people, objects and statements if they were introduced to them while eating a meal.[18] The effect may be due to the fact that good food puts people in a happy mood and can cause them to make faster, more impulsive decisions.[19] More recently, researchers discovered that people who have just consumed caffeinated drinks were more likely to be swayed by arguments about various controversial topics.[20] In short, good evidence that there really is no such thing as a free lunch or an innocent cup of coffee.

Save Your Time, Persuade by Rhyme. In his influential book *The Gay Science*, German philosopher Friedrich Nietzsche argued that rhyming poetry originally appealed to the primitive mind because it appeared to have magical connotations and represented a way of speaking directly with the gods. Although this view has not become universally accepted, recent research does suggest that rhymes can be surprisingly effective. Psychologists Matthew McGlone and Jessica Tofighbakhsh (try finding a rhyme for that) showed people well-known rhyming sayings ('caution and measure will win you treasure', 'life is mostly strife') and some non-rhyming counterparts ('caution and measure will win you riches', 'life is mostly a struggle'), and instructed the readers to rate how accurately they described human behaviour.[21] The rhymes were viewed as significantly more accurate than the non-rhyming statements. The authors suggested this was because they were more memorable, likeable and repeatable. The effect is frequently used in advertising ('Beanz Meanz Heinz', 'A Mars a day helps you work, rest and play'), and has even made its way into the courtroom, when attorney Johnnie Cochran defended O. J. Simpson by using the phrase: 'If the gloves don't fit, you must acquit.'

Peas in a Pod. For persuasion, the research points to a simple fact: similarity works. For example, Randy Garner from Sam Houston State University mailed surveys, varying the information on the cover sheet to ensure that the first name of the addressee either matched or didn't match the experimenter's first name.[22] So, in the 'matching name' condition a participant named Fred Smith might receive a survey from researcher Fred Jones, while in the 'non-matching name' condition participant Julie Green might get one from Amanda White. This remarkably simple manipulation affected the response rate, with 30 per cent in the 'non-matching name' condition returning the survey, compared to 56 per cent when people saw their own first name on the cover. Other work suggests that people are far more likely to support, and agree with, others who appear to be like them. In one study, more than 6,000 American voters rated their own personality and how they perceived the personality of John Kerry and George W. Bush.[23] Both sets of voters agreed that Kerry was far more open to new ideas and concepts than Bush, but that Bush was more loyal and sincere than Kerry. However, exactly the same pattern of traits emerged among voters, with those who voted for Kerry rating themselves as more open-minded than the Bush voters, and Bush supporters seeing themselves as more trustworthy than those who voted for Kerry. Regardless of whether the similarity is dress, speech, background, age, religion, politics, drinking and smoking habits, food preference, opinions, personality or body language, we like people who are like us, and find them far more persuasive than others.

Remember to Mention Your Pet Frog. When it comes to persuading others, try lightening up. In a study conducted by Karen O'Quin and Joel Aronoff, participants were asked to negotiate with a seller over the purchase price of a piece of art.[24] Towards the end of the negotiation, the seller made their final offer in one of two ways: half the time they said they would accept $6,000, while the rest of the time they gave the same final price but added in a little humour ('Well, my final offer is six thousand dollars, and I'll throw in my pet frog'). Those few moments of attempted humour had a big effect, with participants making a much greater compromise in their purchase price whenever they heard about the frog. The effect worked just as well with men and women, regardless of the degree to which the seller's final price was above the amount originally offered by the participant. It seems that the brief humorous aside momentarily put the participant in a good mood, and this encouraged them to be more giving. So, next time you're trying to get what you want, remember to mention your pet frog.

Why Too Many Cooks Leads to No Cooking at All, and What Can Be Done About It

On 13 March 1964, a young woman named Kitty Genovese was returning to her apartment in New York City's borough of Queens when she was the victim of a random and vicious attack. Although she parked her car less than 100 feet from her door, she was overpowered by a total stranger during the short walk to her apartment, and repeatedly stabbed. Despite the ordeal, Genovese managed to scream for help and stagger towards her apartment block. Unfortunately, her attacker caught up with her and inflicted a second set of injuries that proved fatal.

On 27 March, the *New York Times* ran a front-page article about the attack, describing how a large number of 'respectable, law-abiding citizens' had either witnessed or heard the attack, but had not telephoned the police during the assault. The detective in charge of the case was reported as being unable to understand why so many witnesses had done so little. The story was quickly picked up by other media, and most journalists concluded that Genovese's neighbours simply didn't care enough to get involved. They saw the incident as damning evidence of how modern-day American society had lost its way. The tragic story caught the public imagination and has since inspired several books, films and songs, and even formed the basis for a sensitively entitled musical drama *The Screams of Kitty Genovese*.[25]

The witnesses' lack of involvement also puzzled two social psychologists working in New York at the time. Bibb Latané and John Darley were unconvinced that the apparent widespread apathy was due to a lack of empathy, and set about investigating some of the other factors that may have caused the witnesses to turn their backs rather than pick up the telephone. The two researchers reasoned that the large number of witnesses may have played a pivotal role, and carried out a series of ingenious experiments that have since been described in almost every social psychology textbook published in the last thirty years.[26]

In their first study, Latané and Darley arranged for a student to fake an epileptic seizure on the streets of New York, and observed whether passers-by would take the time to help. As they were interested in the effect that the number of witnesses might have on the likelihood of any one of them helping, the researchers restaged the fake seizure again and again in front of different numbers of people. The results were as clear as they were counter-intuitive. As the numbers of witnesses increased, the chances of any one of them helping decreased. The effect was far from trivial, with the student receiving assistance 85 per cent of the time when there was one other person present, but only around 30 per cent of the time when there were five others there.

In another study, the researchers moved off the streets and turned their attention to groups of people sitting in a waiting room.[27] Rather than faking an epileptic seizure, they created another apparent emergency by arranging for smoke to seep under the waiting-room door, suggesting that a fire had broken out in the building. Once again, the larger the group, the smaller the chance of anyone raising the alarm. Seventy-five per cent of people sitting on their own reported the leak, versus a 38 per cent reporting rate when there were three people in the room. Other work revealed exactly the same effect, regardless of whether the need for assistance was large or small. For example, in another experiment, the team arranged for 145 stooges to take 1,497 elevator rides, in each of which they dropped some coins or pencils. In total, 4,813 people shared the elevators with them. When accompanied by just one other person, the researchers' coins and pencils were picked up on 40 per cent of the occasions, whereas when they were sharing the lift with six others, the rate of assistance went down to just 20 per cent.[28]

From helping a stranded motorist to donating blood to reporting a shoplifter or making an emergency telephone call, exactly the same pattern has emerged time and again. It seems that the witnesses to the Kitty Genovese attack were not especially uncaring or selfish – there were just too many of them.

Why should the urge to help others decrease, the more people there are in the room? When faced with a relatively uncommon event, such as a man falling down in the street, we have to decide what's going on. Often, there are several options. Maybe it really is a genuine emergency and the man is having an epileptic fit, or maybe he has just tripped over, or perhaps he is faking it as part of a social-psychology experiment, or maybe he is part of a hidden-camera stunt show, or perhaps he is a mime just about to start his street act. Despite the various possibilities, we have to make a quick decision. But how do we do that? One way is to look at the behaviour of those around us. Are they rushing to help, or continuing to go about their daily business? Are they telephoning for an ambulance, or still chatting with their friends? Unfortunately, because most people are reluctant to stand out from the crowd, everyone looks to everyone else for pointers, and the group can end up deciding on a 'nothing to see here, move along' option. Second, even if there exists a clear and present need for help, there is still the issue of responsibility. In most everyday situations, there is no clear chain of command. Is it your job to help, or should you leave it to the guy over there (not him, the guy behind him)? Everyone in the group thinks in the same way, which can result in no one helping out at all.

The situation is very different when you are on your own. Suddenly, you are carrying all the weight on your shoulders. What if the guy who has just fallen over really is in need of help? What if the building really is on fire? What if that woman in the lift really does need that pencil to put between her teeth before a particularly gloomy meeting? Are you prepared to be the person who turned the other cheek and walked away? Under these circumstances, most people are far more likely to find out if there is a problem and, if necessary, provide a helping hand.

Latané and Darley's ground-breaking studies into what has become known as the bystander effect were initiated by the behaviour of thirty-eight witnesses who saw the tragic murder of Kitty Genovese but didn't lend a helping hand. Interestingly, recent work suggests that the original media reports of the murder may have exaggerated the alleged apathy, with one of the attorneys involved saying that they could only find about half a dozen good witnesses, that none of them actually reported seeing Genovese being stabbed, and at least one claimed that the incident *was* reported to the police while it was happening.[29] However, regardless of the reactions that took place on that particular night, the experiments that followed from the media reports of the murder provided a compelling insight into why being surrounded by strangers in a moment of need provides no guarantee of receiving help.

IN 59 SECONDS OR LESS

The message from the bystander effect is clear – the more people who are around when a person is apparently in need of assistance, the lower the likelihood of any one person actually helping.

So, if you are unfortunate enough to require assistance in the street, what can be done to increase your chances of obtaining help? According to persuasion expert Robert Cialdini, the answer is to pick out a friendly face in the crowd, clearly tell them what is happening, and what they need to do. It might be a question of saying you think you are having a heart attack and they need to call an ambulance, or that you are diabetic and need sugar as soon as possible. In short, anything that short-circuits the diffusion of responsibility underlying the problem, and helps transform a bystander from a faceless member of the crowd into a fully functioning human being.

An understanding of the diffusion of responsibility may also help you to persuade people in other situations. For example, when trying to get people to help you via email, do not copy your message to an entire group. When people see that an email has been sent to lots of others, the same diffusion effect can arise, with everyone thinking that it is everyone else's responsibility to respond.[30] To increase the chances of getting people to help, send the message to each person individually.

Every Penny Helps

Is it possible to increase the amount donated to good causes by creating the perfect charity box? To find out, I teamed up with Borders bookstores and conducted a week-long secret study across the UK. Participating stores were sent four charity boxes. The boxes were identical in shape and size, and all advertised the same charity – the National Literacy Trust. Each carried one of four messages that psychologists believed would be effective: 'Please give generously', 'Every penny helps', 'Every pound helps', and 'You can make a difference'. Managers were asked to place each box at one of four randomly selected tills and monitor the amount collected in each box.

Did our different messages make an impact on the cash donated to charity? Yes. At the end of the experiment, the four types of box contained very different amounts of money. 'Every penny helps' worked best, containing an impressive 62 per cent of all contributions, while 'Every pound helps' trailed into fourth place with just 17 per cent of the total take. Why should such a small change have such a big effect? According to work by psychologist Robert Cialdini from Arizona State University, many people are concerned that putting a very small amount of money into a box will make them look mean, and so end up giving nothing at all.[31] 'Every penny helps' legitimizes, and therefore encourages, the smallest of contributions. In contrast, 'Every pound helps' has the reverse effect – people who would have contributed less are suddenly concerned that their donation will appear paltry, and so end up giving nothing at all.

In another part of the experiment we varied the colour of the boxes, and discovered that red was by far the most effective, perhaps because it elicits a sense of urgency. Interestingly, large variations in donations emerged between regions. When the figures were corrected for differences in numbers of customers, London customers were the most generous, donating over twenty times more than people in the store yielding the lowest return, Birmingham.

Together, the results show that charity boxes can become up to 200 per cent more effective by being painted red, labelled 'Every penny counts' and placed anywhere except Birmingham.

On the Importance of Scratching Backs

According to the Bible, it is better to give than receive. This notion is also supported by research into the psychology of persuasion, albeit in ways that might not have been intended by the good book.

In December 1970, psychologists Phillip Kunz and Michael Woolcott conducted perhaps the simplest social-psychology experiment ever.[32] Over the course of a couple of weeks, they popped some Christmas cards in the post. However, Kunz and Woolcott did not send the cards to their friends, family or colleagues, but instead randomly selected the recipients' names and addresses from a local telephone directory. The two intrepid researchers were interested in the psychology of reciprocity, and wondered whether the act of receiving a greetings card from a total stranger would be enough to persuade people to send a card back. The answer was a resounding yes, with Kunz and Woolcott quickly receiving cards from the majority of those on their random list of complete strangers.

The principle of reciprocity has been explored by those interested in the science of persuasion. Perhaps not surprisingly, the work hasn't tended to focus on persuading strangers to send Christmas cards, but instead examines whether the same technique also influences more important aspects of people's behaviour.

In the 1970s, psychologist Dennis Regan invited people to

help out with an experiment exploring aesthetics and art. Willing volunteers were asked to come along to an exhibition one at a time, and were told that on arrival they would be met by another participant. Together they would then have to rate each of the paintings on show.[33] Now, if you take part in a social-psychology experiment and are asked to meet another participant, you can bet your bottom dollar that your new-found friend is actually working for the experimenter. True to form, this was the case in Regan's study. The stooge had been given very careful instructions. When accompanying the genuine participants round the gallery, he was suddenly to become thirsty and head towards the free drinks table. He would return refreshed, but half the time he would be empty-handed, while on the other half he would carry a bottle of cola that he had picked up for the genuine participant.

Now, if you take part in a psychology experiment, and your fellow 'participant' helps you in any way at all, you can bet the rest of your dollars that you are just moments away from being asked a favour. Again, Regan didn't break with tradition. After all the paintings had been rated, the stooge turned to the genuine participant, explained that he was selling raffle tickets, only had a handful left, that they were 25 cents each, and that if he sold the last few tickets he would win a $50 prize. He popped the question, 'Any would help, the more the better.' Even though the cola had not actually cost the stooge anything, it had a large impact on partici-pants' behaviour, with those in the 'I picked this bottle up for you' group buying twice as many raffle tickets as those who had not been given the cola.

Several other studies have also illustrated how apparently spontaneous favours can elicit a powerful need to reciprocate.

In one especially elegant and effective experiment, psychologist David Strohmetz and his colleagues arranged for waiters to hand customers their bills with or without sweets, and examined the impact on tipping.[34] In the control condition, diners were unlucky enough to receive their bills without any sweets at all. A second group was given a single sweet. Compared to the control group, this simple gesture of kindness resulted in a measly 3 per cent increase in tips. A third group of customers received two sweets each, and, compared to the control group, gave 14 per cent larger tips. Not bad. However, here comes the really clever bit. In the fourth and final condition, the waiters were asked to present the bill to customers along with one sweet each, then, just as they were turning away from the table, reach into their pocket and quickly hand everyone a second sweet. In terms of sweets per customer, everyone ended up with exactly the same number of sweets as those in the third group. But psychologically speaking, this was very, very different. The waiter had just carried out an unnecessary and nice favour, and, because of that, tipping increased by an impressive 23 per cent.

Why do these kinds of small favours produce such big results?

According to sociologists, there are only a handful of rules that are absolutely central to the well-being of any society. These rules have been found in almost every culture, and help ensure the smooth running of communal living. Perhaps the best known of these is 'don't kill other people simply for the fun of it', closely followed by 'try not to have sex with members of your close family or their pets'. Even though a minority of people struggle to adhere to them, it is obvious why both of these rules help gel society together. There are, however, several other rules that operate at a more unconscious level, but are nevertheless equally vital for group welfare. The notion of reciprocation is perhaps the most important of these.

In order to help keep society in one piece, people have to work together and help one another. However, some people will always give more than they take, so how do you know who to help and who to ignore? A key part of making this complex decision involves a surprisingly simple rule of thumb – you help those who have helped you. In other words, I scratch your back and you scratch mine. That way, we both have our backs scratched and all is well with the world. If every occasion of reciprocation were this instant and equal, then there would be very little room for the exploitation that fascinates those studying the psychology of persuasion. Thankfully, from a researcher's point of view, the real world of back-scratching is a little more complex. If I scratch your back, it says that I like and trust you and that I am a nice person deserving of your help when the time comes. These factors combine to create a potent force that often results in people giving significantly more than they receive. In the art-gallery experiment, the bottle of cola was free, but nevertheless persuaded people to put their hands in their pockets and buy raffle tickets. In the restaurant experiment, the extra sweet was worth a few pennies but caused people to leave a significantly larger tip.

We like people who help us, and we help people we like. However, in terms of favours, it is surprising how little it takes for us to like a person, and how much we give on the basis of so little. It seems that if you want to help yourself, you should help others first.

IN 59 SECONDS OR LESS

A large body of research has shown that carrying out a favour for someone often results in them giving significantly more in return. So does that mean that all favours will result in overly giving and helpful behaviour? Additional research has revealed that there are several subtle factors that influence when favours are most effective.

Favours have their strongest effect when they occur between people who don't know each other very well, and when they are small but thoughtful. When people go to a large amount of effort to help someone else, the recipient can often feel an uncomfortable pressure to reciprocate. In a sense, by giving too much at the beginning, one person has placed the other in a difficult position because the law of reciprocity states that they have to give even more in return. Motivation is important, as recipients can often experience a drop in self-esteem if they think they are being helped because they are believed not have the ability to be successful by themselves,[35] or if they attribute the favour to an ulterior motive.[36] So, for maximum persuasion, remember to save your favours for strangers, that it really is the thought that counts, and that it has to appear to come from the heart, not the head.

The degree of reciprocity may, to some extent, depend on cultural factors. In one study, by Michael Morris and his colleagues, people from different countries were asked about the factors that influenced whether they would assist a colleague who asked for help.[37] Americans were heavily influenced by the reciprocity rule

('Has this person helped me in the past?'), Germans were more concerned about whether their actions would be consistent with company rules, the Spanish were driven more by basic rules of friendship and liking and the Chinese were swayed by the status of the co-worker.

Finally, if you want to get maximum return for your investment, ask for the return favour quickly. Francis Flynn from Stanford University surveyed employees in the customer service department of a major US airline and found that favours have their greatest power immediately after they have been provided.[38] It seems that if you leave it too long, people either forget what happened or convince themselves that they didn't really need the help in the first place.

Never Lose Your Wallet Again

A few weeks ago I lost my wallet. I panicked, then calmed down, then carefully retraced my steps and failed to find the wallet, then panicked again, then calmed down again, and finally set about cancelling my credit cards. Unfortunately, I never saw my wallet again. However, on the upside, I now have a nice new wallet that is far superior to my old tatty one. I am very keen that my new wallet and I don't permanently part company, so I wondered what I could put into my new wallet to maximize the chances of it being returned if lost.

It turns out that I am not the first person to think about what might encourage someone to return a lost wallet. In the late 1960s and early 70s, researchers interested in the psychology of helping carried out several studies in which they secretly dropped wallets on busy streets and then monitored the return rates. Perhaps the most prolific of these wallet droppers was psychologist Harvey Hornstein from Columbia University.

Hornstein spent years systematically studying some of the factors that influence the return rates of wallets. In one study, for example, Hornstein examined whether people would be more likely to return a wallet if it elicited positive, rather than negative, feelings.[39] Like many of Hornstein's studies, this experiment involved creating a rather unusual scenario that gave the impression that a wallet had been lost not once, but twice. According to this scenario, the original owner had lost his wallet, someone had found it, attached a short note and placed it in an envelope addressed to the original owner. However, on the way to the postbox, the well-intentioned finder had inadvertently dropped the envelope on the street and thus lost the wallet a second time. Those unknowingly taking part in Hornstein's experiment came across an unsealed envelope containing a wallet with a note wrapped round it, and had to decide whether to post the envelope back to the original owner. Half the notes sounded very positive ('It has been a pleasure to help someone . . . and really has been no problem at all') while the others were far more negative ('I was quite annoyed at having to return it and hope you appreciate the effort I have gone through'). The difference in wording had a significant impact on people's behaviour, with almost 40 per cent of the wallets with positive notes being returned, versus just 12 per cent of those with negative notes.

Although Hornstein's findings are interesting, I somehow couldn't see myself permanently wrapping a happy-sounding note round my wallet. Unfortunately, the same applies to much of the academic work into wallet-dropping: although theoretically sound, it is not especially practical. Unperturbed, I canvassed friends for more useful suggestions about what I might put inside my wallet and received various suggestions, including photographs of a baby, a dog or something that suggested the owner was a thoroughly nice person. To find out which idea was the most effective I turned back time and conducted a Hornstein-esque study.

I bought 240 wallets and filled them with the same set of everyday items, including raffle tickets, discount vouchers and fake membership cards. Next, one of four photographs was added to four batches of forty wallets. The photographs depicted either a smiling baby, a cute puppy, a happy family or a contented elderly couple. Another forty wallets contained a card suggesting that the owner had recently made a contribution to charity, while the final batch of forty acted as a control and contained no additional item. The extra item was inserted behind a clear plastic window in each wallet, making it clearly visible when the wallet was opened. All the wallets were then randomly ordered, and over a period of a couple of weeks were secretly dropped on the streets of Edinburgh in areas of high footfall, but well away from post-boxes, litterbins, vomit and dog faeces.

Within a week 52 per cent of the wallets were returned and a clear pattern emerged. Just 6 per cent of the wallets in the control group, and 8 per cent of those containing the charity card, made their way back. The results from the wallets containing a photograph of the elderly couple, cute puppy or happy-looking family were slightly more impressive, with return rates of 11 per cent, 19 per cent and 21 per cent respectively. However, the winning wallets were those with the photograph of the smiling baby, taking pole position with an impressive 35 per cent return rate.

Why should the photograph of the baby have performed so well? The answer appears to lie deep within our evolutionary past. Brain-scanning scientists at the University of Oxford recently examined what was going on in people's heads when they were shown photographs of either baby or adult faces.[40] Even though all the photographs were matched for attractiveness, activity in the section of the brain directly behind the eyes (officially referred to as the 'medial orbitofrontal cortex') kicked in within a seventh of a second after seeing the baby's, but not adult's, face. The response happened too fast to be consciously controlled, and the part of the brain involved is associated with people receiving a nice reward, such as a big bar of chocolate or a lottery win. Many scientists think that this 'baby-awww' linkage has evolved over thousands of years and promotes the survival of future generations by making people feel good about, and therefore help, vulnerable and defenceless infants. Other research suggests this caring attitude will not just apply to assisting babies, but also increase the likelihood of people helping anyone in need. Seen in this way, participants who opened the wallets containing the photograph of the baby couldn't prevent their brains automatically responding to the image of big eyes, broad forehead and button nose. Within a fraction of a second a deep-seated evolutionary mechanism had caused them rapidly to get in touch with their inner parent, become happier and more caring, and thus increase the likelihood of them returning the wallet.

Whatever the explanation, the practical message is clear: if you want to up the chances of your wallet being returned if lost, obtain a photograph of the cutest, happiest baby you can find, and make sure it is prominently displayed in your wallet.

3. MOTIVATION

The dark side of visualization, how to achieve absolutely
anything by creating the perfect plan, overcoming
procrastination and employing doublethink.

Throughout the past forty years, a large number of books, audio products and training courses have promised to help people look beyond the perils of instant gratification and achieve their long-term goals. From visualization to self-affirmation, from being focused to going with the flow, you pays your money and you takes your choice. There is just one small problem: several scientific studies suggest that many of these exercises don't work. Take, for example, the type of simple visualization exercise I described at the start of this book. As you may remember, you were asked to close your eyes and imagine the new you: to think how great you would feel in those close-fitting jeans, or sitting in a huge office at the top of the corporate ladder, or sipping a cocktail with the warm Caribbean sand between your toes. This type of exercise has been promoted by the self-help industry for years, with claims that it can help people lose weight, stop smoking, find their perfect partner and enjoy increased career success. Unfortunately, a large body of research now suggests that although it might make you feel good, the technique is, at best, ineffective.

In one study, conducted by Lien Pham and Shelley Taylor at the University of California, a group of students were asked to spend a few moments each day visualizing them-selves getting a high grade in an important midterm exam that would take place in a few days' time.[1] They were asked to form a clear image in their mind's eye, and imagine how great it would feel. The study also involved a control group of students who went about their business as usual and were asked not to visualize doing especially well in the exams. The experimenters asked the students in both groups to make a note of the number of hours they studied each day, and monitored their final grades. Even though the daydreaming exercise only lasted a few minutes, it had a significant impact on the students' behaviour, causing them to study less, and obtain lower marks in the exam. The exercise may have made them feel better about themselves, but it did not help them achieve their goals.

In another experiment, Gabriele Oettingen and Thomas Wadden from the University of Pennsylvania followed a group of obese women taking part in a weight-reduction programme.[2] During the work, the women were asked to imagine how they might behave in various food-related scenarios, such as going round to a friend's house and being tempted with tasty pizza. Each of their responses were categorized from highly positive (with, for example, someone stating: 'I would be a good person, and keep well away from the cakes and ice cream') through to highly negative ('I would be straight in there, consuming both my own and other people's portions'). After tracking the women for a year, the results revealed that those with more positive fantasies had lost, on average, 12 kilos less than those with negative fantasies.

Oettingen's work has also shown that the same effects happen in many different situations. In yet another study, she worked with a group of students who admitted to having a serious but secret crush on a classmate, asking them to imagine what would happen in various scenarios, such as arriving early for class, sitting down, then seeing the door open and the apple of their eye enter. Once again, the degree of fantasizing was rated, this time varying between those who seemed to live in a world that would make even the most ardent Mills & Boon reader blush ('Our eyes meet, and we both know that this is the type of love that only happens once in a lifetime'), through to more negative scenarios ('We are both free and single. He turns to me, smiles, and asks how I am. For some reason that I still do not fully understand, I explain that I already have a boyfriend'). Five months later, the results revealed that those with positive fantasies were less likely than the others to have told the desirable classmate about their crush or made any other form of progress towards having a relationship with them.[3]

Exactly the same effect applies to career success. Oettingen asked her final-year students to note down how often they fantasized about getting their dream job after leaving university. A two-year follow-up revealed that the students who had reported frequently fantasizing about success had made fewer job applications, received a lower number of job offers and had significantly smaller salaries than their classmates.

Why should imagining yourself achieving your goals be so bad for you? Researchers have speculated that those who fantasize about how wonderful life could be are ill prepared for the setbacks that frequently occur along the rocky road to success, or maybe they enjoy indulging in escapism and so become reluctant to put in the effort required to achieve their goal. Either way, the message from the research is clear – fantasizing about your perfect world may make you feel better but is unlikely to help transform your dreams into reality.

Fortunately, the results from other research into motivation are not all doom and gloom. A large amount of work has revealed that some techniques do help create permanent and positive changes to people's lives. From weight loss to quitting smoking, changing careers to finding your perfect partner, there are quick and painless techniques that can provide real help. It is all about having the perfect plan, knowing how to beat procrastination and a rather strange form of doublethink.

Creating the Perfect Plan

Think back to when you have attempted to achieve an important goal or ambition. Perhaps losing some weight, getting a new job, revising for an exam or preparing for a key interview. What sorts of techniques did you use? Take a few moments to read each of the following statements, and then tick the 'yes' or 'no' box to indicate which technique(s) you tend to use. Don't spend too long thinking about each statement, and answer as honestly as possible.

		Yes	No
	When attempting to change an important aspect of my life, I tend to:		
1	make a step-by-step plan.	☐	☐
2	motivate myself by focusing on someone I admire for achieving so much (e.g. a celebrity role model or great leader).	☐	☐
3	tell other people about my goals.	☐	☐
4	think about the bad things that will happen if I don't achieve my goal.	☐	☐
5	think about the good things that will happen if I achieve my goal.	☐	☐
6	try to suppress unhelpful thoughts (e.g. not thinking about eating unhealthy food or smoking).	☐	☐
7	reward myself for making progress towards my goal.	☐	☐
8	rely on willpower.	☐	☐

		Yes	No
9	record my progress (e.g. in a journal or on a chart).	❑	❑
10	fantasize about how great my life will be when I achieve my goal.	❑	❑

Now you need to create two scores. Create Score A by awarding yourself 1 point each time you answered 'yes' to questions 1, 3, 5, 7 and 9. Create Score B by giving yourself 1 point each time you answered 'no' to questions 2, 4, 6, 8 and 10. Disregard all other answers. Finally, add together Scores A and B to obtain a number between 0 and 10.

•

A few years ago I conducted two large-scale scientific studies into the psychology of motivation. The project involved tracking more than 5,000 participants from around the world who were attempting to achieve a wide range of aims and ambitions, including losing weight, gaining new qualifications, starting a new relationship, quitting smoking, embarking on a new career and being more environmentally friendly. One group was followed for six months, the other for one year. Towards the start of the project, the vast majority of participants were confident of doing well. At the end of their allotted time period, everyone was asked to describe the techniques they had used to try to achieve their goals, and to report their level of success. By the end, only about 10 per cent of people had successfully achieved their aims and ambitions.

The questionnaire above contains the ten techniques that participants used most frequently. Some sound like good common sense, others frequently appear in self-help books and training courses. However, although the techniques may appear credible, according to our data, half will significantly increase your chances of being successful, while the other half are ineffective. The question is: which are which?

In our experiment, participants who endorsed the even-numbered items in the questionnaire were unlikely to achieve their goals. So, for example, those who adopted a celebrity role model, perhaps putting a picture of Elle Macpherson or Richard Branson on their fridge door, did not tend to drop that all-important clothing size or achieve their business ambitions. Similarly, those relying on will power, using thought suppression to erase images of cream cakes and chocolate sundaes from their mind, focusing on the bad things that would happen if they didn't achieve their goals or spending their time daydreaming, were also wasting their time. All these techniques constitute yet more striking examples of the types of motivational myths that prevent people taking control of their lives.

A different story emerged when we examined the data from the people using the techniques that have an odd number in the questionnaire. Each of these five tools significantly increased the likelihood of people successfully achieving their aims. Let's look at each in turn.

Firstly, the successful participants in our study had a plan. Author Zig Ziglar once famously remarked that people tend not to wander around and then suddenly find themselves at the top of Mount Everest. Likewise, those moving aimlessly through life are unlikely to end up suddenly starting a new business or losing a significant amount of weight. Successful participants broke their overall goal into a series of sub-goals, and thereby created a step-by-step process that helped remove the fear and hesitation often associated with trying to achieve a major life change. These plans were especially powerful when the sub-goals were concrete, measurable and time-based. Whereas successful and unsuccessful participants might have stated that their aim was to find a new job, it was the successful people who quickly went on to describe how they intended to rewrite their CV in week one, and then apply for one new job every two weeks for the next six months. Similarly, although many people said they aimed to enjoy life more, it was the successful ones who explained how they intended to spend two evenings each week with friends and visit one new country each year.

Secondly, successful participants were far more likely than others to tell their friends, family and colleagues about their goals. It seems that although keeping your aims to yourself helps ease the fear of failure, it also makes it too easy to avoid changing your life and drift back into old habits and routines. This is in keeping with several key findings from psychology. People are more likely to stick to their views and promises if they have gone public. In one classic study, students were asked to estimate the length of some lines that had been drawn on a pad, and either make a public commitment to their judgements (by writing them on a slip of paper, signing the paper and handing it to the experimenter), or keep the estimates to themselves.[4] When the participants were informed that their estimates might be wrong, those who had made a public commitment were far more likely to stand by their opinion than those who had not told anyone. Other work suggests that the greater the public declaration, the more motivated people are to achieve their goals.[5] Telling others about your aims helps you achieve them, in part, because friends and family often provide much-needed support when the going gets tough. In fact, some research suggests that having friends at your side makes life seem easier. In a series of studies carried out by Simone Schnall from the University of Plymouth, people were taken to the bottom of a hill and asked to estimate how steep it was and therefore how difficult it would be to climb.[6] When accompanied by a friend, their estimates were around 15 per cent lower than when they were on their own, and even just thinking about a friend when looking at the hill made it seem far more surmountable.

Thirdly, those who ended up making and maintaining permanent changes to their lives frequently tended to remind themselves of the benefits associated with achieving their goals. It wasn't a case of them imagining their perfect selves, but rather having an objective checklist of how life would be better once they obtained their aim. In contrast, unsuccessful participants tended to focus on how failure to change would result in having to endure the negative aspects of their current situation. For example, when asked to list the benefits of getting a new job, successful participants might reflect on finding more fulfilling and well-paid employment, whereas their unsuccessful counterparts might focus on a failure leaving them trapped and unhappy. When looking at weight loss, a successful participant might remark upon how good they would look and feel when they drop a dress size, whereas an unsuccessful participant might talk about how not losing weight would mean continued unhappiness about their appearance. While the former technique encourages participants to look forward to a more positive future, the latter demotivates by fixing on unsatisfactory events and experiences.

Fourth, there was the issue of reward. As part of their planning, successful participants ensured that each of their sub-goals had a reward attached to it. Often it was something small, which never conflicted with the goal itself (no going on a binge of chocolate bars to celebrate a week of healthy eating) but nevertheless gave them something to look forward to and provided a sense of achievement.

Finally, successful participants also tended to make their plans, progress, benefits and rewards as concrete as possible by expressing them in writing. Many people kept a hand-written journal, some used a computer, a few even covered their fridge or noticeboard with graphs or pictures. Either way, the act of writing, typing or drawing significantly boosted their chances of success.

IN 59 SECONDS OR LESS

To achieve your aims and ambitions, there are four key techniques that will help you succeed: having the right kind of plan; telling your friends and family; focusing on the benefits; and rewarding yourself each step of the way. To help incorporate these techniques into your life, I have created a unique motivational journal that can be used when attempting any form of change.

1 What Is Your Overall Goal?

My overall goal is to . . .

2 Create a Step-by-Step Plan

Break your overall goal into a maximum of 5 smaller steps. Each step should be associated with a goal that is concrete, measurable, realistic and time-based. Think about how you will achieve each step and the reward that you will give yourself when you do. The rewards can be anything you like, perhaps sweets, new shoes or clothes, the latest high-tech gadget, a book, dinner out or a massage.

MOTIVATION

Step 1
My first sub-goal is to . . .
I believe I can achieve this goal because . . .
To achieve this sub-goal, I will . . .
This will be achieved by the following date . . .
My reward for achieving this will be . . .

Step 2
My second sub-goal is to . . .
I believe I can achieve this goal because . . .
To achieve this sub-goal, I will . . .
This will be achieved by the following date . . .
My reward for achieving this will be . . .

Step 3
My third sub-goal is to . . .
I believe I can achieve this goal because . . .
To achieve this sub-goal, I will . . .
This will be achieved by the following date . . .
My reward for achieving this will be . . .

Step 4
My fourth sub-goal is to . . .
I believe I can achieve this goal because . . .
To achieve this sub-goal, I will . . .
This will be achieved by the following date . . .
My reward for achieving this will be . . .

Step 5
My fifth sub-goal is to . . .
I believe I can achieve this goal because . . .

To achieve this sub-goal, I will . . .
This will be achieved by the following date . . .
My reward for achieving this will be . . .

3 What Are the Benefits of Achieving Your Overall Goal?

List three important benefits, focusing on how much better life will be for you and those around you. Focus on the benefits associated with your desired future, rather than escaping the negative aspects of your current situation.

Benefit 1:

Benefit 2:

Benefit 3:
----

4 Going Public

Who are you going to tell about your goal and sub-goals? Perhaps your friends, family or colleagues? Could you describe it on a blog or display it somewhere prominent in your house or at the office?

I will go public by:

Procrastination and the Zeigarnik Effect

Research suggests that 24 per cent of people identify themselves as chronic procrastinators. Presumably this figure underestimates the scale of the problem, given that it can only be based on people who completed the questionnaires on time. Regardless of the actual figure, it is obvious that procrastination can be a major problem, causing people to fail to pay bills on time, not complete projects within deadlines and make inadequate preparations for important exams and interviews. Procrastination is a surprisingly complex phenomenon, and can stem from a variety of causes, including the fear of failure, perfectionism, low levels of self-control, a tendency to see projects as a whole rather than breaking them into smaller parts, being prone to boredom, feeling that life is too short to worry about seemingly unimportant tasks and an inability to accurately estimate how long it takes to do things.

However, the problem can be overcome using a technique first uncovered during an informal observation of waiters. According to research lore, in the 1920s a young Russian psychology graduate named Bluma Zeigarnik found herself in a Viennese café taking tea with her supervisor. Being students of human nature, they were watching how the waiters and customers behaved, and happened to notice a curious phenomenon. When a customer asked for the bill, the waiters could easily remember the food that had been ordered. However, if the customer paid the bill, but then queried it a few moments later, the waiters struggled to remember anything about the order. It seemed that the act of paying for the meal brought a sense of closure in the waiter's mind and erased the order from their memories.

Zeigarnik was curious, and returned to the laboratory to test an idea. She asked people to carry out a number of simple tasks (such as stacking up counters or placing toys in a box), but for some tasks she stopped the participants before they had finished. At the end of the experiment, the participants were told to describe all the tasks. As with her observations of waiters, Zeigarnik found that the unfinished tasks stuck in people's minds and so were far easier to remember.[7] According to Zeigarnik, starting any activity causes your mind to experience a kind of psychic anxiety. Once the activity is done and dusted, your mind breathes an unconscious sigh of relief, and all is forgotten. However, if you are somehow prevented from completing the activity, your anxious mind quietly nags away until you have finished what you started.

What has this got to do with procrastination? Procrastinators frequently put off starting certain activities because they are overwhelmed by the size of the job in front of them. However, if they can be persuaded, or can persuade themselves, to work on the activity for 'just a few minutes', they often feel an urge to see it through to completion. Research shows that the 'just a few minutes' rule is a highly effective way of beating procrastination, and could help people finish the most arduous of tasks.[8] It is also a perfect application of Zeigarnik's work – those few minutes of initial activity create an anxious brain that refuses to rest until the job is finished.

Zeigarnik's work on the psychology of unfinished activity is just one example of her fascinating research. On another occasion she attempted to restore movement to patients paralysed by hysteria by having a stooge dress in a military uniform, suddenly enter the room and order the patient to stand. Unfortunately, the results of this study have been lost in the mists of time, although one recent Russian biographer has noted that it is no longer possible to repeat the studies as it is impossible to find anyone in Russia who holds the required reverent attitude toward either military or political figures.[9]

Doublethink

At the start of this section I described how research conducted by Gabriele Oettingen from the University of Pennsylvania showed the negative effects of visualizing yourself having achieved an important goal. Other work, again conducted by Oettingen, suggests that it doesn't take much to turn such fantasies into a tool for good. In fact, all it takes is a little bit of Orwellian doublethink.

In *Nineteen Eighty-Four*, George Orwell introduced the concept of doublethink, describing it as the simultaneous holding of two opposing beliefs in one's mind and yet accepting both. In Orwell's novel, this technique was used by a totalitarian government to continuously rewrite history, and so control the populace. However, recent research has shown that the same type of idea can also be used in a more productive way, helping people to achieve their goals and ambitions. Oettingen speculated that one of the most effective states of mind involves people being optimistic about achieving their goals but also realistic about some of the problems they may encounter. To investigate, she developed an unusual procedure that encouraged people to hold both types of thought in their mind, and she then carried out a series of studies to assess its effectiveness.

The procedure is simple. People are asked to think about something they want to achieve, such as losing weight, learning a new skill or changing their drinking habits. Next, they are told to spend a few moments fantasizing about obtaining the goal, and note the top two benefits that would flow from such an achievement. After this, they are asked to spend another few moments reflecting on the type of barriers and problems they are likely to encounter if they attempt to fulfil their ambition and, again, make a note of the top two issues. Now comes the doublethink. People are asked to reflect on their first benefit, elaborating on how it would make their life more enjoyable. Immediately afterwards, they are asked to think about the biggest hurdle to such success, focusing on what they would do if they encountered the difficulty. Then they repeat the same process for the second most positive aspect of achieving their aim and second greatest potential problem.

In several experiments, Oettingen has discovered that this procedure provides the best of both worlds. When people focused on an existing relationship they wanted to improve, she discovered those engaging in the doublethink were more successful than those who just fantasized or focused on the negatives.[10] Returning to the theme of romance, she applied the doublethink procedure to students harbouring a secret crush. Those who employed the fantasy–reality technique were more successful than those who dreamed about their perfect date or dwelt on the difficulties of revealing their true feelings.[11] Additional work has shown that doublethink is also effective in the workplace, encouraging employees to become involved in training courses, delegate more effectively and improve their time-management skills.[12]

The research shows that it *is* possible to use visualization to motivate. The solution is a question of balance by interleaving the benefits of achievement with a realistic assessment of the problems that could be encountered. In short, doublethink.

IN 59 SECONDS OR LESS

The following exercise is based on the doublethink technique, and can be used to motivate you to achieve your goals and persevere in the face of difficulties.

1. What is Your Goal?

. . . .

2. Potential Benefits and Setbacks

a Write down one word that reflects an important way in which your life would be better if you achieved your goal.

. . . .

b Write down one word that reflects a significant barrier standing in the way of you achieving your goal.

. . . .

c Write down one word that reflects another important way in which your life would be better if you achieved your goal.

. . . .

d Write down one word that reflects another significant barrier that stands in the way of you achieving your goal.

. . . .

3. Elaboration

On a separate document elaborate on your answers to the above.

- Elaborate your answer to question **a**
  Imagine all the benefits that would flow from this achievement.

- Elaborate your answer to question **b**
  Imagine how the obstacle hinders achievement and the steps you would take to deal with it.

- Elaborate your answer to question **c**
  Imagine all of the benefits that would flow from this achievement.

- Elaborate your answer to question **d**
  Imagine how the obstacle hinders achievement and the steps you would take to deal with it.

Dieting and Drinking

Surveys show that most people attempt to diet or cut down on their drinking at some point in their lives. However, the same surveys also suggest that the vast majority fail, often blaming a lack of motivation for their downfall. Part of the problem is that people do not tend to follow their gut instincts when starting and stopping, and are instead unknowingly influenced by a wide range of factors. Brian Wansink from Cornell University has devoted his academic career to understanding some of the more unusual factors at work, and his results illustrate just how much irrationality surrounds the dinner table.

In one study, Wansink and his colleagues speculated that people's decisions about whether to carry on eating might be unconsciously determined by a surprisingly simple question: 'Have I finished my food?'[13] Wansink therefore created a special bottom to a soup bowl by which, via a concealed tube, he could secretly and continuously refill the bowl. Groups of participants sat round a table, chatting and tasting soup for 20 minutes, and then gave their opinion about the soup to the experimenters. Without being aware of the fact, half of them were drinking their soup from a 'bottomless bowl' that was being continuously refilled, while the others had normal bowls.

Remarkably, those with the bottomless bowls consumed more than 75 per cent more soup than those with a normal bowl. In addition, those who consumed more weren't aware of how much they had taken, and said that they were no less hungry than those who had consumed a normal portion.

However, there is some consolation in that by understanding a few of the hidden factors that influence consumption, we can create quick but effective techniques for cutting the extent of our eating and drinking.

IN 59 SECONDS OR LESS

The Power of Slow. Some research suggests that eating more slowly helps people eat less, perhaps because it fools our brains into thinking that we've eaten more, and allows extra time for the body to digest food.[14] In an additional twist on this work, Corby Martin and his colleagues at the Pennington BioMedical Research Centre had overweight participants eat a lunchtime meal at three different speeds: their normal rate; half their normal rate; their normal rate to begin with, followed by half their normal rate.[15] Eating at the slower rate resulted in men, but not women, eating less. However, starting the meal at a normal rate of eating then dropping to the slower rate, caused both men and women to experience a large reduction in their appetite. The normal–slow combination was even more effective than eating slowly all the way through the meal, suggesting that the secret to feeling satisfied is to start at your normal speed, but then savour each and every mouthful.

Make Mine a Tall, Thin One. Brian Wansink and Koert van Ittersum from Cornell University asked students to pour a single shot of whiskey from a full bottle into a glass.[16] Those given a short, wide glass poured, on average, 30 per cent larger shots than those given a taller, narrower glass. It seems that people used the depth of the liquid as an indicator of the amount of liquid in the glass, not noticing that one glass was far wider than the other. The researchers then repeated the experiment with experienced bartenders, and discovered that they poured, on average, 20 per cent larger shots into the short, wide glass. If you want to reduce your drinking, stay away from short, wide glasses, and stick to tall, narrow ones.

Out of Sight, Out of Mind. Research shows that just placing food or drink out of sight or moving it a few metres away can have a big effect on consumption. In a series of studies, experimenters strategically placed jars of chocolates around an office and carefully counted how many were consumed.[17] In one condition they compared placing the jars on people's desks with moving them just two metres away. In another, they placed the chocolates in either transparent or opaque jars. Putting the chocolates on people's desks resulted in staff consuming an average of six more chocolates each day, with the chocolates in transparent jars eaten 46 per cent more quickly than those in opaque jars. A similar principle applies to food around the house. In another study (described in the snappily entitled paper 'When are Stockpiled Products Consumed Faster? A Convenience-Salience Frame-work of Post-Purchase Consumption Incidence and Quantity'), researchers stockpiled people's homes with either large or moderate quantities of ready-to-eat meals, and discovered that the food was eaten at twice the rate in more heavily stockpiled homes.[18] To cut intake, make sure that tempting foods are out of sight, and in a place that is difficult to access, such as a top cupboard or basement.

Focus, Focus, Focus. People eat significantly more when they are distracted at mealtimes and therefore not paying attention to their food. In one experiment, the amount of attention that cinema goers paid to a film was related to how much popcorn they consumed. Those who were more absorbed by the movie ate significantly larger amounts.[19] In another experiment, people who listened to a detective story during their lunch break ate 15 per cent more food than those who sat in silence.[20] Distractions while eating, such as watching television, reading a magazine or even chatting with others encourage people to consume more.

Beware of Large Crockery. Is the amount you eat influenced by the size of bowls and spoons? A few years ago, Brian Wansink invited a group of friends to a party, and secretly conducted an experiment.[21] Each guest was randomly handed either a 17- or 34-ounce bowl and a 2- or 3-ounce spoon. The guests then helped themselves to ice cream. However, seconds before they took their first mouthful, researchers snatched away the bowls and weighed them. The results revealed that those given the large spoons and large bowls had, on average, taken 14 per cent and 31 per cent more ice cream than their modestly equipped companions. Andrew Geier and his colleagues from the University of Pennsylvania have demonstrated that the effect is not confined to ice creams and parties.[22] In their study, a bowl of M&M sweets was left in the hallway of an apartment building, along with a spoon and a sign saying: 'Eat your fill: please use the spoon to serve yourself'. On some days the experimenters placed a tablespoon-sized scoop next to the bowl; on others they left a larger scoop. The findings revealed that using the larger spoon caused people to take almost twice as many M&Ms from the bowl. Try cutting down on your eating by replacing your crockery and cutlery.

Keep a Food Diary. Research conducted by the Kaiser Permanente's Center for Health Research suggests that making a note of how much you eat can help you lose weight.[23] During the study, participants who kept daily food records lost twice as much weight as those who kept none. You don't need to turn into Samuel Pepys to gain the benefits; just scribbling down what you eat on a Post-It note or sending yourself an email has the same effect. According to the theory, becoming aware of what you are eating on a daily basis will help you break old habits and consume less.

Regret and Reflection. Not happy with your body, but finding it difficult to motivate yourself to go to the gym? Try harnessing the power of regret and avoiding reflection. Research conducted by Charles Abraham and Paschal Sheeran has shown that just a few moments thinking about how much you will regret *not* going to the gym will help motivate you to climb off the couch and onto an exercise bike.[24] And once you get there, try avoiding those imposing floor-to-ceiling mirrors. Other work, by Kathleen Martin Ginis and her colleagues, from McMaster University, involved people pedalling on an exercise cycle either in front of a mirror or a bare wall. The results revealed that those who constantly saw themselves in the mirror ended up feeling significantly less revitalized and more exhausted than those in front of the wall. Researchers believe that the mirrors may encourage people to focus on their less than perfect bodies, and consequently do more harm than good.[25]

Use More Energy. Think about how you could burn more calories by making small changes to your everyday routines. It might be something as simple as using wax polish rather than a spray during housework (rubbing is far more energy-consuming than spraying), ensuring you have to use the stairs more (don't take the lift at work, or alternate floors when doing housework), or listening to upbeat music to encourage vigorous movement when you are walking or mowing the lawn.

Mirror, Mirror on the Kitchen Wall. Work conducted by Stacey Sentyrz and Brad Bushman from Iowa State University, suggests that placing a mirror in your kitchen may help you shed pounds.[26] In several studies, participants were given the opportunity to eat healthy or unhealthy food. In one study, in a supermarket, almost 1,000 shoppers were presented with the option of trying new types of full-fat or no-fat margarine. Half the time a mirror was strategically placed behind the spreads to ensure the participants could see their own reflection; the other half it was removed. The presence of the mirror resulted in a remarkable 32 per cent reduction in trying the full-fat margarine. The researchers argue that seeing your own reflection makes you more aware of your body.

The Pitfalls of Diet Packs. Supermarket aisles are frequently full of small-portion 'diet packs' of sweets and crisps that will help you control your craving and so eat less. But will buying such packs really help you cut down consumption? To find out, researchers at Tilburg University in the Netherlands gave participants either two bags of crisps or nine diet packs, and asked them to watch TV.[27] Before tucking into their treats and TV, participants were weighed in front of a mirror to create a 'dieting mindset'. The results revealed that participants given the diet bags ate twice as many crisps as those given the large bags. The researchers speculated that the participants given the diet bags felt they didn't need to exercise so much self-control and thus ended up eating more.

The Benefits of Writing Your Own Eulogy

In Charles Dickens' *A Christmas Carol*, Ebenezer Scrooge is visited by three ghostly figures. The first two, the ghosts of Christmas Past and Christmas Present, show how Scrooge's selfishness have made his life lonely and miserable. It is only when the ghost of Christmas Future appears and leads him to his ill-kept and forgotten grave that Scrooge finally changes his character and becomes a far more giving and compassionate person. Dickens looked at the effect of taking a long-term view, and the contemplation of life after death, but a large number of psychologists have done the same, and their findings suggest that Scrooge's fictional transformation can also occur in real life.

In one study, people were stopped in the street and asked to use a ten-point scale to rate how they felt about their favourite charities ('How beneficial is this charity to society?', 'How much do you think society needs this charity?' and 'How desirable is this charity to you personally?').[28] Some of the people were stopped as they walked past a funeral home, while others were stopped a few blocks later in front of a nondescript building. When interviewing people in front of the funeral home, researchers positioned themselves in such a way to ensure participants were forced to face a large sign reading 'Howe's Mortuary'. The results revealed a Scrooge-like effect, with those facing up to their own death feeling far more benevolent than those standing in front of the nondescript building.

Christopher Peterson from the University of Michigan believes encouraging people to consider how they would like to be remembered after their death has various motivational benefits, including helping them to identify their long-term goals, and assess the degree to which they are progressing towards making those goals a reality.[29] So, with no further ado, let's evoke your own ghost of Christmas future.

Imagine a close friend standing up at your funeral and presenting your eulogy. Write the script for your friend. What would you really like them to say about you? Feel free to avoid any sense of modesty, but keep it realistic. How would you want them to describe your personality, achievements, personal strengths, family life, professional success and behaviour towards others? When you have finished, take a long and honest look at the eulogy for your ideal self. Does your present lifestyle and behaviour justify the comments, or is there work to be done?

4. CREATIVITY

Exploding the myth of brainstorming,
how to get in touch with your inner Leonardo by
merely glancing at modern art, lying down,
and putting a plant on your desk.

In the early 1940s, advertising executive Alex Osborn argued that it was possible to enhance creativity by putting a group of people in a room and having them follow a set of simple rules. For example, coming up with as many thoughts as possible, encouraging wild and exaggerated ideas, and not criticizing or evaluating anyone's comments. When selling his approach to businesses, Osborn claimed that 'the average person thinks up twice as many ideas when working with a group than when working alone', and, perhaps not surprisingly, his novel approach quickly conquered the world.[1] Over the years, organizations around the globe have encouraged their employees to tackle key problems using this approach.

Researchers have gone to a great deal of trouble to test the efficacy of group brainstorming. In a typical experiment, participants arrive in a group. Half of them are randomly chosen to be in the 'work as a group' condition and are placed in one room. They are given standard brainstorming rules and have to come up with ideas to help solve a specific problem (perhaps design a new ad campaign, or find ways of easing traffic congestion). The other half of the participants are asked to sit alone in separate rooms, are given exactly the same instructions and tasks and asked to generate ideas on their own. Researchers then tally the quantity of ideas produced under the different conditions, and then experts rate their quality. So do such studies show that group brainstorming is more effective than individuals working alone? Many scientists are far from convinced. Brian Mullen from the University of Kent at Canterbury and his colleagues analysed twenty studies that tested the efficacy of group brainstorming in this way, and were amazed to discover that in the vast majority of the experiments, the participants working on their own produced a higher quantity and quality of ideas than those working in groups.[2]

Other research suggests that group brainstorming may fail, in part, because of a phenomenon known as 'social loafing'. In the late 1880s, a French agricultural engineer named Max Ringelmann became obsessed with trying to make workers as efficient as possible.[3] After carrying out hundreds of experiments, he inadvertently stumbled across an unexpected effect that would inspire a century of psychological research. One of Ringelmann's studies involved asking people to pull on a rope and lift increasingly heavy weights. Perhaps not unreasonably, Ringelmann expected people in groups to work harder than those on their own. But the results revealed the opposite pattern. When working alone, individuals lifted around 85 kilos, but managed only 65 kilos when placed in a group. Additional work revealed that the phenomenon, like the bystander effect described in the Persuasion chapter on p. 64, is largely due to a diffusion of responsibility.[4] When people work on their own, their success or failure is entirely due to their own abilities and hard work. If they do well, the glory is theirs. If they fail, they carry the can. However, add other people to the situation and suddenly everyone stops trying so hard, safe in the knowledge that, though they will not receive personal praise if the group does well, they can always blame others if it performs badly.

Research shows that this phenomenon occurs in many different situations. Ask people to make as much noise as possible, and they make more on their own than in a group. Ask them to add up rows of numbers and the more people involved, the lower the work rate. Ask them to come up with ideas and people are more creative away from the crowd. It is a universal phenomenon, emerging in work conducted across the world, including America, India, Thailand and Japan.

In short, a large body of research now suggests that for more than seventy years, people using group brainstorming may have inadvertently been stifling, not stimulating, their creative juices. When working together they aren't as motivated to put in the time and energy needed to generate great ideas, and end up spending more time thinking inside the box.

So, when it comes to creativity, is it simply a case of keeping away from the pack? No. In fact, other work shows that if you really want to get in touch with your inner Leonardo da Vinci, there are several quick and surprisingly powerful techniques available. All it takes is a glance at the right type of modern art, lying down on the job, doing nothing or putting a plant on your desk.

Testing Creativity

Psychologists have developed lots of weird and wonderful ways of testing for creativity. People can be presented with a brick and given a few minutes to create as many uses for it as possible. They could be given a pencil and a squared sheet of paper and asked to make each square into a different object (e.g. a television, fish tank, book etc.). In both cases, the number of responses would be counted and judged for originality in comparison to the responses from all those taking part. Researchers also often use various types of visual and verbal lateral-thinking problems. Try the following questions to test your creativity.

1) Can you add a single line to the following equation to make it correct? (There is just one rule – you are not allowed to place the line over the equals sign like this: ≠, thus converting it into a 'not equals' sign.)

$$I0 \ I0 \ II = I0.50$$

2) Joanna and Jackie were born on the same day of the same month of the same year. They have the same mother and father, yet they are not twins. How is that possible?

3) A man has married twenty different women in the same town. All are still alive and he never divorced any of them. Polygamy is unlawful, yet the man has not broken the law. How is this possible?

4   A man walks into an antique shop and offers to
    sell a beautiful bronze coin. One side of the coin
    contains a wonderful image of a Roman emperor's
    head, while the other shows the date as 500 BC.
    The antique dealer instantly knows that the coin
    does not date back to 500 BC. Why?

Answers

1) This is all about time. By adding a short line over the
    second 'I', you convert the number 'I0' into the word
    'TO' and now the equation reads ten to eleven, which
    is the same as ten fifty.

    I0 TO II = I0.50

2) Joanna and Jackie are part of a set of triplets.

3) The man is a minister and so presided over the wedding
    ceremonies.

4) The year 500 BC predates the birth of Christ, and thus
    a coin from that time would not be inscribed with an
    abbreviation for before Christ.

Listening to the Quiet Guy

Surrealist Salvador Dalí would sometimes generate ideas for his paintings by using a rather unusual technique. He would lie on a couch and put a glass on the floor, then carefully place one end of a spoon on the edge of the glass and lightly hold the other end in his hand. As he drifted off to sleep, Dalí would naturally relax his hand and release the spoon. The sound of the spoon falling into the glass would wake him up, and he would immediately sketch the bizarre images that had just started to drift through his half-asleep semi-conscious mind. In view of the impractical nature of so many of his ideas (think lobster telephone), this technique clearly might not be for everyone, but that is not to say that your unconscious mind is not a powerhouse of creative thought.

In fact, several studies suggest that when it comes to innovative ways of looking at the world, there may be lots more going on in your unconscious mind than you realize. In a simple experimental demonstration of this, Stephen Smith from Texas A&M University presented volunteers with picture-word puzzles that suggest common phrases, and asked them to solve as many as possible.[5] So, for example, they might be asked to identify the phrase indicated in the following set of words.

YOU JUST ME

The answer is 'just between you and me'. Now that you have the general idea, try these three:

SALE SALE SALE SALE

STAND
I

BRO   KEN

The answers are 'for sale', 'I understand', and 'broken in half'. In Smith's experiment, if a puzzle was unsolved, the volunteers were told to relax for 15 minutes, and then try the puzzles again. More than a third were solved at the second attempt. While relaxing, the volunteers had not been working on the puzzles consciously. But their unconscious thoughts had devised new and helpful perspectives on the puzzles.

Recent work suggests that you don't even need to spend 15 minutes away from a problem. Instead, you can achieve the same results in just a few moments. Psychologists Ap Dijksterhuis and Teun Meurs from the University of Amsterdam have carried out a series of unusual and fascinating experiments into creativity and the unconscious.[6] Their ideas about the nature of the unconscious mind and creativity are simple to understand. Imagine two men in a room. One of them is highly creative, but very shy. The other is clever, not as creative and far more domineering. Now imagine going into the room and asking them to come up with ideas for a campaign to advertise a new type of chocolate bar. True to form, the loud but not especially creative man dominates the conversation. He does not allow his quieter counterpart to contribute, and the ideas produced are good but not very innovative.

Now let's imagine a slightly different scenario. Again you walk into the room and ask for campaign ideas. However, this time you distract the loud man by getting him to watch a film. Under these circumstances, the quiet man is able to make his voice heard, and you walk away with a completely different, and far more creative, set of ideas. In many ways, this is a good analogy for the relationship between your mind and creativity. The quiet guy represents your unconscious mind. It is capable of wonderful ideas, but is often difficult to hear. The loud guy represents your conscious mind – clever, not as innovative, but difficult to get out of your head.

Ap Dijksterhuis conducted a series of experiments to find out whether people might become more creative if they had their conscious minds distracted. In perhaps the best-known of these, volunteers were asked to devise new and creative names for pasta. To help them, the experimenters started by presenting them with five new names, all of which ended with the letter 'i', thus sounding like typical pasta possibilities. Some of the volunteers were then given 3 minutes to think about it before listing their ideas. In terms of the 'two guys in the room' analogy, these volunteers were listening to the comments of the loud and not especially creative guy in their heads. Another group of volunteers were asked to forget about the pasta and instead spend 3 minutes carrying out a mentally taxing task by carefully tracking a dot as it moved round a computer screen and clicking a space bar whenever it changed colour. In terms of the room analogy, this task was designed to distract the loud guy, and give the quiet man a chance to have his voice heard. Only after completing this difficult and attention-sapping task were they asked to list some new names for pasta.

The researchers developed a simple, no-nonsense and ingenious way of deciding whether the pasta names suggested by volunteers should be categorized as creative or uncreative. They worked through all the suggestions, carefully counting the number of times they produced a pasta name ending in 'i', versus another letter. As the five examples given at the start of the experiment all ended with 'i', they concluded that any suggestion also ending in 'i' was evidence of people simply following the crowd and being uncreative, whereas those ideas ending in another letter were more innovative.

The results were remarkable. The volunteers who had been consciously thinking about the task produced more pasta names ending in 'i' than those who had been busy chasing a dot around a computer screen. In contrast, when the more unusual pasta names were examined, the dot-chasing volunteers produced almost twice as many suggestions as those in the other groups. It was experimental evidence that once the loud man is distracted, the quiet, creative guy has a chance to be heard. Exactly as predicted by the 'Two Men In a Room' theory.

These startling findings have yielded a considerable insight into the relationship between creativity and the unconscious. Volunteers in the 'follow the dot' condition felt as if all their attention and mental effort was fully engaged in tracking a dot as it moved round a computer screen. However, their unconscious mind was working on the problem at hand. Perhaps more importantly, it wasn't just reproducing the same work as their conscious mind, but thinking about things in a very different way. It was being innovative. It was making new connections. It was creating truly original ideas.

Many standard texts on creativity emphasize the value of

relaxation. They tell people to take it easy and empty their mind of thoughts. Dutch research suggests exactly the opposite. Genuine creativity can come from spending just a few moments occupying your conscious mind, and thus preventing it from interfering with the important and innovative thoughts in your unconscious. Everyone can be more creative; it is just a case of keeping the loud guy in your head busy, and giving the quiet guy a chance to speak up.

IN 59 SECONDS OR LESS

When you next want to come up with a creative solution to a problem, try the following technique and then see what pops into your mind. If the word-search puzzle below is not for you, try tackling a difficult crossword puzzle, sudoko or any other task that fully occupies your conscious mind.

A What problem are you trying to solve?

B Find the ten target words below inside the grid opposite. The words might run horizontally, vertically or diagonally and be either forwards or backwards. There may also be an overlap between the words.

SIXTY
SECONDS
CREATIVITY
BOOST
QUICK
RAPID
THINK
CHANGE
NEW
FRESH

Answers on page 126

Y	V	S	N	S	H	Y	E	X
T	F	R	E	S	H	E	S	D
I	S	Q	H	D	G	T	I	A
V	E	R	A	N	S	S	F	Y
I	T	E	A	O	Q	E	T	T
T	T	H	O	C	U	X	H	O
A	C	B	E	E	I	C	I	N
E	H	I	Q	S	C	H	N	I
R	A	P	I	D	K	E	K	A
C	S	I	T	Q	W	T	T	B

C Now, without thinking too much about it, jot down below the various thoughts and possible solutions that come to you in answer to your problem.

Getting in Touch With Your Inner Gorilla

A few years ago I wrote a book about creativity called *Did You Spot the Gorilla?* It outlined four techniques designed to help people think and behave in more flexible and unusual ways. Here are summaries of each of the techniques and some exercises designed to help implement them.

Priming. Prime your mind by working feverishly on a problem, but then give yourself a release of effort by doing something completely different. During the release period, feed your mind with new and diverse ideas by, for example, visiting a museum or art gallery, flicking through magazines or newspapers, going on a train or car journey or randomly searching the internet. But don't push it. Simply immerse yourself in novel ideas and experiences, and leave it up to your brain to find connections and create seemingly serendipitous events.

Perspective. Changing perspective helps produce novel solutions. Try imagining how a child, idiot, friend, artist or accountant would approach the problem. Alternatively, think about two analogous situations by applying the 'is like' rule (e.g. attracting more people to my business *is like* a street entertainer trying to attract a crowd). How is the problem solved in these situations, and can this idea be applied to your problem? Finally, think about doing the exact opposite of every solution you have created so far.

Play. When you are being too serious your brain becomes constrained. Jump-start your creativity by having some fun. Take a break for 15 minutes, watch a funny film, incorporate the words 'cheese' and 'pie' into your next meeting or telephone call, or digitally alter a photograph of a colleague so that he or she looks more like an owl.

Perceive. When the world becomes too familiar, your brain reverts to automatic pilot and stops seeing what is right in front of your eyes. Try switching your mind to manual by becoming more curious about the world. Ask yourself an interesting question each week. How do elephants communicate over hundreds of miles? Why do people laugh? Why are bananas yellow? How cmoe yuor bairn is albe to udnertsnad tihs snetence eevn tghouh olny the frist and lsat ltetres of ecah wrod are crreoct? Invest some time and energy trying to discover possible answers to the question, if only for the sake of finding out.

Nature Calls

In 1948, George deMestral went for a stroll in the country-side in his native Switzerland. When he returned home he noticed that his clothing was covered in tiny cockleburs. As he set about the annoying task of removing them one by one, deMestral decided to figure out why they stuck to his clothing. Close examination revealed that the cockleburs were covered in tiny hooks that easily attached themselves to the loops within fabric. Inspired by this simple concept, deMestral wondered whether the same idea could be used to attach other surfaces together, a thought that eventually resulted in him inventing Velcro.

DeMestral's story is frequently cited as evidence for one of the most important principles underlying creativity: the realization that an idea or technique from one situation can be applied to another. This principle certainly appears to account for many famous examples of breakthrough think-ing, including, for example, Frank Lloyd Wright finding inspiration for the design of a church roof by noticing the shape of his hands at prayer. However, there may have been another hidden, but equally important, factor at work.

A significant amount of research has examined the effects of the natural environment on people's thinking and behav-iour. The work shows that even a small amount of shrubbery can have a surprisingly large impact on making the world a better place. The recovery rates of patients in hospitals is significantly increased when they are able to see trees out of their ward windows,[7] and prisoners whose cell windows overlook farmland and forests report fewer medical problems than others.[8] The effects are not just constrained to prisoners and patients, but instead influence everyone's lives. Other studies have examined the relationship between greenery and crime. In perhaps the most ingenious of these, researchers focused their attention on a large public housing development in Chicago.[9] The development was especially interesting for two reasons. First, some sections contained a relatively large number of shrubs and trees, whilst other sections resembled the proverbial concrete jungle. Second, the residents had been randomly assigned to apartments in the development, thus ensuring that any differences in crime rates in the two types of areas could not be due to income, background or any other factors. The study provided impressive results. Areas of the development containing greenery were associated with 48 per cent fewer property crimes and 52 per cent fewer violent crimes than those containing nothing but concrete. The researchers speculated that the greenery may have helped put people in a good mood and therefore make them less likely to commit crime.

In the same way that greenery seems to reduce anti-social behaviour, so it also seems to make people more creative. In a series of experiments, Japanese psychologists Seiji Shibata and Naoto Suzuki asked people to carry out various creativity exercises in carefully controlled office environments. In one study, some of the offices contained a pot plant that had been carefully positioned in front of, or to the side of, the participant, while others were devoid of any greenery. In another study the researchers carefully compared the effect of replacing the plant with a similarly sized magazine rack. Time and again, the researchers discovered that the addition of the pot plant enhanced people's creativity. The results from these artificial studies appear to stand up to scrutiny in more realistic settings. An eight-month study of creativity in the workplace conducted by Robert Ulrich from Texas A&M University showed that adding flowers and plants to an office resulted in a 15 per cent increase in ideas from male employees, and more flexible solutions to problems from their female counterparts. In another study, researchers discovered that children engage in significantly more creative play when they are in courtyards containing greenery versus comparatively barren outdoor spaces.[10] Why should a little nature have these effects?

According to some theorists, the explanation dates back thousands of years. Evolutionary psychologists attempt to explain behaviour on the basis of how it might have helped people thrive and survive through generations. In their opinion, being confronted with healthy trees and plants might initiate an ancient feeling of calm because it suggests there will be an abundance of nearby food, which eases the worry about where the next meal is coming from. Such pleasant feelings then make people more helpful, happy and creative.

So is a long country walk or well-placed pot plant the minimum needed to get your creative juices flowing? Andrew Elliot and his colleagues from the University of Rochester carried out an unusual study in which they looked at the relationship between creativity and the near subliminal presentation of colour.[11] The researchers thought that as the colour red is commonly associated with a sense of danger and error (think red traffic lights and teachers' red pens), whereas green is associated with positivity and relaxation (think green traffic lights and nature), the merest suggestion of such colours might hinder or help creativity. They presented participants with a booklet containing some standard anagrams, writing the participant's code number in the corner of each page of the booklet using either red or green ink. They asked the participants to check that the number on each page was correct and then told them to work through the booklet. Remarkably, even though everyone saw the numbers for just a few seconds, those who were exposed to the red ink only solved a third of the anagrams, compared to those who saw the green ink. The evidence suggests that for creativity, you are better off going green.

IN 59 SECONDS OR LESS

To inspire creative thoughts, place plants and flowers in a room, and, if possible, ensure that windows look out on trees and grass, not concrete and steel. Don't try to fake it. Pictures of waterfalls do not aid innovation, and even high-definition screens showing live-camera feeds from natural scenes do not make people feel more relaxed.[12] So, if you really cannot introduce nature into a space, head for the nearest green spot. Also, when decorating rooms to inspire creative and innovative thinking, avoid red and go for green. The same concept applies if you are trying to get creative juices flowing for others – prime them with the colour green (green folder covers, green chairs or even your clothing).

Musical Chairs

There are two schools of thought relating to group dynamics and creativity. One believes in not changing team membership, arguing that people then feel more comfortable with one another, and so are happier to suggest the type of weird and wonderful ideas that are the hallmark of creativity. In contrast, the other thinks that it is better to generate new patterns of thinking by constantly mixing membership up.

To find out which position is the best, Charlan Nemeth and Margaret Ormiston from the University of California conducted a revealing study.[13] In the first part of the experiment, groups of people were asked to think of new ways to solve real problems, such as boosting tourism in the San Francisco Bay area. Next, the membership of half of those groups was kept constant, while the people in the other half were changed in order to create totally new teams. Those who remained together rated their groups as friendlier and more creative than those who had been asked to move around. However, from the perspective of creativity, the results contradicted this, with the newly formed groups generating significantly more ideas, which were later judged to be more creative.

Other work suggests that even one new person can make a difference. In a study conducted by Hoon-Seok Choi and Leigh Thompson, three-person groups were first asked to think of as many uses as possible for a cardboard box.[14] Next, the experimenters kept the membership of half of the groups constant, and changed just one person in the other half of the groups. When asked to repeat the cardboard-box task, the groups containing one new member devised significantly more creative uses for the box. Further analyses showed that the newcomer had helped increase the creativity of the two original team members.

So, in respect of group creativity, the message is clear: play musical chairs. Even though a team may have worked well together in the past, maximize the potential for new and exciting thoughts by altering members as often as possible.

The Power of Small

Can small cues have a surprisingly large impact on the way people think? In work conducted by Ap Dijksterhuis and Ad van Knippenberg from the University of Nijmegen in Holland, participants jotted down a few sentences describing either a typical football hooligan or a typical professor.[15] Surprisingly, when then asked a series of general-knowledge questions, those who had spent time thinking about a typical football hooligan answered 46 per cent of the questions correctly, whereas those who had spent a few moments reflecting on a typical professor attained a mark of 60 per cent. Other studies have shown that similar types of priming effects occur in many different situations. Sit people in front of computer wallpaper containing dollar symbols and they behave in a more selfish and unfriendly way, giving less money to charity and sitting further away from others.[16] Give interviewers a cup of iced coffee and they unknowingly rate interviewees as colder and less pleasant.[17] Add a faint smell of cleaning fluid to the air and people tidy up more thoroughly.[18] Put a briefcase on a table during a meeting and people suddenly become more competitive.[19] The evidence points to a little counting for a lot.

Priming can also quickly make people more creative. In a study conducted by psychologist Jens Förster from the International University Bremen, Germany, participants were asked to jot down a few sentences about the behaviour, lifestyle and appearance of a typical punk (chosen because punks were, as the researchers put it, 'anarchic and radical'), while others did exactly the same for a typical engineer ('conservative and logical').[20] Everyone was then given a standard test of creativity. The results revealed that those who had spent just a few seconds thinking about the punk were significantly more creative than those who had put time into thinking about the typical engineer. Without people being aware of it, their ability to be creative was dramatically altered by a few quick and simple thoughts. Interestingly, the effect only works with generic stereotypes such as punks and engineers. Ask people to spend a few moments thinking about a famous figure, such Leonardo da Vinci, and more likely than not their creative juices suddenly run dry.[21] It seems that if the bar is set too high, people unconsciously compare their own meagre skills against those of a genius, become disheartened and stop trying.

In 2005, Förster conducted a new type of creativity priming experiment that has real implications for instant change. He speculated that merely glancing at a piece of modern art designed to evoke a sense of unconventionality would unconsciously inspire viewers to become more creative. To test his idea, Förster asked participants to perform a standard creativity task ('think of as many uses for a brick as possible') while seated in front of one of two specially created art prints. The two prints were about a metre square, almost identical, and consisted of twelve large crosses against a light-green background. In one picture all the crosses were dark green, while in the other eleven were dark green and one was yellow. The researchers speculated that the unconscious mind would perceive this single yellow cross as breaking away from its more conservative and conventional green cousins, and this would encourage more radical and creative thinking. The results were astounding. Even though the participants didn't consciously notice the picture, those seated in front of the 'creative' picture produced significantly more uses for the brick. A panel of experts judged their responses as far more creative. The message is clear – if you want to fast-track a group or individual to think more creatively, use the power of visual priming.

But other work suggests that instant creativity is not just about sitting in front of an unusual modern-art print. It is also about how you use your body. There is a strong link between anxiety and creativity. When people feel worried, they become very focused, concentrate on the task at hand, become risk-averse, rely on well-established habits and routines and see the world through less creative eyes. In contrast, when people feel at ease in a situation, they are more likely to explore new and unusual ways of thinking and behaving, see the bigger picture, take risks, and think and act more creatively.

In view of this link, it should, theoretically, be possible to increase people's creativity by making them feel more at ease. Using willing volunteers, researchers have tested a variety of anxiety-reducing procedures, including lengthy relaxation exercises, funny films and listening to Vivaldi's *The Four Seasons*. The results suggest that people have more creative and interesting ideas when they feel comfortable in their surroundings, although induction techniques for the effect have tended to be somewhat time consuming. With speed always of the essence, a few years ago, psychologists Ronald Friedman and Jens Förster created a quick and unusual technique for making people feel relaxed. A rewarding side effect was the discovery that their technique also enhanced creativity.[22]

When you like an object, you sometimes pull it towards you. Similarly, when you dislike it, you tend to push it away. You have been carrying out these simple pull–push behaviours from birth, and probably repeat them on an almost daily basis. As a result, strong associations will have become ingrained in your brain, with the act of pulling being associated with a positive feeling and pushing being seen as far more negative. Friedman and Förster wondered whether getting people to carry out these actions for just a few moments might be enough to trigger the feelings associated with them, and therefore affect people's creative thinking.

They asked willing volunteers to sit at a table and complete standard creativity tasks, like devising as many uses for everyday objects as possible, or solving some classic lateral-thinking puzzles. Half the volunteers were asked to place their right hand under the table and gently pull the table towards them, giving their brains a subtle signal that they liked their surroundings. The other half were asked to place their right hand on the top of the table and push down, thus unconsciously giving the impression that they felt under threat. The pushes and pulls were gentle enough not to move the table, and none of the volunteers had any idea that pushing and pulling might affect their creativity. While gently pushing or pulling with one hand, the creativity task was completed with the other. Friedman and Förster found that for creative ideas about everyday objects, or generating the important 'A-ha!' moments, those people pulling scored significantly higher than those pushing.

It is a simple, strange but effective technique. It is also not the only piece of research to reveal the strange effects your body can have on creativity in the brain. Another experiment, conducted by Ron Friedman and Andrew Elliot from the University of Rochester, involved asking people to tackle difficult anagrams with either their arms crossed or resting on their thighs.[23] In the same way that pushing and pulling is unconsciously associated with liking and disliking, so folding your arms is commonly associated with stubbornness and perseverance. Would this simple act be enough to convince the participants to spend longer trying to solve the anagrams? Yes. The volunteers with their arms folded struggled for nearly twice as long as those with their hands on their thighs. Perhaps more importantly, because of this, they ended up solving significantly more anagrams.

Other work provides scientific justification for perhaps the most popular act of all – lying down on the job. An experiment conducted by Darren Lipnicki and Don Byrne from the Australian National University involved asking participants to try to solve a series of five-letter anagrams while either standing up or lying down on a mattress.[24] The anagrams were a mixed bunch – some were relatively simple ('gip' into 'pig') while others were tough ('nodru' into 'round'). Interestingly, the volunteers solved the puzzles around 10 per cent faster when horizontal, and thus achieved a higher score in the allotted time. What caused the difference?

The answer, according to Lipnicki and Byrne, might have to do with a small section of the brain referred to as the locus coeruleus (Latin for 'blue spot'). When activated, a modest amount of thought produces a stress hormone called noradrenaline that, in turn, increases heart rate, blood flow around the body and triggers the release of energy. When you stand up, gravity draws blood away from the upper body, which subsequently increases activity in the locus coeruleus, whereas lying down decreases its activity. Some researchers think that noradrenaline may also impair the brain's ability to engage in certain types of thinking, including the creativity and flexibility required to solve anagrams. It seems that the act of adopting an upright or supine (Latin for 'can't be bothered') position dramatically affects the chemicals racing through your body, and causes your brain to operate in quite different ways, including its ability to think outside of the box.

IN 59 SECONDS OR LESS

Priming. To prime your mind into thinking creatively, spend a few moments describing a typical musician or artist. List their behaviours, lifestyle and appearance. Or, following on from Förster's work into creativity and patterns, use the following designs to help produce original ideas. They can be turned into examples of modern art and used to adorn the walls of boardrooms and

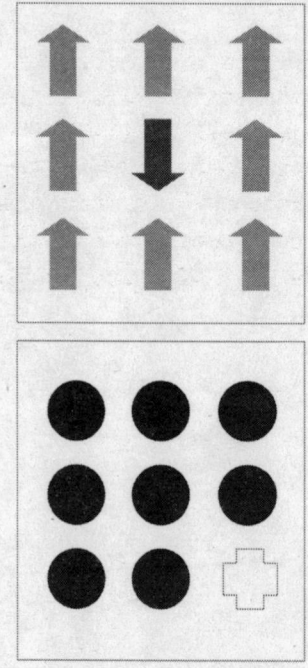

meeting spaces. Alternatively, they can be loaded on computers as wallpaper or even used as subtle background designs on the pads people use to scribble their ideas. Whatever you choose, creating creativity has never been so quick or easy.

Bodywork. The next time you are trying to be creative in a meeting, gently lean forward and pull against the table. When the going gets tough, cross your arms to help perseverance in the face of failure, and if that doesn't work, lie down. If anyone accuses you of being lazy, quietly explain that you are employing your locus coeruleus in the war against rigid thinking.

5. ATTRACTION

Why you shouldn't play hard to get, how the
subtle art of seduction involves the simplest of touches,
rollercoaster rides and artificial Christmas trees.

Imagine being handed a jar containing ten biscuits, being asked to remove one, take a nibble and rating it for quality and taste. Now imagine being asked to perform exactly the same task but this time being handed a jar containing just two biscuits. It would seem reasonable to think that the initial number of biscuits in each jar wouldn't affect your ratings. Reasonable but wrong. According to work conducted by psychologist Stephen Worchel from the University of Hawaii at Hilo, biscuits taken from a jar that is almost empty taste significantly better than identical cookies taken from a full jar.[1]

Why should this be the case? How much we desire and treasure an object depends, in part, on how easy it is to obtain. A jar crammed full of biscuits suggests that the contents are plentiful. In contrast, a nearly empty jar suggests that the cookies are scarce, and therefore significantly more desirable. In Worchel's experiment, this simple idea had unconsciously affected how participants perceived the availability of the cookies, and how good they tasted.

Exactly the same effect explains why collectors spend millions on limited editions, why people are attracted to books or films that have been banned and why retailers are quick to point out limited stocks. But does it also apply to dating? When trying to attract a potential partner, is it better to actively pursue a desired date or play hard to get?

It is a question that has taxed some of the world's greatest minds. The classical Greek philosopher Socrates, when advising the prostitute Theodota on the best way to attract men, came down firmly in favour of the 'treat them mean, keep them keen' hypothesis, noting:

> They will appreciate your favours most highly if you wait till they ask for them. The sweetest meats, you see, if served before they are wanted seem sour, and to those who had enough they are positively nauseating: but even poor fare is very welcome when offered to a hungry man.

A few hundred years later, the great Roman poet Ovid was moved to agree:

> Fool. If you feel no need to guard your girl for her own sake, guard her for mine, so I may want her more. Easy things nobody wants, but what is forbidden is tempting . . . Anyone who can love the wife of an indolent cuckold, I should suppose, would steal buckets of sand from the shore.

The wise words of Socrates and Ovid are echoed in many modern-day books about dating. Time and again, people are advised to play it cool and make any potential love of their life do the running. But does playing hard to get really work?

To find out, Elaine Hatfield from the University of Hawaii and her colleagues conducted a series of fascinating and, at times, downright odd studies.[2] In the first of these, students were shown photographs and brief biographies of teenaged couples and asked to rate how desirable they found each member of the couple. The biographies had been carefully constructed to ensure that some of the teenagers appeared to have fallen for their partner after only a couple of dates (think 'easy'), while others had taken much longer ('hard to get'). Contrary to the researchers' expectations, the students gave much higher ratings to those people who had declared their undying love within moments of meeting their partner, leading them to conclude that 'all the world does love a lover'. Undaunted, the researchers undertook a second, slightly more realistic study.

This time, the research team asked a group of women who had signed up with a dating agency to help out. Whenever a guy telephoned them for a date, they were asked to respond in one of two ways. On half the calls they were to accept immediately ('easy'), while the rest of the time they would pause for precisely 3 seconds before saying yes ('hard to get'). After the call, all the guys were told that they had taken part in an experiment ('she was faking it') and asked to rate their dates. Once again, the team discovered that playing hard to get did not affect the ratings. The team then wondered whether the experimental 3-second pause had been ambiguous, and decided to make things a little more clear-cut. In yet another study, the women with the dating agency either rapidly accepted any offer of a date ('easy'), or paused, explained that they get received countless offers, and then rather begrudgingly arranged for just a coffee ('hard to get'). This time, the results revealed . . . absolutely no effect.

Desperate, the researchers did what many people do when the going gets tough in the heady world of dating – they turned to prostitution.

In a remarkable and little-known social-psychology experiment, the researchers persuaded a group of prostitutes to chat with their clients in one of two ways. While pouring them a drink and before getting down to business, they would either say nothing ('easy'), or casually explain that they were starting college soon and so would only be seeing the customers they liked best ('hard to get'). The research team then secretly monitored how many times each client contacted the prostitute during the following month and, yet again, found no relationship between the prostitute playing hard to get and return rate.

To discover why playing hard to get should prove to be such a myth, Hatfield and the team asked a group of men whether they would rather date someone who seemed eager to have a relationship or someone who made others do all of the running. Most said that there were pros and cons for each option. According to the interviewees, easy women were relaxing and fun to be with, but could be an embarrassment in public. In contrast, hard-to-get women were great for the ego, but were often unfriendly, cold and had a tendency to humiliate you in front of your friends. As a result of the interviews, the researchers speculated that the best strategy would be to give a potential date the impression that, in general, you were hard to get (and therefore a scarce resource worth having), but really enthusiastic about him or her. They tested this notion using some of the same techniques (although this time not involving the prostitutes), and found overwhelming evidence to support their ideas.

However, being able to attract a mate is not just about providing the magic 'I am choosy, and I have chosen you' impression. Instead, research into the psychology of dating has uncovered a number of equally quick but effective ways of making your attraction to someone a mutual affair. All you need is a simple touch, an afternoon at a theme park and the confidence to ask people about their favourite pizza topping.

The Power of Touch

French psychologist Nicolas Guéguen has spent his career investigating some of the more unusual aspects of everyday life, and perhaps none is more unusual than his ground-breaking work into breasts. For years, psychologists have been fascinated by the impact of women's chests on male brains, and have carried out a series of studies that have scientifically proven that men are attracted to women with large breasts. This work, although fascinating and (not altogether) surprising, suffers from one significant draw-back. Most of it has been undertaken in the relatively artificial confines of the laboratory, and has involved presenting men with photographs of women with various-sized breasts, and asking them to select the ones they find most attractive. As a result, whenever this work was presented at academic conferences, other scientists would ask the same question time and again: 'Yes, that's all very well, but does men's preference for large-breasted women actually exist in real life?'

Enter Nicolas Guéguen.

Guéguen decided to conduct two studies investigating breast size and male behaviour in more realistic settings. One of these, subsequently described in his paper 'Women's Bust Size and Men's Courtship Solicitation', involved systematically changing the apparent size of a young woman's breasts and examining the number of times she was approached by men in a nightclub.[3] The woman (who, according to the experimental report, was selected because she had an A-cup bust size, and had been rated by male students as having average physical attractiveness) was asked to sit in a night-club for an hour and look longingly at the dance floor. Meanwhile, a hidden researcher carefully counted the number of men who asked her to dance. Over the course of twelve weeks, the experimenters used latex inserts to vary the woman's bust size between a B and C cup. The effect was as dramatic as it was predictable. Without the help of the latex insert, she was approached by men thirteen times over the course of a night. When she moved up to an artificial B cup this rose to nineteen, while the fake C cup resulted in a staggering forty-four approaches.

Of course, it could easily be argued that the researchers stacked the deck in their favour. After all, most of the men in the nightclub were probably there to meet women, and would have had the time to look at several people before making an approach. What would happen if these factors were removed? What if the context was far less sexual, and men had only a few seconds to make up their minds? To find out, Guéguen conducted another experiment: 'Bust Size and Hitchhiking: A Field Study'.[4] This time, the woman with the highly variable breasts was asked to stand at the side of a busy road and try to thumb a lift. Meanwhile, two researchers sat in a car on the opposite side of the road and secretly counted the number of male and female drivers who drove by, and the number who stopped to offer the woman a ride. After 100 cars had passed, the experimental hitchhiker added or removed latex to alter the size of her breasts. The results from 426 women drivers revealed that bust size had no impact on whether they stopped, with around 9 per cent pulling up regardless of whether they had been presented with an A, B or C cup. In stark contrast, the pattern from 774 male drivers was completely different. 15 per cent stopped to pick up the women without latex inserts, compared to 18 per cent when she transformed into a B cup, and 24 per cent when confronted with a C cup. The researchers concluded that in the male mind, breast size looms large even when men are not in an overtly sexual setting.

Another aspect of Guéguen's work has examined the power of touch.[5] A large number of studies have shown that touching someone on the upper arm for just a second or two can have a surprisingly large effect on how much help they then provide. In one experiment, American researchers approached people in the street and asked them for a dime. A brief touch on the upper arm increased the likelihood of getting the money by 20 per cent. Similar work has shown that the same subtle touch also significantly increases the likelihood of people signing petitions, leaving a tip for wait-ing staff, participating in a taste supermarket test (which then, in turn, increased the chances of them buying the product), drinking more in a bar, and becoming involved in charity work. Could it, however, also dramatically increase the chances of success in courtship?

To find out, Guéguen arranged for a twenty-year-old man to approach 120 women in a nightclub over a three-week period. The approaches were carefully controlled to ensure consistency across all 120 women. Each took place when slow songs were being played and involved the man walking up to a woman and saying, 'Hello, my name's Antoine. Do you want to dance?' Half the time the request was accom-panied by a light touch on the top of the woman's arm, and the remaining times the young man kept his hands to himself. If the woman declined, the man said, 'Too bad, maybe another time?' then moved two or three metres away and tried his luck with another woman. If the woman accepted, the man explained that she had just taken part in an experiment, and handed her a sheet containing additional details about the study. And who says romance is dead?

In a second study by Guéguen, one of three male researchers approached women in the street and attempted to obtain their telephone number.[6] Apparently all three had to be good-looking because, according to the report describing the work, 'pre-test evaluation showed that it was difficult to obtain the phone number from young women in the street' ('honestly, it is part of a scientific experiment, officer'). The men approached a total of 240 women, told them they were really pretty, suggested going for a drink later in the day, and asked for their telephone number. As before, half the time the men touched the woman lightly on the arm as they delivered their chat-up line. The men were then instructed to wait 10 seconds, smile and gaze at the woman. If the woman declined the kind offer, she was allowed to walk away. If she accepted, the researcher quickly explained that the whole thing had been an experiment, handed her an information sheet, and delivered one final scripted line: 'Thanks for your participation and I'm sorry that I have taken up your time. Perhaps we could meet another time. Bye.'

The results from both experiments were impressive. In the nightclub, women accepted the offer of a dance 43 per cent of the time when not being touched on the arm, and 65 per cent after even the briefest of touches. In the street, the research team obtained offers of telephone numbers from

10 per cent of women with no physical contact, and almost 20 per cent when touching. In both cases, a brief touch dramatically increased success.

Why is such a touch so effective when flirting? Many psychologists believe that the answer is to do with sex and status. A large body of research supports the not especially surprising fact that women find high-status men more attractive than their low-status counterparts. From an evolutionary perspective, those men represent ideal mates because they are able to provide for the couple, and any potential offspring, in times of need. But how do women decide on the status of a stranger within a few moments of meeting him?

The answer, in part, is touch. There is considerable evidence that a gentle touch is perceived as a sign of high status.[7] For example, ask people to look at photographs of one person touching another, and they consistently rate the 'toucher' as far more dominant than the 'touchee'. This is especially true of that all-important male to female touch on the upper arm. Most women don't consciously register the touch, but unconsciously it makes them think more highly of their potential beau.

Women frequently accuse men of being shallow, and too easily influenced by a pair of large breasts. Guéguen's adventures with hitchhiking and latex certainly suggest that this is the case. However, his work on the psychology of female seduction shows that women's romantic decision-making can also be swayed by physical factors, providing they signal high status. Perhaps the real message is that deep down we are all a tad more shallow than we might like to admit.

IN 59 SECONDS OR LESS

If you want to get someone to help you out, try the briefest of touches on the upper arm. The same behaviour also increases the likelihood of a woman finding a man attractive, providing that the touch is short, constrained to the upper arm and delivered at the same time as a compliment or request. Do be careful, however, because it is easy to get this terribly wrong. Touching is a strong social signal and even a few inches can make all the difference between the recipient inviting you in for coffee or calling the police.

Assess Your Loving Style

More than thirty years of psychological research has revealed that most people adopt one of several very different 'loving' styles in their romantic relationships. This style does not tend to change throughout a person's life, and plays a key role in determining their relationships. The following questionnaire will give you an insight into how you score on the three main loving styles.[8]

Take a few moments to read the following nine statements and assign each of them a rating to indicate the degree to which they describe you. Some of the statements refer to a specific relationship, while others refer to your general beliefs. Whenever possible, answer the questions with your current partner in mind or, if you are not in a relationship, answer with your most recent partner in mind. If you have not been in a relationship, answer in a way that is consistent with how you believe you would think and behave. Don't spend too long thinking about each statement, and answer honestly.

Rating

1 = strongly disagree to 5 = strongly agree

1	I was attracted to my partner within moments of meeting him/her.	1 2 3 4 5
2	When it comes to relationships, I find a certain type of person attractive and my partner fits that ideal.	1 2 3 4 5

3	My partner and I simply feel like we were meant for one another.	1 2 3 4 5
4	I value loving relationships that grow out of strong friendships.	1 2 3 4 5
5	I cannot say exactly when I fell in love; it seemed to happen over a relatively long period of time.	1 2 3 4 5
6	Love is not a mysterious sensation but rather an extreme form of caring and friendship.	1 2 3 4 5
7	My partner would not be happy if they knew some of the things that I get up to.	1 2 3 4 5
8	I like the idea of playing the field with several different partners.	1 2 3 4 5
9	I tend to bounce back from failed love affairs quite easily.	1 2 3 4 5

Scoring: This type of questionnaire measures the three main types of loving styles. Based on concepts first proposed by the famous Greek philosopher Plato, these are commonly referred to by psychologists, rather catchily, as 'Eros'(Greek for 'desire'), 'Ludus' ('game playing') and 'Storge' ('affection'). To produce your score for each style, add your scores together for the following statements:

Statements 1, 2 and 3 = Eros

Statements 4, 5 and 6 = Storge

Statements 7, 8 and 9 = Ludus

The largest of the three scores indicates your main loving style.

Eros. These lovers have very strong thoughts about the type of physical and psychological characteristics they desire in a partner. When they encounter a match, they frequently experience love at first sight and, all being well, engage in an emotionally intense relationship. Such relationships tend to survive for a few years but often falter as the love of their life changes over time and no longer matches their strict criteria. When this happens, the passionate Eros lover again sets off in search of their perfect soulmate. Extroverted and giving, these passionate lovers feel secure in their relationships and are willing to get emotionally close to others. They tend to become infatuated during the initial stages of any relationship, and while in the grip of passionate love would not dream of infidelity.

Storge. These lovers value trust over lust. Instead of having a perfect partner in mind, they slowly develop a network of friends in the hope that affection will transform into deep commitment and love. Once committed, they are intensely loyal and supportive and only tend to form one or two long-term romantic relationships throughout their life. Highly altruistic and trusting, they have often been brought up in a large family and feel comfortable with the idea of depending on others for support.

Ludus. These lovers have no ideal type in mind, but instead are happy to play the field. They strive for novelty and thrills, are uncomfortable with commitment and quickly move from one short-term relationship to another. Summed up by the expression 'they fancy the face they face', these roving lovers enjoy the thrill of the chase and display little in the way of loyalty or commitment. More neurotic and self-conscious than most, they have little sympathy for the feelings of others. They are risk-takers whose loving style is often driven by a fear of being abandoned by a partner – a situation they avoid by not getting too close to anyone.

Research suggests that psychological similarity is a good predictor of long-term satisfaction in a relationship, so couples sharing a loving style will have a better chance of staying together than those with very different styles.

The Science of Speed Dating

Speed dating is not complicated. During the course of an evening, you meet a series of complete strangers, face to face. Each encounter lasts just a few minutes, during which time you have to decide whether you ever want to see your 'date' again. Apparently invented in the late 1990s by an American rabbi as a way to help Jewish singletons find a partner, the idea rapidly spread from one country to another, and now represents one of the most popular ways of meeting potential soulmates. But what is the best way of using these vital few moments to impress a possible love of your life in 3 minutes or under? Subtly mention your Ferrari? Bare your soul and hope for the best? According to the latest research into the mysteries of attraction, it is more about pizza toppings, mirroring, avoiding spread betting and modesty.

A few years ago, for the Edinburgh International Science Festival, I teamed up with fellow psychologists James Houran and Caroline Watt, to examine the best chat-up lines when speed dating. We assembled fifty single men and fifty single women, randomly paired them together, and asked the pairs to spend 3 minutes chatting. We then told everyone to make quick notes about the lines they had used to impress one another, rate their potential beau for attractiveness and then try again with another person. To uncover the best type of chat-up lines, we compared the conversations of participants rated as very desirable by their dates with those seen as especially undesirable.

Those who obtained few dates from the evening tended to employ old chestnuts like 'Do you come here often?', or struggled to impress with comments like 'I have a PhD in computing.' Those more skilled in seduction encouraged their dates to talk about themselves in a fun and offbeat way, with the top-rated male's best line being: 'If you were on *Stars In Their Eyes*, who would you be?', while the top-rated female asked: 'If you were a pizza topping, what would you be?' These types of lines are successful because at a speed-dating event people frequently feel they are trapped in *Groundhog Day*, having the same conversations again and again. Getting people to open up and talk about themselves in a creative, funny and unusual way promotes a sense of closeness and attraction.

In addition, there is the small matter of 'monkey see, monkey do'. Research shows that we all have an unconscious tendency to mimic others. Without realizing it, we copy the facial expressions, posture and speech patterns of the people we meet. Most psychologists think that such mimicry aids communication by helping people think and feel the same way. However, the degree to which a person mirrors our own behaviours also has a surprisingly large influence on how we feel about them.

The power of this effect was beautifully illustrated in a simple but elegant study conducted by Dutch psychologist Rick van Baaren and his colleagues at the University of Nijmegen.[9] The research team descended on a small restaurant and asked a waitress to help them. After showing customers to their table, the waitress was asked to take their order in one of two ways. Half the time she was instructed to politely listen and generally be positive by using phrases such as 'okay' and 'coming right up'. For the other half she was asked to repeat the order back to the customers. Repeating the order proved to have a remarkable effect on the tips customers left.

Those who had been subjected to hearing their own words repeated left 70 per cent larger tips than those in the 'polite and positive' group. Additional work has shown that mimicry does not just result in larger tips. Another study conducted by the same team showed it also affects the degree to which we find others attractive.[10] In that experiment, an individual posed as a market researcher, stopped people in the street and asked whether they would be kind enough to take part in a survey. Half the time the experimenter unobtrusively copied the person's posture and gestures as they answered the questions, and half of the time he behaved normally. When questioned later, the first group subjected to the mirroring reported feeling a much closer emotional bond with the experimenter, yet had no idea that their own behaviour was being copied. The message here is: in order to help convince someone that the chemistry is right, mirror their movements. Lean forward when they lean forward, cross your legs when they cross theirs, and hold your hands in the same position as they do. Without them realizing it, these small but important movements will help make the target of your affections feel you share that certain, as the French say, *je ne sais quoi*.

So is a successful speed date simply about pizza toppings and mirroring? No. Other work suggests that it is also about being selective. A few years ago, Paul Eastwick and his colleagues from the Northwestern University, staged a series of experimental speed-dating sessions involving more than 150 students.[11] After each date, the students were asked to rate how attractive they found their partner. The results revealed that people who reported finding a large number of daters desirable tended to be rated as undesirable by others. You might think that this finding was caused by a small group of especially ugly people trying to increase their chances of success by ticking the 'yes' box to everyone they met. First, I can't believe you would be so judgmental, and second, according to the data, you would be wrong. The researchers had a group of people rate all the participants for attractiveness, and the same pattern emerged for attractive and unattractive people. Instead, it seems that the speed-dating equivalent of spread betting can be picked up by daters within moments and is a big turn-off. In general, liking lots of others usually means that people will like you. In a more romantic context, potential dates want to feel special, and seem especially skilled at detecting those who are there to play the field.

Finally, a word of warning for men: be careful not to fall into the 'too good to be true' trap. Psychologist Simon Chu and his colleagues from the University of Central Lancashire asked a group of women to look at photographs and brief descriptions of sixty men and rate their attractiveness as possible long-term partners.[12] As part of the description, the researchers systematically varied the men's alleged jobs, deliberately choosing careers that implied either high ('company director'), medium ('travel agent') or low ('waiter') status. Overall, the good-looking men were rated as more attractive than others. Likewise, those in high-status jobs were generally seen as more desirable than those with smaller pay packets. No great surprises there. However, the important finding was that good-looking men in high-status jobs were seen as relatively unattractive long-term propositions. Chu and his colleagues argue that women might well avoid these types of men because they are likely to prove attractive to many other women, and so might be especially likely to be unfaithful. The findings suggest that for speed dating, if you are a good-looking guy, have a great job, a huge bank balance and lavish lifestyle, and you are looking for a long-term partner, keep at least some of your assets under wraps.

IN 59 SECONDS OR LESS

In speed dating you have only moments to impress. So, to make best use of the short time available, think of lines that get the other person to talk about themselves in a creative, fun and unusual way. Mimic (within reason) the way they sit, how they use their hands, their speech patterns and facial expressions. Avoid spread betting. Rather than tick the 'yes, I would like to see you again' box for lots of people in the hope of obtaining the maximum number of dates, focus on the one or two people where there appears to be genuine chemistry. Finally, if you are a great-looking and highly successful guy, remember that for many women your looks and status might make you fall into the 'too good to be true' category. Assuming that adding a prosthetic scar or two is out of the question, be prepared to play down your successes. Of course, for all other guys, the theory represents a great way of coping with rejection – if one woman after another turns you down, convince yourself that you are too damn handsome and successful for your own good!

Sex and Sport

When attempting to impress women, men often make a special effort to present themselves as especially caring and altruistic creatures. However, research suggests that they may have it all wrong.[13] When women were asked to indicate the traits that they found most desirable in friends, short- and long-term partners, most did place kindness high on their shopping lists. However, each and every time it was trumped by bravery. It seems that when it comes to love, women value courage and a willingness to take risks over kindness and altruism. So, instead of men making a special effort to woo women by describing their tireless work for charity, they should perhaps consider mentioning their love of skydiving, the importance of standing up for what you think is right and following your heart no matter where it leads.

The effect emerged in an online survey that I conducted with fitness expert Sam Murphy to explore the relationship between sport and attraction. Are men more impressed by women who play football or climb mountains? Do women go for bodybuilders or yoga fanatics? More than 6,000 people reported which sporting activities would make a member of the opposite sex more attractive. Results revealed that 57 per cent of women found climbing attractive, making it the sexiest sport from a female perspective. This was closely followed by extreme sports (56 per cent), football (52 per cent) and hiking (51 per cent). Bottom of their list came golf and aerobics, with just 13 per cent and 9 per cent of the vote respectively. In contrast, men were most attracted to women into aerobics (70 per cent), followed by yoga (65 per cent) and going to the gym (64 per cent). Bottom of their list came golf (18 per cent), rugby (6 per cent) and bodybuilding (5 per cent).

Women's choices appear to reflect the type of psychological qualities they find attractive – such as bravery and a willingness to take on challenges – while men appear to be looking for a woman who is physically fit, but will not challenge their ego by being overly strong. No one, it seems, is attracted by golfers.

How to Construct the Perfect First Date

In 1975, Senator William Proxmire created the 'Golden Fleece' award to highlight instances wherein the US government had, in the Senator's opinion, frittered away public money on frivolous causes. Proxmire gave his first award to the National Science Foundation for supporting a study into why people fall in love, noting: 'I believe that 200 million Americans want to leave some things in life a mystery, and right at the top of the list of things we don't want to know is why a man falls in love with a woman, and vice versa.' Fortunately, his opinion was not widely shared, and over the years psychologists have investigated many aspects of love and attraction. Some of the most intriguing work examines the psychology lurking behind that all-important initial encounter.

First dates can be a tad tricky. Where is the best place for a romantic encounter? What should you talk about? Should you appear really keen from the very start, or play hard to get? Worry not, help is at hand. During the past thirty years researchers have tackled these questions and uncovered several quick and easy techniques designed to help Cupid's arrow find its target.

Let us first consider the thorny issue of where best to take a potential partner. You might think that a quiet restaurant or a walk in the countryside are both good bets. However, according to research conducted by psychologists Donald Dutton and Arthur Aron, you would be way off the mark.[14]

Prior to their research, several experiments had already confirmed what poets had long suspected: when people find someone attractive, their hearts beat faster. Dutton and Aron thought that the opposite could also be true: in other words, people whose hearts are beating faster might be more likely to find someone attractive.

To find out if this was the case, they arranged for a female experimenter to approach men on one of two very different bridges across the Capilano River in British Columbia. One bridge was swaying precariously in the wind about 200 feet above the rocks, while the other was much lower and far more solid. After asking a few simple survey questions, the experimenter offered the men her telephone number in case they would like to find out more about her work. Those crossing the precarious footbridge had higher heart rates than those on the lower bridge. When approached by the young woman, they unconsciously attributed their increased heart rate to her rather than the bridge, fooled themselves into thinking that they found her attractive, and were far more likely to make a special effort to call her.

Of course, it is one thing to obtain this effect with strangers on bridges, but does it work with real couples in a more realistic setting? A few years ago, psychologists Cindy Meston and Penny Frohlich from the University of Texas decided to find out. They visited two large theme parks in Texas and waited near several roller coasters armed with little more than a clipboard and photographs of an average-looking man and woman. They interviewed romantically involved couples either a few moments before or after they had scared themselves silly on the ride. The researchers asked them to assign a number between one and seven to indicate how attractive they found both the person that they were with, and the people in the photographs. The experimenters anticipated that those who had finished the ride would have higher heart beats than those preparing for it, and, according to the 'heart beating faster = find person attractive' theory, would give higher attractiveness ratings.

Describing their findings in a paper entitled 'Love At First Fright', the researchers admitted that only some of their predictions were supported.[15] Those rating the photographs after the ride did find the people in the pictures significantly more attractive than those waiting in line. However, a different pattern emerged when it came to people rating one another, with people finding the person they were with slightly less attractive after the ride. When speculating about why this might be the case, the researchers wondered whether these ratings may have been influenced by the embarrassment of their partner finding out they had just been given a lower than expected attractiveness rating ('What exactly did you mean when you said that you would give me one?'). They also considered the possibility that people may look less attractive after a roller coaster ride due to 'sweating, messy hair and post-anxiety expressions'. However, similar work, examining whether a comparable effect occurs when couples watch exciting films has provided more clear-cut evidence in support of the theory. In this work, researchers secretly observed couples leaving different kinds of films, and discovered that those who had just seen a suspense thriller were especially likely to be holding hands and touching one another.[16]

Of course, the perfect date is not just about getting your heart beat racing. There is also the important issue of what you say, and when you say it.

A few years ago, psychologist Arthur Aron (he of the two bridges) and his colleagues also examined whether it was possible to place people on the fast track to attraction by getting them to chat about certain topics.[17] Obviously, the more couples get to know one another, the more likely they are to disclose personal information. Aron and his team wondered whether the reverse was also true: namely, could the act of disclosing personal information to another person make you feel especially close to that person? The work involved people who didn't know one another being paired together and instructed to chat about increasingly private aspects of their lives. By asking each other a series of preset questions, each couple was given 45 minutes to play the 'Sharing Game'. The list started with normal conversational openings frequently used at dinner parties ('If you could meet anyone in history, who would it be?), then quickly moved into 'drunk with a close friend' territory ('Do you have a hunch about how, and when, you are going to die?'), before finally getting into 'young couple trying to be intimate' land ('When did you last cry in front of someone?).

Aron knew that chatting about any subject might promote closeness, so he had other pairs of strangers work their way through a control list of small-talk questions ('What are the advantages and disadvantages of artificial Christmas trees?', 'Do you prefer digital clocks or the kind with hands?'). At the end of the sessions, each pair was asked to rate how attractive they found each other. Perhaps not surprisingly, the pairs who had been made to chat about Christmas trees and clocks did not feel they had developed that vital sense of chemistry. In contrast, those who had played the Sharing Game developed the types of intimacy that usually takes months or years.

In fact, the researchers noticed several participants exchanging telephone numbers after the end of the study.

So, when it comes to that all-important first date, go somewhere scary and don't be afraid of intimate conversation. Common sense says your date may find you a tad strange. Science suggests you will be irresistible.

IN 59 SECONDS OR LESS

Beat Fast my Still Heart. To help promote the chances of a successful date, choose an activity that is likely to get the heart racing. Avoid slow-moving classical-music concerts, country walks and wind chimes. Instead, look towards suspense-filled films, theme parks and cycle rides. The theory is that your date will attribute their racing heart to you, rather than the activity, convincing themselves you have that special something.

The Sharing Game. When it comes to playing the Sharing Games, it is a case of taking one step at a time. However, providing that each extra stage seems appropriate, the research suggests that disclosing personal information about yourself and encouraging your date to do the same can significantly speed up those all-important feelings of intimacy. Here are ten questions based on items from Aron's Sharing Game to help the process:

1 Imagine hosting the perfect dinner party. You can invite anyone who has ever lived. Who would you ask?
2 When did you last talk to yourself?
3 Name two ways in which you consider yourself lucky.
4 Name something you have always wanted to do, and explain why you haven't done it yet.
5 Imagine your house or apartment caught fire. You can only save one object. What would it be?
6 Describe one of the happiest days of your life.

7 Imagine you are going to become close friends with your date. What is the most important thing for him or her to know about you?

8 Tell your date two things you really like about him or her.

9 Describe one of the most embarrassing moments in your life.

10 Describe a personal problem and ask your date's advice on how best to handle it.

5 Quick Tips for Dating

Reflected Glory. Research shows that women rate a man as more attractive after they've seen another woman smiling at him or having a good time in his company.[18] So, if you want to impress women in a bar or at a party, ask a good female friend to come along and openly laugh at your jokes, and then have them quietly slip away. And swear them to secrecy.

Your Eyes are Bigger Than Your Stomach. Many evolutionary psychologists believe that hungry men should show a preference for bigger women because their size suggests access to food. To test this idea, researchers asked male students entering or leaving a university dining hall to rate the attractiveness of full-length photographs of different-sized women.[19] Hungry students rated the heavier women as more desirable. So, if you are female, 'traditionally built' and interested in a guy, suggest going for that all-important drink before a meal, not after. Or try meeting a couple of hours before eating, and then insist he only has a light salad.

Disagree Then Agree. You might think that constant praise and head-nodding is the way to a person's heart. However, research suggests that this may not be true, with people tending to be more attracted to those who start off lukewarm and then become more positive towards the end of the date.[20] So, instead of rushing in at a hundred smiles an hour from the very start of the evening, try playing slightly hard to get for the first hour or so and then turn on the charm towards home time. Also, rather than trying to chat about things you both like, try to talk about things you both dislike. Describing their work in the snappily entitled paper, 'Interpersonal Chemistry Through Negativity: Bonding by Sharing Negative Attitudes About Others', researchers discovered that people feel closer to each other when they agree about dislikes rather than likes.[21]

Faking a Genuine Smile. More than a century ago, scientists discovered that although authentic and fake smiles involve the sides of the mouth being pulled up, only a genuine smile causes crinkling around the sides of the eyes. More recent research has started to explore the subtle science of smiling, including trying to identify the signals that make a smile appear particularly flirtatious. Initial work suggests that smiles that take longer to spread over a person's face (over half a second) are seen as very attractive, especially when accompanied with a slight head tilt towards a partner.[22]

Love or Lust. Gian Gonzaga and his colleagues videotaped couples talking about their first date, and then asked them to rate whether the discussion was more associated with love or lust.[23] When the couples decided it was about the joys of love, the tape showed they leant towards each other, nodded and smiled. But when they thought about lust, they were more likely to stick out their tongues and lick their lips. So if you want to know what your date has on their mind, look for these key signals. Whereas nodding and smiling might signal liking and possible love, the odd licking of the lips suggests it might be your lucky night.

Previous Partners. It is always a tricky moment on any date. You are getting on well, and then the issue of previous relationships rears its ugly head. Suddenly, a whole series of questions run through your mind: is it better to pretend to be picky and suggest you have only had one or two sexual partners? Alternatively, should you appear more experienced and go with a much larger number of lovers? According to work conducted by Doug Kendrick at Arizona State University, it is all a question of balance.[24] Kendrick presented college students with profiles of people with different numbers of partners and had them rate each person's desirability. The results revealed that for women, increasing a man's number of previous partners from zero to two made them more desirable, but anything over two was seen as unattractive. In contrast, for men, woman became more and more desirable each time their number of previous partners increased from zero to four, but anything over that was a turn-off.

6. STRESS

Why not to kick and scream, how to reduce resentment
in seconds, harness the power of a four-legged friend,
and think your way to low blood pressure.

The famous psychoanalyst Sigmund Freud believed that the psyche is composed of three main components: the id, ego and superego. The id is the animalistic portion of your mind that is impulsive and driven by basic instincts, the super-ego represents the more moral side of things, while the ego attempts to arbitrate between these two opposing forces. Most of the time, the three parts agree with one another and all is fine and dandy. However, once in a while, a major disagreement breaks out and, as is so often the case in life, it usually comes down to sex and violence.

To help fully appreciate Freud's idea, imagine locking a horny teenage boy (think id), a priest (superego) and an accountant (ego) in a room with a pornographic magazine. The teenager, representing your animalistic side, would jump on the magazine, while the priest would attempt to rip it out of his immoral grasp and dispose of it. The accountant would then face an uphill struggle getting them to agree on the best way forward. Eventually, all three would calm down, discuss the issue, and perhaps decide that it would be best to pretend that the magazine didn't exist. That way, the teenager wouldn't be tempted to look at the naughty photographs, and the priest wouldn't have to lecture him constantly about the importance of morality. Happy with the clever compromise, the three might hide the magazine under the carpet and try to forget about it. Unfortunately, that is easier said than done.

Day after day the teenager would be tempted to take a peek, but every time he lifted the carpet, the priest would wag his finger. Eventually, the tension would build, making everyone feel more and more anxious.

According to Freud, we are frequently caught up in struggles between our inner teenager and priest, with one arguing for what we want to do and the other for what we ought to do. The teenager wants to have an extramarital affair, and the priest points out the importance of our marriage vows. The teenager wants to strike out at someone who has upset them, and the priest votes in favour of forgiveness. The teenager wants to go ahead with a dodgy business deal, and the priest emphasizes the need to be a good law-abiding citizen. Most of the time, we end up pretending these problems don't exist, and try to bury them deep within the unconscious. However, the mental stress caused by having to keep our conceptual pornographic magazines hidden under the carpet builds, and eventually can make us feel frustrated, anxious and angry.

Many psychologists have argued that the best solution is to release these repressed feelings in a safe and socially acceptable way. Punch a pillow. Shout and scream. Stamp your feet. Anything to help calm down your inner teenager before he kicks in the door. This cathartic approach to anger management has gained wide acceptance, but was Freud correct?

For several years, psychologists have examined the effects of putting people under stress and then encouraging them to shout and scream. A few years ago, Brad Bushman from Iowa State University carried out an experiment whereby 600 students were asked to produce an essay describing their views on abortion.[1] These essays were then taken away and allegedly given to another student for evaluation. In reality, the experimenters evaluated all the essays themselves, and made sure the students received bad marks, negative feedback and a handwritten note saying: 'This is one of the worst essays I have read.' Perhaps not surprisingly, the students were annoyed with the way in which their essays had been evaluated, and were furious with their fictitious evaluator.

Some of the students were then given an opportunity to get their aggressive feelings out of their system. They were given a pair of boxing gloves, shown a photograph of the person who had allegedly marked their essay, and told to think about that person while they hit a 70-pound punch bag. Although the students were left alone with the bag while venting their aggression, an intercom system allowed the experimenters to secretly count the number of times they hit the bag. In contrast, another group of students were not introduced to the boxing gloves and punch bag, but instead were asked to sit in a quiet room for 2 minutes.

Afterwards, everyone completed a standard mood questionnaire that measured, among other things, how angry, annoyed and frustrated they felt. Finally, games were played between pairs, with the victor winning the right to administer a loud blast of noise into the face of the loser. The winner decided how long and how loud each blast would be, and a computer carefully recorded their choices.

Did the people who punched the bag feel less aggressive than those who had sat quietly in the room? Did the 'punchers' feel more inclined to generate louder blasts?

Those who had donned the boxing gloves and punched as hard as they could felt far more aggressive afterwards, and administered longer and louder blasts of noise into the faces of their fellow participants. The results revealed large differences in the final mood and blasting behaviour between the two groups, and this results pattern has been proven frequently. The venting of anger does not extinguish the flame. In fact, as Brad Bushman remarks in his paper, it is far more likely to pour petrol onto the fire.

If punching and screaming don't help quell feelings of stress and frustration, what does? And what can be done to create a more relaxed view of life? Are lengthy anger-management courses or hours of deep meditation the answer? In fact, there are some simple and fast solutions, which include the ability to find benefits by doing nothing and harnessing the positive power of a four-legged friend.

In Search of Benefits

Everyone will experience negative events at some point in their lives. Perhaps you will contract an illness, endure the break-up of a long-term relationship, discover that your partner has had an affair, or maybe a close friend will spread hurtful gossip about you. Quite understandably, such events usually cause people to feel anxious, upset and down. People often reflect on the past, wishing things could be different. If another person is responsible for their suffering, thoughts might turn to revenge and retribution. Oftentimes, such experiences lead to feelings of anger, bitterness and aggression. Given that putting on boxing gloves and hitting a punch bag is likely to make the situation worse rather than better, what is the best way of dealing with such emotions?

One possibility is simply to behave in a way that is incompatible with being angry. Watch a funny film, go to a party, play with a puppy, tackle a difficult crossword puzzle. Alternatively, you could distract yourself by exercising, creating an art project or spending an evening with friends or family. However, although such behaviour may help reduce feelings of stress caused by relatively minor hassles, it is unlikely to provide a lasting solution to more serious sources of long-term frustration. However, a more effective solution does not require lengthy sessions with a therapist or hours talking over the issues with those around you. Instead, it takes minutes not months, and has been shown to help people who have lost their possessions due to fire, suffered bereavement, experienced a heart attack, been the victims of disaster or been diagnosed with rheumatoid arthritis.[2] It is called 'benefit finding'.

The procedure can be illustrated by research conducted by Michael McCullough and his colleagues from the University of Miami.[3] Over 300 undergraduates were first asked to choose an incident in their lives when someone had hurt or offended them. From infidelity to insults, rejection to abandonment, the students all came out with something that had been eating away at them.

A third of the participants were then asked to spend a few minutes describing the event in detail, focusing on how angry they felt and how the experience had had a negative effect on their lives. A second group were asked to do the same thing, but focus on the benefits that had flowed from the experience, including, for example, becoming a stronger or wiser person. The final group were simply asked to describe the plans they had for the following day.

At the end of the study, everyone was asked to complete a questionnaire that measured their thoughts and feelings towards the person who had upset and hurt them. The results revealed that just a few minutes focusing on the benefits that flowed from the seemingly hurtful experience helped participants deal with the anger and upset caused by the situation. They felt significantly more forgiving towards those who had hurt them, and were less likely to seek revenge or avoid them.

Finding the benefits that have flowed from negative life events may seem like wishful thinking. However, there is some evidence that such benefits may be genuine. For example, research shows that certain positive character traits, such as gratitude, hope, kindness, leadership and teamwork increased in Americans following the 9/11 terrorist attacks.[4] In addition, other work has shown that having had a serious physical illness can result in increased levels of bravery, curiosity, fairness, humour and an appreciation of beauty.[5]

When it comes to anger management, putting on the boxing gloves or punching a pillow are far more likely to increase, not decrease, feelings of aggression. Instead, it is possible to significantly reduce such feelings by focusing on the benefits that have risen from the seemingly negative events underlying your anger.

IN 59 SECONDS OR LESS

When you experience an event that has the potential to make you feel angry, try the following exercise to ease the pain and help you move on.

Spend a few moments thinking about the positive aspects of the event you found hurtful. For example, did the event help you . . .

- grow stronger or become aware of personal strengths that you didn't realize you had?
- appreciate aspects of your life more than before?
- become a wiser person or strengthen important relationships?
- become more skilled at communicating your feelings, more confident or encourage you to end a bad relationship?
- develop into a more compassionate or forgiving person?
- strengthen your relationship with a person who hurt you?

Write down how you have benefited from the experience, and how your life is better as a result of what happened. Do not withhold anything and be as honest as possible.

4 x 15-Second Tips for Conquering Stress

When you sense danger, your body gears up for action as you prepare to either run away or stand your ground. Unfortunately, the stress of modern-day life can result in this system being triggered constantly. Whether it is not being able to find a parking space or an argument with the kids, most people hit the 'fight or flight' button on an all too regular basis. Although mild amounts of stress may help some people focus on the task at hand, constant problems can take their toll, eventually sending the stress meter rocketing and causing increased blood pressure, concentration difficulties, worry, weight gain and a weakening of the immune system. However, there are several quick and easy ways of bringing your blood pressure back to planet earth.

Help Yourself by Praying for Others. Research conducted by Neal Krause from the University of Michigan suggests that praying for others might be good for one's health.[6] After interviewing more than 1,000 people about the nature of their prayers, finances and health, Krause discovered that praying for others helped reduce the financial stresses and strains of the person doing the praying and improved their well-being. Interestingly, praying for material things, such as a new car or better house, offered no such protection.

Study the Classics. Sky Chafin and colleagues from the University of California have examined which music best reduces blood pressure after a stressful event.[7] Their work involved making people anxious by making them count down aloud from 2,397 in sets of 13, i.e. 2,397, 2,384 . . . To make matters worse, every 30 seconds, the experimenter harassed the participant with negative feedback ('come on, get a move on') and urged them to speed up. Afterwards, some of the participants were left alone to recover in silence, while others were played either classical music (Pachelbel's Canon, Vivaldi's *The Four Seasons*: 'Spring', Movement 1), jazz (including 'Flamenco Sketches' by Miles Davis) or pop music (Sarah McLachlan's 'Angel', Dave Matthews Band's 'Crash Into Me'). Blood-pressure readings revealed that listening to pop or jazz has the same restorative effect as total silence. In contrast, those made to listen to Pachelbel and Vivaldi relaxed much more quickly, their blood pressure dropping back to normal levels in far less time.

Here Comes the Sun. Matthew Keller and colleagues from the Virginia Institute for Psychiatric and Behavioral Genetics have looked at the relationship between the sun and emotion.[8] The team discovered that hot weather, indicated by higher temperature and barometric pressure, caused people to be in a better mood and improved their memory, but only if they had spent more than 30 minutes outside. People who had spent less than the magic half-hour in the sun were actually in a poorer mood than usual. Perhaps, as the authors suggest, people resent being cooped up when the weather is pleasant.

Get in Touch with Your Inner Clown. Laugh, and the whole world laughs with you; cry, and you increase your chances of a heart attack. Well, at least that is the general conclusion from research examining laughter and relaxation. People who spontaneously use humour to cope with stress have particularly healthy immune systems, are 40 per cent less likely to suffer heart attacks and strokes, experience less pain during dental surgery and live 4.5 years longer than average.[9] In 2005, Michael Miller and his colleagues from the University of Maryland showed people scenes from films that were likely to make them feel anxious (such as the opening 30 minutes of *Saving Private Ryan*) or laugh (such as the 'orgasm' scene from *When Harry Met Sally*). Participants' blood flow dropped by about 35 per cent after watching the stress-inducing films, but rose by 22 per cent following the more humorous material. On the basis of the results, the researchers recommend that people laugh for at least 15 minutes each day.

Paws for Thought

There are many ways in which a dog can make you feel better. One could, for example, chop the dog up and use it as the basis for a hearty stew. But would eating the stew really make you feel good or leave a guilty aftertaste? To find out, researchers from the University of . . . Just kidding; to my knowledge, scientists have yet to explore the psychological impact of eating dog stew. They have, however, examined other ways in which you might benefit from a four-legged friend.

Some of the best-known research was conducted by Erika Friedmann and her colleagues from the University of Maryland and investigated the possible relationship between dog ownership and cardiovascular functioning.[10] After carefully following the recovery rates of patients who had suffered a heart attack, Friedmann discovered that, compared to people without a canine pal, dog owners were almost nine times more likely to be alive twelve months later. This remarkable result encouraged scientists to explore other possible benefits of canine companionship, resulting in studies showing that dog owners coped well with everyday stress, were relaxed about life, had high self-esteem and were less likely to be diagnosed with depression.[11]

The magnitude of these benefits should not be underestimated. One study measured the blood pressure and heart rate of dog owners as they carried out two stressful tasks (counting backwards in threes from a four-digit number and holding their hand in a bucket of iced water) while in the presence of their pet or spouse.[12] The participants had lower heart rates and blood pressure and made far fewer errors on the counting task in the presence of their dog than their partner. Scientific evidence, if any were needed, that your dog is better for your health than your husband or wife.

Interestingly, the same cannot be said for cats, with some studies showing that living with a cat may help alleviate negative moods but is unlikely to make you feel especially good,[13] and others suggesting that cat owners may actually be more likely than others to die in the twelve months following a heart attack.[14]

Promising as they may seem, there is one huge problem with these types of studies. Although dog ownership is related to having a more relaxed attitude to life and a healthier cardiovascular system, it doesn't necessarily mean that having a dog is the cause of this. People who own a dog may have a certain type of personality and it could be this that is responsible for them living longer and less stressful lives.

To help sift correlation from causation, Karen Allen from the State University of New York at Buffalo conducted a much-needed study.[15] Allen assembled a group of city stockbrokers suffering from hypertension and randomly divided them into two groups, one of which was given a dog to look after. Both groups then had their blood pressure monitored over a six-month period. The results revealed that the stockbrokers with dogs were significantly more relaxed than those in the control group. In fact, when it came to helping alleviate the effects of mental stress, the dogs proved more effective than one of the most commonly used drugs to treat hypertension. More importantly, as the people were randomly assigned to the 'dog' and 'no dog' condition, there was no difference in personality between the groups, and so this could not account for the findings. Interestingly, in addition to feeling less stressed, the hard-nosed city types had become emotionally attached to their animals, with none of them accepting the opportunity of returning their new-found friend at the end of the study.

Several theories have been proposed to explain why owning a dog should be good for you. It could be that the exercise associated with daily walking benefits your physical and psychological health. Others have argued that dogs act as the ultimate 'non-judgemental friend', patiently listening to your innermost thoughts, and never passing on your secrets to others. Seen in this way, dogs are like a devoted therapist, albeit one with woolly ears, a wet nose and low fees. An alternative theory is that simply touching or stroking a dog could have a calming and beneficial effect, with evidence showing that even a nurse holding a patient's hand significantly lowers the patient's heart rate.[16]

However, most researchers acknowledge that one of the most important factors centres on the social benefits of owning a dog. Spend time in a park frequented by people out walking their dogs and you will quickly see how man's best friend encourages strangers to talk to one another ('Aw . . . how cute . . . what breed is he?', 'What a lovely dog . . . how old is she?', 'Look at what I've just trodden in . . . did he do that?'). A large body of research has demonstrated that spending time with other people is a major source of happiness and health, and dogs' inadvertent but effective ability to bring people together is likely to play a major role in promoting the well-being of their owners.

But just how good are dogs at initiating such meetings, and what kind of dog works best when networking? To find out, animal psychologist Deborah Wells from Queen's University Belfast arranged for a researcher to give up several lunch hours in order to walk back and forth along the same stretch of road with a variety of dogs.[17] Each walk continued until the researcher had passed 300 people coming in the opposite direction. Another experimenter, walking a few paces behind, secretly noted whether each passer-by looked at the researcher, smiled at her or stopped to talk. For three of the trips the researcher was accompanied by a yellow Labrador puppy, an adult Labrador or an adult Rottweiler. As a control experiment, on three other days she walked alone, carried a 20-inch-high brown teddy bear (chosen to have attention-grabbing big brown eyes, short limbs and a high forehead) or a yucca plant.

From 1,800 passers-by and 211 conversations later, the results revealed that the teddy bear and plant initiated lots of looking, but did not result in very much smiling and almost no chatting. In contrast, the dogs caused people to look, smile and chat. The Rottweiler produced a very low chat rate, presumably because people associate the breed with aggression and liked the idea of keeping their throats intact and fully functional. In contrast, around 1 in 10 people stopped to chat to the researcher when she was with the adult or puppy Labrador.

This work is not the only study to support the notion that people talk to those with animals. Previous work found that a female experimenter sitting on a park bench received more attention from passers-by when she had a pet rabbit or turtle at her side, compared to when she sat alone blowing bubbles or next to a working television set.[18]

IN 59 SECONDS OR LESS

There are two key messages from this research. First, owning a dog helps relieve the stresses and strains of everyday life, in part because it promotes social contact. Second, to maximize the chances of such meetings, choose a Labrador rather than a Rottweiler, teddy bear, yucca plant, television set or bubble mixture.

However, if your lifestyle is incompatible with owning a dog, there are still two things that you can do to gain the benefits of a four-legged friend.

i-dog. You could consider getting a robotic rather than a real dog. Recent research by Marian Banks and her colleagues from the Saint Louis University School of Medicine examined the effects of robot and real dogs on patient loneliness in long-term care facilities.[19] The research team took either a living dog or a Sony AIBO to each facility on a weekly basis, spending around 30 minutes with patients on each visit. During the course of eight weeks, patients formed the same strength of emotional bond with both types of dog and both helped alleviate feelings of loneliness to the same extent.

Tune into Dog TV. In an innovative study, Deborah Wells examined whether merely looking at a video of an animal can have the same type of calming and restorative effects created by being in its company.[20] She created three short videotapes (ten fish swimming around a plant-filled aquarium, ten budgerigars in an aviary and ten monkeys sitting in trees), and took participants' blood pressure before and after watching the videos. In one control condition, Wells organized a group of people to watch a video of a well-known soap opera, and in another to watch a blank television screen. Two main findings emerged. First, physiologically speaking, watching the soap opera was almost identical to staring at a blank television screen. Second, compared to the two control conditions, all three animal videos made the participants feel much more relaxed. To help reduce your heart rate and blood pressure in less than a minute, go online and watch a video of a cute animal.

Lower Your Blood Pressure
By Doing Nothing

A few years ago, I conducted an unusual experiment into the psychology of alcohol consumption as part of a television programme. The study involved a group of students spending an evening in a bar with their mates. It was easy to persuade people to participate because the drinks were on the house, and the only downside was that throughout the course of the evening our guinea pigs were asked to participate in a few short tests. On the night of the experiment, everyone arrived and the first round of testing began. Each student was presented with a list of numbers and asked to remember as many as possible, walk along a line marked on the floor and undergo a reaction-time test that involved holding a ruler between their first finger and thumb, then dropping it and asking them to catch it the moment they saw it move.

Having completed the initial tests, we quickly moved onto the desirable part of the evening – drinking. Each student was randomly assigned to a blue or red group, given an appropriate badge and told that they were more than welcome to make good use of the free bar. There was, however, just one rule – each person had to go to the bar and order their own drink and was not to get any drinks for their friends. Throughout the evening we frequently interrupted the flow of conversation, pulling people away for testing and having them carry out the same memory, balance and reaction tests as before.

As the amount of alcohol flowing through their veins increased, so people became much louder, significantly more jolly and far more flirtatious. The test results provided an objective measure of change, and by the end of the evening most people struggled to recall any list of numbers that contained more than one digit, consistently failed even to find the line marked on the floor, and closed their fingers a good 60 seconds after the ruler had clattered to the ground. OK, so I am exaggerating for comic effect, but you get the idea. However, by far the most fascinating result was the similarity in scores between those wearing red and blue badges, because both groups had been deliberately duped.

Both groups seemed to suffer significant memory impairment, experience increased difficulty balancing on the line and constantly let the ruler slip through the fingers.

But what the students in the blue group didn't know was that they hadn't touched a drop of alcohol throughout the entire evening. Before the experiment started, we had secretly stocked half the bar with drinks that contained no alcohol, but nevertheless looked, smelled and tasted like the real thing. The bar staff had been under strict instructions to look at the colour of the each person's badge and provide those in the red group with genuine alcohol and those in the blue group with the non-alcoholic fakes. Despite not a single drop of liquor passing their lips, those with blue badges managed to produce all the symptoms commonly associated with having a few too many. Were they faking their reactions? No. They had convinced themselves that they had been drinking, and this thought was enough to convince their brains and bodies to think and behave in a 'drunk' way. At the end of the evening we explained the ruse. They laughed, instantly sobered up, and left the bar in an orderly and amused fashion.

This simple experiment demonstrates the power of the placebo. Our participants believed they were drunk and so thought and acted in a way that was consistent with their beliefs. Exactly the same type of effect has emerged in medical experiments, when people exposed to fake poison ivy have developed genuine rashes, those given caffeine-free coffee become more alert, and patients who underwent a fake knee operation reported reduced pain from their 'healed' tendons. In fact, experiments comparing the effects of genuine drugs to sugared pills show that between 60 and 90 per cent of drugs depend, to some extent, on the placebo effect for their effectiveness.[21]

Exercise is an effective way of reducing blood pressure, but how much of this relationship is all in the mind? In a groundbreaking and innovative study, Alia Crum and Ellen Langer from Harvard University enlisted the help of more than eighty hotel-room attendants selected from seven hotels.[22] They knew that the attendants were a physically active lot. They cleaned and serviced an average of fifteen rooms each day, with each room taking about 25 minutes, and were constantly undertaking the type of lifting, carrying and climbing that would make even the most dedicated gym-goer green with envy. However, Crum and Langer speculated that even though their attendants were leading an active life, they might not realize that this was the case, and wondered what would happen if they were told how physically beneficial their job was for them. Would they come to believe that they were fit people, and could this belief cause significant changes to their weight and blood pressure?

The research team randomly allocated the attendants in each hotel to one of two conditions. Those in one condition were informed about the upside of exercise, and told about the number of calories they burnt during a day. The experimenters had done their maths, and so could tell the attendants that a 15-minute sheet-changing session consumed 40 calories, that the same amount of time vacuuming used 50, and that a quarter of an hour scrubbing a bathroom lost another 60. To help make the information stick in their minds, everyone in the group was given a handout containing the important facts and figures, and the researchers placed a poster carrying the same information on a noticeboard in the staff lounge. The control group of attendants were also given the general information about the benefits of exercise, but not told about the calories they burnt. Everyone then completed a questionnaire about how much they tended to exercise outside work and their diet, drinking and smoking habits, and underwent a series of health tests.

A month later, the researchers returned. The hotel managers confirmed that the workloads of the attendants in the 'Wow, your job involves lots of exercise' group and the control group had remained constant. The experimenters then asked everyone to complete the same questionnaires and health tests as before, and set about analysing the data. The two groups had not taken additional exercise outside work, nor had they changed their eating, smoking or drinking habits. As a result, there were no actual changes in their lifestyle that would suggest that one group should have become any fitter than the other.

The researchers turned their attention to the health tests. Remarkably, those who had been told about how many calories they burnt on a daily basis had lost a significant amount of weight, lowered their body mass index and waist-to-hip ratio, and experienced a decrease in blood pressure. The control attendants showed no similar improvements.

So what caused this health boost? Crum and Langer believe that it is all connected to the power of the placebo. By reminding the attendants of the amount of exercise they took on a daily basis, they altered their beliefs about themselves, and their bodies responded to make these beliefs a reality. It seems in the same way that people slur their words when they think they are drunk or develop a rash when they think that they are ill, so merely thinking about your normal daily exercise can make you healthier.

Whatever the explanation for this mysterious effect, when it comes to improving your health, you may already be putting in the necessary effort. It is just a case of realizing it.

IN 59 SECONDS OR LESS

Crum and Langer's research is controversial but, if valid, suggests that being conscious of the fuel-burning activities you do every day is good for you. The following chart gives an approximate number of calories burnt by someone of average weight carrying out a range of normal activities (people with higher or lower weight will burn proportionately more or less calories). Use the chart to calculate the approximate number of calories you burn each day.

Keep the chart handy to remind yourself of the 'invisible' exercise you undertake each day of your life, and, according to the theory, you should see your stress levels drop by doing nothing.

STRESS

Activity	A Calories burnt per minute	B Do you carry out this activity during a typical week?	C If so, for roughly how many minutes each week?	D Total number of calories burnt (Column A x Column C)
Normal walking	3			
Brisk walking	6			
Cycling	5			
Light housework	4			
Ironing	3			
Washing-up	3			
Mowing the lawn	5.5			
Washing the car	5.5			
Mopping the floor	5.5			
Gardening	5			
Reading a book	1.5			
Shopping	3			
Sitting at a desk	1.5			
Watching TV	1.5			
Sexual intercourse	2			
Driving	1.5			
Sleeping	1			
Talking on telephone	1			
Eating	0.5			
Having a shower	5			
Standing up	1.5			
Walking up and down stairs	8			
Playing with kids	4			
			TOTAL:	

7. RELATIONSHIPS

The perils of 'active listening', why Velcro can help
couples stick together, words speak louder than actions and
a single photograph can make all the difference.

According to some experts, the bedrock of successful marital relationships involves a form of interaction that has come to be labelled 'active listening'. This style of communication involves partners paraphrasing, and then attempting to empathize with, each other. Imagine, for example, that during a counselling session, a wife explains that she is furious with her husband because he regularly gets drunk, comes home smelling of alcohol and sits in front of the television until the small hours. According to the tenets of active listening, the husband would put his wife's concerns into his own words, and then try his very best to understand why she feels so angry with him. This intuitively pleasing technique is very popular, and has given rise to the phrase 'I hear what you are saying'. But is active listening really essential to successful relationships, or is this yet another mind myth?

In the 1990s, psychologist and world-renowned expert on marital stability John Gottman and his colleagues from the University of Washington were eager to find out, and conducted a lengthy and elaborate study.[1] They recruited more than a hundred newly-wed couples, invited them to the lab and asked them to sit in front of a camera and chat for 15 minutes about a topic of ongoing disagreement. The research team then examined every second of the footage, analysing each comment. Over the next six years, the experimenters contacted the couples to find out if they were still together and, if so, how happy they were in their relationship.

To test the effectiveness of active listening, they looked at every instance in which one person on the film expressed any negative emotion or comment, such as 'I am unhappy with your behaviour', or 'I can't stand the way you talk to my parents'. The team recorded how the partner responded, looking for the types of comments associated with active listening, such as paraphrases indicating understanding or empathy. By comparing the frequency of such comments from the conversations of couples who had stayed together with those who had divorced, and those who were in happy and unhappy relationships, the team could scientifically evaluate the power of active listening.

Gottman and his team were surprised and shocked by their own findings. Instances of active listening were few and far between, and didn't predict whether a couple would be successful and happy. According to their results, active listening was unrelated to marital bliss.

Amazed by the results, the team turned to another set of videos for a second opinion. In a previous study they had followed another group of couples over the course of thirteen years, and set about carrying out the same types of analyses on these tapes. They found a similar pattern in the data, which suggested even the most successful, long-term and happy couples rarely engaged in anything that resembled active listening.

According to Gottman, trying to paraphrase and empathize with your partner when they are being critical is a bridge too far, and requires a kind of 'emotional gymnastics' that few can achieve. Although the team's findings and conclusions proved controversial, especially with many relationship counsellors who appeared wedded to the notion of active listening, other research also failed to provide evidence that active listening forms the cornerstone to a successful relationship.[2]

So, if listening and responding to a partner's comments is not the best way forward, what is? The Gottman study suggests that couples in long-term and happy heterosexual relationships tend to exhibit a very particular pattern in times of conflict. The female usually raises a difficult issue, presents an analysis of the problem and suggests some possible solutions. Males who are able to accept some of these ideas, and therefore show a sense of power-sharing with their partner, are far more likely to maintain a successful relationship. In contrast, couples in which the males react by stonewalling or even showing contempt are especially likely to break up.

Teaching couples to change the way they respond to one another when the going gets tough is possible, but time-consuming and difficult. However, there are several techniques that are surprisingly quick to learn and can also help people live happily ever after. All that's required is the ability to write a love letter, place a photograph above the fireplace and turn back the hands of time to your very first date.

IN 59 SECONDS OR LESS

Assess Your Relationship

According to research conducted by John Gottman, the degree to which you know the trivial minutiae of your partner's life is a good predictor of how long your relationship will last. The following fun quiz will help evaluate how well you and your partner know each other. One person should answer the questions by trying to guess the answer your partner will give. Your partner then tells you the actual answer, and you award yourself one point for each correct response. You then swap roles and repeat the process. Finally, add your two scores together, which will result in a total between 0 and 20.

Question
1 In general, which of the following types of film would your partner most enjoy? Horror, comedy, action, drama.
2 What was your partner's first job?
3 In general, which of the following types of sport would your partner most enjoy watching on TV? Snooker, rugby, boxing, athletics.
4 Where was your partner born?
5 Which of the following classic books would your partner most prefer to read? *Moby Dick, A Tale of Two Cities, A Room With A View, Frankenstein.*

6 What is your partner's collar size (male) or dress size (female)?

7 In general, which of the following types of holiday would your partner most prefer? Beach, skiing, walking, city.

8 What is the first name of your partner's closest friend (excluding yourself)?

9 Which of the following world leaders would your partner most like to meet? Adolf Hitler, J. F. Kennedy, Mahatma Gandhi, Winston Churchill.

10 What colour are your partner's eyes?

The Importance of Bonding

In the late 1980s, researcher James Laird from Clark University in Massachusetts and his colleagues advertised for people to take part in an unusual experiment into the possible existence of extra-sensory perception.[3] Male and female participants who didn't know one another were scheduled to arrive at the laboratory at the same time, and were taken through a rather unusual procedure. A researcher explained that it was important for the two participants to undergo a rapport-building exercise prior to the telepathy test, and they were asked to spend a few moments looking into each other's eyes. They were then taken to separate rooms, and one of them was presented with a series of simple pictures while the other tried, 'psychically', to guess the nature of the images.

At the end of the study, Laird looked at his data and discovered no evidence for psychic powers. Was he disappointed? Not at all. In reality, the study had nothing to do with extra-sensory perception, and the alleged telepathy test was just an elaborate cover story that allowed the team to conduct a groundbreaking study into the psychology of love.

Many people believe that falling in love is a highly complex affair that depends on a complicated mixture of looks, personality, chemistry and chance. However, Laird had other ideas. He wondered whether this unique and mysterious sensation might be much more straightforward than it first appeared, and whether it was possible to manufacture the feeling in just a few carefully engineered moments. His hypothesis was simple. It was obvious from everyday life that couples in love spent a significant amount of time looking into each other's eyes. Laird wanted to know whether the reverse was also true. Would it be possible to create a feeling of love by having people spend a few moments gazing at each other?

Normally, staring at strangers is, at best, perceived as peculiar and at worst aggressive. Because of this, Laird had to create an artificial but believable reason for prolonged eye contact, and eventually designed the telepathy-test cover story. Without realizing it, the participants in his fake ESP experiment were made to look into each other's eyes and were therefore behaving as if they found each other attractive. Laird thought this would be enough to kick-start feelings of love and affection.

After the fake telepathy study had ended, all of the participants were asked to rate their amorous feelings towards their experimental partner. Remarkably, the data proved Laird right, with participants reporting genuine feelings of affection and attraction for their new-found soulmate.

The study represents a novel approach to understanding the psychology of affection. According to this view of human behaviour, not only do our thoughts and feelings affect the way we act, but the way we act influences our thoughts and feelings.

Laird is not alone in exploring ways in which this approach can help researchers better understand matters of the heart. Another study, carried out by Arthur Aron and his colleagues from the State University of New York at Stony

Brook, suggests that the same type of approach can also help bring couples closer together.[4] The start of any romantic relationship is usually a time of great excitement, with people enjoying the novelty of experiencing life with a new partner. Fast-forward twenty years, and often a very different picture emerges. Now, the couple know each other very well, and life has become far more routine. The same restaurants, the same holiday destinations and the same conversations. Although familiarity can be comforting, it can also induce a sense of boredom and is unlikely to make hearts race the way they once did.

Aron wondered whether, in the same way that gazing into another person's eyes induces attraction, getting couples to experience the thrill of courtship could help them rekindle the romance in their relationship. Specifically, would getting them to break the monotony of married life by doing something new and fun result in them finding one another more attractive? In an initial study, Aron placed newspaper adverts asking for couples to participate in an experiment exploring the 'factors that affect relationships'.

When volunteers arrived at the lab, each couple completed a questionnaire about their relationship and were randomly assigned to one of two groups. The experimenters then cleared away the tables and chairs, rolled out some gym mats and started the next part of the study.

For half of the couples, the researchers produced a roll of Velcro tape and explained that they were about to take part in a rather strange game. If the couples' eyes lit up and they exchanged knowing glances, the researchers quickly put the Velcro away and asked them to leave. For everyone else, the team used tape to secure one person's right wrist to the left wrist of their partner, and also strap their right and left ankles together.

After resisting the temptation to hum Lionel Richie's 'Stuck On You', the researchers placed a 1-metre high foam obstacle in the middle of the room, and handed each couple a large pillow. Each couple had to get on their hands and knees, crawl up to the obstacle, climb over it, crawl to the other side of the room, turn around, scamper back to the obstacle, climb over it again and return to their starting position. To make things a little more interesting, they were asked to support the pillow between their bodies at all times (no hands, arms or teeth allowed) and only had 60 seconds to complete the course. To make sure that no one finished disappointed, the research team removed participants' watches ('we don't want them getting scratched during the frivolity'), and pretended that everyone completed the task in the allotted time.

The couples in the other group were asked to do something far more mundane. One of them was asked to get on their hands and knees, given a ball and told to roll it to a designated spot in the centre of the room. Their partner was asked to watch from the side of the room and, when the ball made it to the spot, exchange places with their partner, and roll the ball back to the starting position.

The experimenters assumed that the vast majority of couples would not have spent very much time crawling over a large foam obstacle, so the experience would be novel, fun and relatively exciting. It was a chance for them to work together to achieve a goal, and an opportunity to see each other from a new and unusual perspective. Conceptually speaking, it was like the type of experience they used to have when they first met and life was much more exciting. In contrast, those in the other group were acting as a control, performing a task that was far more mundane and didn't involve any joint effort.

At the end of the experiment, all of the couples filled in several questionnaires (including the rather unromantically named 'Romantic Love Symptom Check List'), rating, for example, the degree to which their partner made them 'tingle' and 'burst with happiness'. As predicted, the couples who had conquered the giant foam obstacle were far more loving towards one another than those who had completed the ball-rolling task. Just a few minutes carrying out a new and fun joint activity appeared to have worked wonders.

Encouraged by these initial results, Aron and his team repeated the study, but this time using a different measure of marital satisfaction to the post-experiment questionnaire. At the end of this study, the experimenters filmed each couple chatting about planning their next holiday, or how they might make significant home improvements. Another set of researchers then watched the films and carefully counted every instance where one member of the couple demonstrated some form of hostility. The Velcro couples made significantly more positive comments than the ball rollers.

Aron's findings demonstrate yet another way in which our behaviour exerts a powerful influence over how we think and feel. In the same way that gazing into the eyes of a complete stranger can induce feelings of mutual attraction, so carrying out the activities associated with early courtship can help rekindle past passions.

According to this work, keeping the romance alive could just be a question of having a roll of Velcro tape, a large foam obstacle and an open mind.

IN 59 SECONDS OR LESS

Aron's work suggests that long-term couples will feel more attracted to one another when they regularly engage in novel and exciting joint activities which involve working together to achieve a goal. This finding is supported by the results of several surveys showing that long-term couples who are happy in their relationship are more likely to take part in leisure activities that involve both partners, are relatively unpredictable, exciting and active rather than passive.

So, regardless of whether it is playing sport, amateur dramatics, rock climbing, visiting new places, learning a new dance or travelling to unusual holiday destinations, couples who face life's foam obstacles together, stick together.

Romance Made Simple

I recently conducted a large-scale online survey examining the psychology of romantic gestures. Working with writer Rachael Armstrong, I produced a questionnaire containing descriptions of a wide variety of romantic gestures, including, for example, 'running your partner a relaxing bath after they have had a bad day at work', 'offering them your coat when they are cold', and 'whisking your partner away somewhere exciting for the weekend'. Over 1,500 people from the UK and US completed the survey, and the results help reveal the secret psychology underlying romance. Women frequently complain about men not being the most romantic of creatures. But did the survey confirm their suspicions?

Women were asked to look at the list and indicate how frequently their own partner had carried out each of the romantic gestures. The findings made for depressing reading. For example, 55 per cent of women said their partners had never run them a bath after a hard day at work, 45 per cent had not been offered a coat when cold, and 53 per cent had never been whisked away for an exciting weekend. Objective evidence to support long-standing female complaints about unromantic men. But what might the underlying reason be for this poor showing?

In another part of the survey, male respondents were asked to look at the list of romantic gestures and, using a ten-point scale, rate how romantic they thought a woman would find it if her partner carried out each of the gestures. In contrast, female respondents were asked to use the same scale to indicate how romantic they thought it would be if their partner carried out each of the romantic acts. The results revealed that men severely underestimate the romantic value of even the simplest act.

For example, only 11 per cent of men, compared with 25 per cent of women, awarded the maximum score to the item 'tell her that she is the most wonderful woman that you have ever met'. Likewise, 8 per cent of men but 22 per cent of women assigned 10 out of 10 to 'run her a relaxing bath after she has had a bad day at work'. The same pattern emerged with almost the entire list, suggesting that men's reluctance to carry out a romantic gesture or two may not stem from laziness or a lack of caring, but because they underestimate how romantic behaviour is perceived by women.

Finally, the survey findings were also able to lend a helping hand to those men who wanted to engage in some heartfelt wooing, by identifying the gestures that women view as most and least romantic. The top-ten list of gestures is shown below, along with the percentage of women who assigned each gesture maximum marks on the 'how romantic is this' scale.

1 Cover her eyes and lead her to a lovely surprise – *40 per cent*.
2 Whisk her away somewhere exciting for the weekend – *40 per cent*.

3 Write a song or poem about her – *28 per cent*.
4 Tell her that she is the most wonderful woman that you have ever met – *25 per cent*.
5 Run her a relaxing bath after she has had a bad day at work – *22 per cent*.
6 Send her a romantic text or email or leave a note around the house – *22 per cent*.
7 Wake her up with breakfast in bed – *22 per cent*.
8 Offer her a coat when she is cold – *18 per cent*.
9 Send her a large bouquet of flowers or box of chocolates to her workplace – *16 per cent*.
10 Make her a compilation of her favourite music – *12 per cent*.

Interestingly, it seems that gestures that reflect a form of escapism and surprise top the list, followed by those that reflect thoughtfulness, with blatant acts of materialism trailing into last place. Scientific evidence, perhaps, that when it comes to romance, it really is the thought that counts.

Five to One: When Words Speak Louder Than Actions

Try to spot the unhappy face in the diagram below.

For most people, the task is surprisingly easy, with the unhappy face seeming to jump out from the crowd. Research shows that, conceptually speaking, the same effect influences many aspects of our everyday lives. When it comes to the way we think and behave, negative events and experiences are far more noticeable and have a greater impact than their positive counterparts.[5] Put people in a bad mood and they can easily remember negative life events, such as the break-up of a relationship or being made redundant, but cheer them up and they find it far harder to recall their first kiss or best holiday. A single act of lying or dishonesty often has a disproportionate effect on a person's reputation, and can quickly undo the years of hard work that have gone into building up a positive image.

Dale Carnegie's seminal book *How To Win Friends and Influence People* argued that the same principle applies to the comments we make to friends and partners. According to Carnegie, even the slightest hint of criticism has an enormously damaging effect on relationships, and he urged his readers to shower their nearest and dearest with lavish praise. Over the years, many writers have echoed Carnegie's thoughts, including, for example, American humorist Helen Rowland, who once noted: 'A woman's flattery may inflate a man's head a little, but her criticism goes straight to his heart, and contracts it so that it can never again hold quite so much love for her.'

But are these assertions supported by the findings from modern-day science?

As discussed earlier, psychologist John Gottman has spent over thirty years exploring the key factors that predict whether a couple will stick together or drift apart.[6] Much of his work has involved examining the comments made by couples when they chat with each other about their relationship. Over the years he has become especially interested in the role played by positive comments (reflecting, for example, agreement, understanding or forgiveness), and negative ones (involving hostility, criticism or contempt). By carefully recording the frequency of these, and then tracking the success or otherwise of the relationship, Gottman was able to figure out the ratio of positive to negative comments that predicted the downfall of a partnership. His findings make for fascinating reading, and firmly endorse the thoughts of Carnegie. For a relationship to succeed, the frequency of positive comments has to outweigh the number of negative remarks by about five to one. In other words, it takes five instances of agreement and support to undo the harm caused by a single criticism.

In addition to proving the power of negativity, Gottman's work has also examined why hostility and criticism are so destructive. Analysing how people reacted to positive and negative comments revealed two very different patterns. When one person made a supportive remark ('Nice tie'), their partner tended to respond with a positive comment of their own ('Thanks; nice dress'). However, the pattern was far from reliable, and an entire succession of positive remarks ('Nice tie, and really like your shirt and lovely sweater too') often failed to produce a single pleasant reply ('What time is it?'). In contrast, the response to negative comments was far more predictable, with the smallest of criticisms ('Are you sure about that tie?') often provoking a hail of negativity ('Well, I like it, even if you don't. And why should I care what you think about my tie? It's not as if you have the best dress sense in the world. I mean take that dress, you look like a scarecrow that has let itself go. That's it, I am out of here'). Relationships thrive and survive on mutual support and agreement, and even the briefest of bitter-tasting comments need to be sweetened with a significant amount of love and attention.

Having partners monitor and modify the language they use when they speak to one another is difficult and would require a relatively large amount of time and effort. However, researchers have discovered quick, but nevertheless effective, ways of using words to improve relationships.

Take, for example, the work conducted by psychologists Richard Slatcher and James Pennebaker from the University of Texas at Austin.[7] Slatcher and Pennebaker knew that previous research suggested that getting people who have experienced a traumatic event to write about their thoughts and feelings helped prevent the onset of depression and enhanced their immune system. But, they wondered, could it also improve the quality of people's relationships? To find out, they recruited over eighty newly formed couples and randomly assigned one member of each couple to one of two groups. Those in one group were asked to spend 20 minutes a day for three consecutive days writing about their thoughts and feelings concerning their current relationship. In contrast, those in the other group were asked to spend the same amount of time writing about what they had been up to that day. Three months later, the researchers contacted all the participants and asked them whether their relationship was still ongoing. Remarkably, the simple act of one member of the relationship writing about their feelings for their partner had had a significant effect. 77 per cent of those who had engaged in such 'expressive' writing were still dating their partners, compared to just 52 per cent of those who had written about their daily activities.

To help find out what lay behind this dramatic difference,

the researchers collected and analysed the text messages that the couples had sent to one another during the three-month assessment period. By carefully counting all the positive and negative words in the messages, they discovered that the texts from those who had carried out the expressive writing exercise contained significantly more positive words than the messages from those who had written about their daily lives. In short, the results demonstrate how a seemingly small activity can have a surprisingly large impact. Spending just 20 minutes a day for three days writing about their relation-ship had a long-term impact both on the language that they used to communicate with their partner, and on the likelihood of them sticking together.

Other research has suggested that it doesn't even take 20 minutes a day for three days to improve the health of your relationship. Take a look at the illustration below.

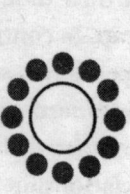 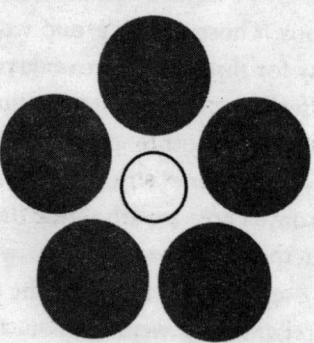

The white circle on the left appears to be larger than the white circle on the right. In fact, the two of them are identi-cal, but they appear to be different sizes because our brains automatically compare each of the circles to their surroundings. The left white circle is surrounded by small circles and so, in comparison, appears to be relatively large. In contrast, the right circle is surrounded by large circles and therefore appears to be relatively small.

Bram Buunk from the University of Groningen and his colleagues wondered whether the same type of 'comparative thinking' could be used to enhance the way in which people viewed their relationships.[8] To find out, Buunk recruited participants who were in long-term relationships, and asked them to think about their partner in one of two ways. One group were simply asked to jot down a few words explaining why they thought that their relationship was good. In contrast, a second group were asked first to think about other relationships they believed were not as good as their own, and then note down why theirs was better. Conceptually, the second group's task is similar to the situation on the left side of the illustration. As predicted, by mentally surrounding their relationship with smaller circles, participants felt far more positive about their partner.

Finally, work by psychologists Sandra Murray and John Holmes suggests that even one word can make all of the difference.[9] In their study, people were interviewed about their partner's most positive and negative qualities. The research team then followed participants for a year, monitoring which relationships stayed the course and which fell by the wayside. They next examined the different types of language the people in the successful and unsuccessful relationships had used during the interview. Perhaps the most important difference came down to just one word – 'but'. When talking about their partner's greatest faults, those in successful relationships tended to qualify any criticism. Her husband was lazy, but that gave the two of them reason to laugh. His wife was a terrible cook, but it meant they ate out lots. He was introverted, but expressed his love in other ways. She was sometimes thought-less, but that was due to a rather difficult childhood. That one simple word was able to help reduce the negative effect of their partner's alleged faults, and keep the relationship on an even keel.

IN 59 SECONDS OR LESS

The following three-day task is similar to those used in experimental studies showing that spending time writing about a relationship has several physical and psychological benefits, and can help improve the longevity of the relationship.

DAY 1
Spend 10 minutes writing down your deepest feelings about your current romantic relationship. Feel free to explore your emotions and thoughts.

DAY 2
Think about someone you know who is in a relationship in some way inferior to your own. Write down three important reasons why your relationship is better than theirs.

1 ....

2 ....

3 ....

DAY 3
Write down one important positive quality your partner has, and why this quality means so much to you.

Now write down something you consider to be a fault in your partner (perhaps something about their personality, habits or behaviour), and then list one way in which this fault could be considered redeeming or endearing.

A Room with a Cue

Imagine that you have just walked into the living room of a complete stranger. You know nothing about the person, and have just a few moments to look around and try to understand something about their personality. Take a look at those art prints on the walls and the photographs above the fireplace. Notice how their books and CDs are scattered all over the place – what does that tell you? Do you think that the person living here is an extrovert or introvert? An anxious person or someone who is more relaxed about life? Are they in a relationship and, if so, are they genuinely happy with their partner? OK, time to leave. The fictitious owner is coming back soon, and if they find you here they will be furious.

Psychologists have recently started to take a serious interest in whether it is possible to tell something about a person's personality and relationships from their homes and offices. For example, a few years ago, Sam Gosling from the University of Texas at Austin arranged for people to complete standard personality questionnaires, and then sent a team of trained observers to record carefully many aspects of their living and work spaces.[10] Were the rooms cluttered or well organised? What kinds of posters did they have on the wall? Did they have pot plants and, if so, how many? The research showed that, for example, the bedrooms of creative people did not have any more books and magazines than others, but their reading matter was drawn from a greater variety of genres. Likewise, when it came to the workplace, extroverts' offices were judged as warmer and more inviting than those of their introverted colleagues. Gosling concluded that many aspects of people's personalities were reflected in their surroundings.

Other work has examined what you can tell about a person's relationship from their surroundings. Time for another exercise. This one only really works if you are currently in a relationship, so you will have to sit this one out if you are single. Sorry about that. On the plus side, it is quite quick, so you won't have long to wait.

First of all, decide which room in your house you tend to use to entertain guests. OK, now imagine sitting in the middle of that room and looking around (of course, if you happen to be in the room, simply look around). On a piece of paper, make a list of your five favourite objects in the room. This can include posters, art prints, tables, chairs, sculptures, pot plants, toys or gadgets. Anything that really appeals to you. Next, think about how you acquired each object on the list. If your partner bought the object, or it was a joint purchase, place a tick against it. You should end up with a list of five objects, and a number of ticks between zero and five.

What does the number of ticks say about your relationship? According to psychologist Andrew Lohmann from Claremont Graduate University and his colleagues, a great deal.[11] Lohmann recruited more than a hundred couples, and asked them to complete the 'tick the joint objects in the room' task and also to assess how close they felt to their partner. The results revealed that a large number of ticks was associated with a closer and healthier relationship, a tendency to view the relationship as a long-term partnership, and a greater willingness to expend time and effort to make it work. So, next time you pop round to a friend's house, you might want to ask about how they came to own some of the most prominent objects in the room – it may reveal more about their relationship than they realize.

The presence of objects that remind a person of their relationship may, for example, bring back happy memories, and so make them feel good. Or they might remind them of a particularly emotional or amusing episode in their relationship. However, according to some recent research, they might be doing far more. In an ingenious study exploring the power of love, Jon Maner from Florida State University and his colleagues recruited more than a hundred students who were in committed relationships, asked them to look at photographs of members of the opposite sex and then choose the one they thought was the most physically attractive.[12] One group were then asked to write an essay about a time they felt a strong sense of love for their partner, while a control group were allowed to write about anything they wanted.

While producing their essays, all the students were told to forget about the photograph of the attractive person they had selected earlier. In addition, they were told that if the image happened to pop into their minds, they were to place a tick in the margin of their essay. Asking people not to think about something usually encourages them to dwell on it. This was certainly the case with the control group, who ticked their margins at an average rate of four ticks per page. However, people writing about being in love found it much easier to push the attractive image out of their mind, resulting in an average of only one tick every two pages.

Later in the experiment, everyone was asked to remember as much as possible about their chosen photograph. Those in the 'love' group tended to remember the more general aspects of the image, such as the colour of a person's dress or the location of the shot, and tended to forget the features related to their physical attractiveness, such as having come-to-bed eyes or a wonderful smile. In fact, the students in love remembered, on average, only about two-thirds as many attractive features compared to the control group.

These findings suggest that even a few minutes thinking about the love you feel for a partner drastically reduces the appeal of attractive members of the opposite sex. According to the research team, this may be a mechanism that has evolved over thousands of years to help keep couples together. On a more practical level, it suggests that any object that helps remind you of your partner may be having an important psychological effect. From photos to a wedding ring or a necklace brought on that fun trip abroad, it is all about helping you prefer your partner to the competition.

IN 59 SECONDS OR LESS

Surrounding yourself with objects that remind you of your partner is good for your relationship. It could be something you wear, such as a ring, pendant or necklace. Or perhaps keeping a gift from your partner on show in the home or office. Or maybe place a photograph of the two of you in a prominent location or in a wallet or purse. Either way, remember these objects are not just a token of love, but serve an important psychological function. Not only do they usually evoke happy memories and positive thoughts, but they also activate a deep-seated evolutionary mechanism that helps makes temptation far less tempting.

8. DECISION MAKING

Why two heads are no better than one,
how never to regret a decision again, protect yourself
against hidden persuaders, and tell when someone
is lying to you.

When people have an important decision to make in the workplace, they often arrange to discuss the issues with a group of well-informed and level-headed colleagues. On the face of it, it seems a reasonable plan. After all, when making up your mind, it is easy to imagine how consulting people with a variety of backgrounds, experience and expertise could help provide a more considered and balanced perspective. But are several heads really better than one? Psychologists have conducted hundreds of experiments into this issue, and their findings have surprised even the most ardent supporters of group consultations.

Perhaps the best-known strand of this work was initiated in the early 1960s by MIT graduate James Stoner, who examined the important issue of risk taking.[1] It will come as no great surprise to discover that research shows some people like to live life on the edge, while others are more risk averse. However, Stoner wondered whether people tended to make more (or less) risky decisions when part of a group and, to find out, he devised a simple but brilliant experiment.

In the first part of his study, Stoner asked people to play the role of a life coach. They were presented with various scenarios in which someone faced a dilemma, and asked to choose which of several options offered the best way forward. Stoner had carefully constructed the options to ensure that each represented a different level of risk. For example, one scenario was about a writer named Helen, who earned her living writing cheap thrillers. Helen had recently had an idea for a novel, but to pursue the idea she would have to put her cheap thrillers on the back burner, and face a drop in income. On the positive side, the novel might be her big break and she could earn a large amount of money. On the down side, the novel might be a complete flop and she would have wasted a great deal of time and effort. Participants were asked to think about Helen's dilemma, and then indicate how certain she should be that the novel was going to be a success before she gave up her regular income from the cheap thrillers.

If a participant was very conservative, they might indicate that Helen needed to be almost 100 per cent certain. If the participant felt much more positively towards risk, they might indicate that even a 10 per cent likelihood of success was acceptable.

Stoner then placed participants into small groups of about five people. The groups were told to discuss the scenarios and reach a consensus. His results clearly showed that the decisions made by groups tended to be far riskier than those made by individuals. Time and again, the groups would advise Helen to drop everything and start work on the novel, while individuals would urge her to stick with the thriller writing. Hundreds of further studies have shown that this effect is not so much about making riskier decisions per se, but polarization. In Stoner's classic studies, various factors caused the group to make riskier decisions, but in other experiments groups have become more conservative than individuals. In short, being in a group exaggerates people's opinions, causing them to make a more extreme decision than they would on their own. Depending on the initial inclinations of the individuals in the group, the final decision can be extremely risky, or extremely conservative.

This curious phenomenon has emerged in many different situations, often with worrying consequences. Gather together a group of racially prejudiced people, and they make even more extreme decisions about racially charged issues.[2] Arrange a meeting of business people who are open to investing in failing projects, and they become even more likely to throw good money after bad.[3] Have aggressive teenagers hang out together, and the gang are far more likely to act violently. Allow those with strong religious or political ideologies to spend time in one another's company, and they form more extreme and often violent viewpoints. The effect even emerges on the internet, with individuals participating in discussion lists and chat rooms voicing more extreme opinions and attitudes than they would normally.

What causes this strange, but highly consistent, phenomenon? Teaming up with people who share your attitudes and opinions reinforces your existing beliefs in several ways. You hear new arguments, and find yourself openly expressing a position that you may have only vaguely considered before. You may have been secretly harbouring thoughts because you believed them to be unusual, extreme or socially unacceptable. However, surrounded by other like-minded people, these secret thoughts often find a way of bubbling to the surface, which in turn encourages others to share their extreme feelings with you.

Polarization is not the only phenomenon of 'groupthink' that can influence the hearts and minds of individuals when they get together.[4] Other studies have shown that, compared to individuals, groups tend to be more dogmatic, better able to justify irrational actions, more likely to see their actions as highly moral and have a tendency to form stereotypical views of outsiders. In addition, when strong-willed people lead group discussions, they can pressurize others into conforming, encourage self-censorship and create an illusion of unanimity.

Two heads are not necessarily better than one. Over fifty years of research suggests that irrational thinking occurs when people try to reach decisions in groups, and this can lead to a polarization of opinions and a highly biased assessment of a situation.

If groups are not the answer, what is the best way of making up your mind? According to the research, it is a question of avoiding the various errors and pitfalls that often cloud our thinking. The difficulty is that many of the techniques that underlie rational decision making involve a thorough understanding of probability and logic. However, some of these can be learnt in just a few moments. Take, for example, how to guard against the most common tricks used by sales people, how to decide whether someone is lying, and how to ensure that you never, ever regret a decision again.

Getting Your Foot in the Door, and the Door in Your Face

Let's start with a quick question: imagine being offered two jobs. In terms of working hours, duties, location and career prospects, Job A is absolutely identical to Job B. In fact, the only difference between the two positions is the disparity between your salary and that of your future co-workers. In Job A, your annual pay will be £50,000 and your colleagues will be earning £30,000. In Job B, you will be earning £60,000, and your fellow employees will be on £80,000. Would you be tempted by Job A or Job B? Surveys show that the majority of people opt for Job A.[5]

Seen in purely financial terms, the decision is completely irrational because Job B pays £10,000 more. However, if the scientific study of human nature tells us anything, it is that we are far from rational creatures. Instead, we are social animals easily persuaded by a whole host of factors, including how we feel, how we see ourselves and how we appear to others. Although, objectively speaking, Job B pays more than Job A, in Job A we are earning £20,000 more than our fellow employees, and the feeling of superiority evoked by the pay difference proves more than enough to compensate for the extra earnings that come with Job B.

This subtle, and often unconscious, effect can also influence our buying behaviour.

I can still remember the very first time I saw a demonstrator working in a large department store. I was eight years old, and my parents had taken me to London. We had wandered into the store, and I had become mesmerized by the man enthusiastically demonstrating the very latest breakthrough in kitchen-knife technology. This wonderful piece of equipment was able to do everything you could possibly want from a knife, and several things you probably didn't want, including the ability to cut an empty cola can in half. Towards the end of the pitch, the nice man calmly informed us that the knife retailed for £10.

But then something strange happened. Right before our very eyes, he suddenly transformed into a man who could not prevent himself offering an amazing deal. Actually, the knife was going to be just £8 . . . no . . . £5. And then, because we had been such a great crowd, he was prepared to sell it to us for only £3. Just when we couldn't believe our good fortune, like the end of a carefully choreographed fireworks display, the real explosions started. He was going to give us a second identical knife for no extra cost, throw in five smaller knives for free and put them all in a leatherette case that usually retailed for over £10. Each amazingly generous step surprised and delighted the crowd. More importantly, it persuaded the majority of people, including my parents, to purchase some knives that they had had no intention of buying when they had first walked into the store. Still, it was a lesson learnt. When we got home I attempted to use the wonder knife to cut through an empty cola can and the handle fell off.

My parents and I had been fooled by a technique researchers refer to as 'that's not all'. Without prompting, the sales person keeps making the deal better and better until it becomes totally irresistible. Even the smallest of reductions or tiniest of additions are effective. In one study, 40 per cent of people bought a cupcake and two cookies together for 75 cents, but 73 per cent put their hands in their pockets when the cupcake was advertised as 75 cents and the two cookies were suddenly added for 'free'.[6]

In addition to examining these frequently used principles of persuasion, psychologists have also explored other more unusual, but nevertheless still highly effective, techniques. There is, for example, the so-called 'pique' technique, wherein a strange request makes people pay more attention, and increases the likelihood of compliance. In one study, carried out by Michael Santos and his colleagues from the University of California, a beggar (actually a researcher) asked passers-by if they could spare a quarter or 37 cents.[7] Significantly more people gave away their money when confronted with the unusual request.

Related to this is the 'disrupt then reframe' technique, in which you momentarily surprise a person in order to shake them out of autopilot, and then present a normal request. In a series of studies, experimenters went from door to door selling paper pads for charity.[8] In one condition they stated 'They sell for $3. It's a bargain.' In the 'disrupt then reframe' condition they said, 'They sell for 300 pennies . . . that's $3. It's a bargain.' This strange and surprising change almost doubled sales.

However, much of the work into quick but effective techniques has focused on two principles: getting your foot in the door, and the door in your face.

In the early 1960s, Stanford psychologists Jonathan Freedman and Scott Fraser carried out a groundbreaking experiment into persuasion.[9] The research team started by randomly telephoning more than 150 women and pretending to be from the California Consumers' Group. The researcher asked if they would mind taking part in an unusual survey about their use of household products for a publication called *The Guide*. Unlike their competitors, *The Guide* liked to really get to the bottom of things. So, would it be possible, asked the researcher, for a team of six men to come and spend a couple of hours rooting through their cupboards? The search was going to be thorough: it would involve going into every storage area to catalogue all the soap, washing-up liquid, cleaning fluid and bleach that they could get their hands on. Perhaps not surprisingly, less than a quarter of the women agreed to this forensic-style search. This was, however, only part of the experiment. Another group of women received a similar call, but instead of requesting access to all areas, the researcher asked if they would mind taking part in a quick telephone survey about the household products they preferred. Almost everyone agreed. However, three days later, they received a second call asking if they would mind if the six-man search team investigated their cupboards. Under these circumstances, over half of the women agreed.

In a follow-up experiment, the same team wanted to see if they could persuade people to place a very large sign proclaiming 'Drive Carefully' in their front gardens. Even though the sign was apparently designed to help cut speeding in the area, almost no residents accepted the offer. The researchers then approached a second set of residents and asked them to display a much smaller sign that was just three inches square, and almost everyone accepted. Two weeks later, the researchers returned and asked whether they would now mind replacing the small sign with the large placard.

An amazing 76 per cent had no objections, and accepted the proposition.

These experiments demonstrate the power of the 'foot in the door' technique. People are far more likely to agree to a big request if they have already agreed to a small one.

Over forty years of research has shown that the technique works in many different situations.[10] Get people to make modest donations to charity, and larger ones will follow. Get employees to agree little changes in working conditions, and bigger ones are accepted more easily. Get them to change normal light bulbs for low-energy ones and increase the likelihood of far more significant energy-efficient lifestyle changes.

Finally, when researchers are not getting their foot in the door, they are encouraging people to slam it in their faces. Whereas the foot in the door is about starting low and gradually working up, this technique involves beginning with an outrageous request, receiving a firm 'no', and then getting people to agree to a much more modest offer. Perhaps the best-known work into the principle has been carried out by Robert Cialdini and his colleagues from Arizona State University.[11] In his classic study, a research team posed as members of the County Youth Counseling Program, and asked students whether they would mind taking a group of juvenile delinquents to the zoo for the day. They were not surprised to discover that less than 20 per cent of the students accepted the offer of a day out with the animals.

Unperturbed, the research team adopted a different tactic. This time, they approached another group of people with a much larger request, asking whether, for the next two years, they would mind donating 2 hours of their time each week to help counsel the juvenile delinquents. Once again, their request met with widespread refusal. However, once people had turned them down, the research team returned with a far more modest request. Yes, you guessed it – how did they feel about just taking the juvenile delinquents for a day out at the zoo? Under these circumstances, over half of the students agreed.

In another example, French researchers arranged for a young woman to find herself without any money in a restaurant, and so have to ask other customers to help pay her bill.[12] When she asked for just a few francs, only 10 per cent of people offered the money. However, when she started off asking for them to cover the entire bill, and then moved on to requesting just a few francs, 75 per cent of people put their hands in their pockets. Once again, this technique is effective in many different situations. From negotiating about house prices to working hours, salary to overdraft limits, if you are selling, it pays to start high.

Persuasion is all about getting your foot in the door, the door in your face, surprising people with an unusual request, and offering an endless stream of bargains. More importantly, research shows that these techniques can be learnt in exactly 47 seconds. Actually, 30 seconds tops. And that includes a free set of smaller knives.

IN 59 SECONDS OR LESS

We are not the rational creatures that we like to think we are, and can be easily persuaded by a variety of quick, and effective, techniques. Beware of people using the 'that's not all' principle, offering unprompted discounts and bargains to get you to part with your money. Likewise, be wary of those who start small and build up, or start big and quickly back down to a more 'reasonable' offer. Of course, it is also possible to use exactly the same techniques to influence others. That's fine, but as Obi-Wan Kenobi once famously noted, your new-found force can have a strong influence on the weak-minded, so do be careful to use it only for good.

Never Regret a Decision Again

> When making a decision of minor importance, I have always found it advantageous to consider all the pros and cons. In vital matters however . . . the decision should come from the unconscious, from somewhere within.
>
> Sigmund Freud

Imagine your boss telling you they think their office looks a little uncultured, and asking if you would be good enough to a buy an expensive-looking modern-art print to liven up the walls. You put on your coat and drive to the local gallery, only to find that they only have the four prints overleaf in stock.

How do you make up your mind? One possibility is to think about the pros and cons of each piece in terms of your boss's personality, the company image and the existing office décor. Alternatively, you could just trust your gut instinct, and choose the print that 'feels' right. Or you could rely on a different technique that, according to recent research, is significantly more likely to result in a good decision.

A few years ago, psychologists Ap Dijksterhuis and Zeger van Olden carried out a remarkable experiment using the same type of poster-choosing procedure.[13] In their study, participants were asked to come into the lab, look at five posters and use one of three techniques to help choose the poster they

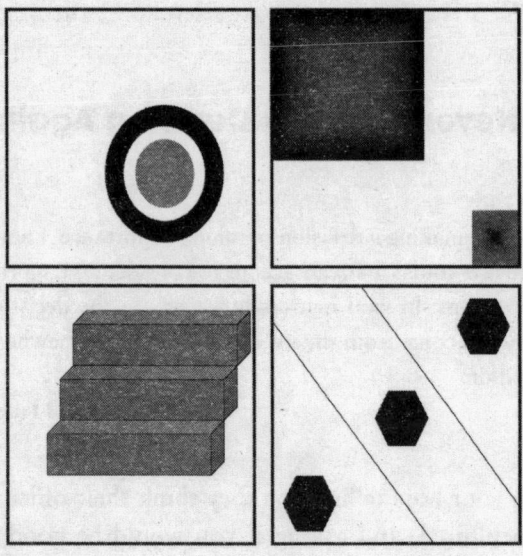

liked best. One group were asked to study each of the posters for about a minute-and-a-half, list some key reasons why they liked and disliked each one, carefully analyse their thoughts, and then select the winning poster. A second group glanced at all five posters, and chose the one they liked best. Those in the third group were shown the posters quickly, asked to spend 5 minutes solving difficult anagrams, briefly shown the posters a second time, and then asked to make their choice. After making their decision, all the participants rated the degree to which they liked all five posters.

After everyone had made their selection and ratings, the experimenters carried out an act of unprecedented generosity, giving them their favourite poster as a free gift for taking part in the study. Finally, just as each person left the laboratory clutching their rolled-up booty, the experimenter casually remarked that it would be good to have their telephone number, just in case there had been a problem with the data storage and they needed to rerun the study.

Now, if you take part in a study and a researcher explains they need your telephone number in case of a hard-disk failure, they are up to something. The most likely scenario is that the experiment is far from over, and they intend to call you at a future date. The call may take a number of forms. Your telephone might ring in the dead of night, and a market researcher might ask if you would mind taking part in a survey about soap. Alternatively, you might get a call from an alleged long-lost friend wondering if you want to meet. Or, as happened here, one of the team might call to say hello, and ask how you are getting on with your poster.

About a month after the experiment, the researchers contacted the participants and asked them how satisfied they were with their poster, and how many euros they would be prepared to sell it for. When they had originally chosen their poster in the laboratory, the participants who had been asked to carefully consider the pros and cons of each print were confident they had made the right choice. In fact, they were far more confident that those who had made their choice within moments of seeing the posters, or those who had been asked to solve anagrams and then decide. However, four weeks later, a very different picture emerged. The participants who had spent time solving anagrams and then chose their poster were the happiest with their choices and wanted significantly more money to part with their cherished print.

You might argue that the choices made in these types of studies are unlike the complicated choices that people have to make in real life. In fact, the researchers have obtained the same curious effect again and again.[14] Whether it is deciding which apartment to rent, car to buy or which shares to invest in, people who are shown the options but then kept busy working on a difficult mental activity make better decisions than others.

Why should this be the case? Dijksterhuis and van Olden claim this is about harnessing the power of your unconscious mind. When having to decide between options that only differ in one or two ways, your conscious mind is very good at studying the situation in a rational, level-headed fashion and deciding the best course of action. However, it only has a limited ability to juggle a small number of facts and figures at any one time, and so is not so good when the going gets complex. Then, instead of looking at the situation as a whole, the conscious mind tends to focus on the most obvious elements and, in doing so, can miss the bigger picture. In contrast, your unconscious mind is much better at dealing with the complex decisions that pervade many aspects of our lives. Given time, it slowly works through all the factors, and eventually provides a more balanced decision. Dijksterhuis and van Olden's explanation for the effect, referred to as the Unconscious Thought Theory, argues for a kind of middle ground for making complex decisions. Thinking too hard about an issue is, in many ways, as bad as making an instant choice. Instead, it is all a question of knowing what needs to be decided, then distracting your conscious mind and allowing your unconscious to work away. And how do you get your unconscious mind to work on a problem? Well, just as we saw in the section on boosting creativity, one technique involves keeping the conscious mind busy with a distracting but difficult task, like solving anagrams or counting backwards in threes.

DECISION MAKING

Solving anagrams prior to an important decision is, of course, not the only way of helping ensure you won't regret a decision. In fact, according to other research, there is an even quicker way of maximizing the likelihood of you regretting *rien*.

At Cornell University, Thomas Gilovich has been studying the psychology of regret for over a decade. His findings make for fascinating reading.[15] Much of his work has involved asking people to look back over their lives and describe their biggest regret. Around 75 per cent of respondents regret not doing something, with the top three slots taken by not studying hard enough at school, not taking advantage of an important opportunity and failing to spend enough time with friends and family. In contrast, only 25 per cent of people regret doing something, such as making a bad career decision, marrying someone they didn't love or having a child at the wrong point in their lives.

It seems that part of the problem is it's relatively easy to see the negative consequences of something that's happened. You made a poor career decision and so were stuck in a job you didn't enjoy. You had kids when you were very young and so couldn't go out with friends. You married the wrong person and constantly argued. The negative consequences are known, and although the potential for regret may still be substantial, it is limited. However, the situation is completely different when it comes to things that didn't happen. Suddenly, the possible positive benefits seem almost endless. What would have happened if you had accepted that job offer, been brave enough to ask the love of your life on a date or spent more time at school studying? Under these circumstances you are limited only by the power of your imagination.

Gilovich's fascinating work provides scientific support for the words of the seventeenth-century American poet John Greenleaf Whittier, who once noted, 'For of all sad words of tongue or pen, the saddest are these: It might have been.'

IN 59 SECONDS OR LESS

Anagrams and the Unconscious Mind. When making straight-forward decisions, stick with the conscious mind by thinking about the pros and cons and assessing the situation in a rational, level-headed way. However, for more complex choices, try giving your conscious mind a rest and letting your unconscious work. The following exercise is based on the research of Dijksterhuis and van Olden, and is designed to help the decision-making process.

A What decisions do you have to make?

B Work through as many of these anagrams as possible in 5 minutes. If you get stuck, don't struggle for too long and instead move onto the next one.

Anagram	Clue	Your answer
1 Open change	European city	....
2 A motto	Well-known vegetable	....
3 Past eight	Popular in Italy	....
4 Noon leap	European general	....
5 Ring late	Three sides	....
6 Lithe cats	Track and field	....

7	Did train	Island holiday location	....
8	Eat	Time for . . .	....
9	Loaded inn	Flower	....
10	Cool cheat	Better than diamonds for many women	....
11	Neat grain	South American country	....
12	Lob aloft	Game of two halves	....
13	Groan	Popular in churches	....
14	Cried	Alcoholic drink	....
15	Cheap	Soft fruit	....

C Now, without thinking too much about the problem, write down your decision here . . .

Anagram answers
1 Copenhagen 2 Tomato 3 Spaghetti 4 Napoleon 5 Triangle 6 Athletics
7 Trinidad 8 Tea 9 Dandelion 10 Chocolate 11 Argentina 12 Football
13 Organ 14 Cider 15 Peach

Ring-Fencing Regret. Research shows that when most people look back on their lives, they tend to regret things they didn't do. However, once you understand this, there are quick and effective techniques that can be used to help avoid feelings of regret.

First, to help prevent regret in the first place, adopt a 'will do' attitude to opportunity. As writer Max Lucado once suggested, 'Go to the effort. Invest the time. Write the letter. Make the apology. Take the trip. Purchase the gift. Do it. The seized opportunity renders joy. The neglected brings regret.' Second, if you do regret not doing something, see if there is anything you can do to remedy the situation. Write the letter, make that telephone call, spend more time with the family, mend broken relationships, go back to college and get the grades. Use the regret as a wake-up call and way of motivating yourself. Finally, if it really isn't possible to do anything to make things better, make a mental picture of a ring fence round the imaginary 'what might have been' benefits that might otherwise occupy your thoughts. Instead of dwelling on the positive things that might have happened, spend time thinking about three benefits of your current situation and three negative consequences that could have occurred had you taken the decision that's causing the regret.

Are You a Maximizer or Satisficer?

Take a few moments to read the following ten statements, and assign each a rating to indicate the degree to which they describe you.[16] Don't spend too long thinking about each statement and answer honestly.

Rating

1 = strongly disagree to 5 = strongly agree

1 When watching television, I tend to channel   1 2 3 4 5
   hop rather than stick with just one
   programme.

2 I tend to find shopping difficult because I   1 2 3 4 5
   won't buy something unless it is exactly
   what I want.

3 I take a long time to choose a rental video   1 2 3 4 5
   or DVD because I like to consider lots of
   possible films.

4 I sometimes think about the opportunities   1 2 3 4 5
   that have passed me by in life.

5 I like to consider all the options before   1 2 3 4 5
   making a decision.

6 I don't like making decisions that are   1 2 3 4 5
   irreversible.

7 When I have made a decision, I often   1 2 3 4 5
   wonder how things would have worked
   out if I had made a different choice.

8 I find it difficult to settle for second best.   1 2 3 4 5

9 When on the internet, I tend to surf around,   1 2 3 4 5
quickly skipping from one page to another.

10 I rarely feel happy with what I have because   1 2 3 4 5
I find it easy to imagine getting something
better.

To score the questionnaire, add up your ratings. Low scores run between 10 and 20, medium scores between 21 and 39, high scores between 40 and 50.

Research suggests that people often approach many aspects of their lives using one of two fundamental strategies – maximizing or satisficing. Extreme maximizers tend to check all available options constantly to make sure they have picked the best one. In contrast, extreme satisficers only look until they have found something that fulfils their needs. As a result, maximizers objectively achieve more, but take longer to find what they want, and tend to be less happy because of a tendency to dwell on how things could have been.

For example, in one study looking at job-hunting, researchers categorized over 500 students from eleven universities as maximizers or satisficers, and then tracked them as they tried to find employment.[17] The maximizers ended with salaries that were, on average, 20 per cent higher than the satisficers, but they were also less satisfied with their job search, and were more prone to regret, pessimism, anxiety and depression.

If you are a maximizer, and find yourself wasting too much time searching for the perfect product, you might find it helpful to limit the resources you put into some activities (e.g. only give yourself 30 minutes to find your friend a birthday card) or make certain decisions irreversible (e.g. by throwing away receipts).[18]

There is an old adage that happiness is about wanting what you have, not having what you want. It seems that for the maximizer, even when they get what they want, they may not always want what they get.

How to Decide Whether People Are Telling You the Truth, the Whole Truth and Nothing but the Truth

How do you think people tend to behave when they lie to you? Take a look at the list of behaviours in the table below, and place a tick in either the 'True' or 'False' column after every statement.

When people lie, they tend to . . .	True	False
avoid eye contact	❑	❑
smile more	❑	❑
squirm in their seats or, if they are standing up, shift from foot to foot	❑	❑
develop sweaty hands and faces	❑	❑
cover their mouths with their hands	❑	❑
give long and rambling answers to questions	❑	❑
give answers that sound unstructured and jumbled	❑	❑
nod their head more	❑	❑
gesture more	❑	❑
grow longer noses	❑	❑

People are often surprisingly economical with the truth. In a survey I conducted with the *Daily Telegraph*, a quarter of respondents claimed to have told a lie within the last 24 hours. Other work suggests that an impressive 90 per cent of people say they have lied on a date, and about 40 per cent of the population are happy to lie to their friends. Deception is also a major problem in the workplace, with surveys suggesting that 80 per cent of people have lied during a job interview, and almost 50 per cent of employees have told at least one important 'porky pie' to their boss.[19]

In view of the prevalence of lying, it is not surprising that all sorts of techniques have been developed in an attempt to detect such fibbery. In ancient times, there was, for example, the ever-popular red-hot poker test. In a procedure that could reasonably be described as hell on earth, a poker would be placed into a fierce fire, removed, and the accused forced to lick it three times. The theory was that the innocent would have a sufficient amount of saliva on their tongues to prevent burning, whereas the guilty would have much drier tongues and thus become somewhat attached to the poker.

According to the history books, a similar, but less barbaric, technique was used during the Spanish Inquisition. On these occasions, the accused would be made to eat some barley bread and cheese, while those around prayed that the Angel Gabriel would prevent the person from successfully swallowing the food if they had lied. To my knowledge, neither of these techniques has been subjected to proper scientific testing, in part, I am guessing, because it would be tricky to obtain the necessary informed consent from participants and the Angel Gabriel. However, if such studies were to be carried out, any positive findings would support one of the most commonly held theories about lying – the Anxiety Hypothesis.

According to this idea, people become very nervous when they lie, and so develop a variety of anxiety-related symptoms, including a drying of the mouth which could cause them to become stuck to red-hot pokers and find it difficult to swallow barley bread. Although intuitively appealing, obtaining reliable proof for the theory has proved far from easy, with some research suggesting that liars are no more stressed than those telling the truth. In a recent study, for example, conducted by Richard Gramzow from the University of Southampton and his colleagues, students were first connected to machinery that measured their heart rate, and then interviewed about their recent exam performance.[20] The interview involved the students describing the grades they had obtained over the years, and comparing their own skills and abilities with classmates. What the students didn't know was that after the interview the experimenters were going to obtain their actual exam results, and so would be able to identify which students had been telling the truth and which had been exaggerating. Interestingly, the results revealed that nearly half the students had exaggerated their academic achievements. Even more interestingly, the heart-rate data showed that those who had raised their grades for the occasion were no more stressed than their honest colleagues. If anything, they were slightly more relaxed.

The results from studies using high-tech anxiety measuring machinery are, at best, mixed. However, that hasn't stopped the public accepting the idea that people become terribly tense when they are economical with the truth. Perhaps driven by the countless films and television programmes showing liars with sweaty palms and racing hearts, most believe that the best signs of deceit are those associated with increased anxiety.

Teams of researchers have spent hours carefully comparing films of known liars and truth tellers, with trained observers carefully coding every smile, blink and gesture. Each minute of footage takes about an hour to analyse, but the resulting data allows researchers to compare the behaviour associated with a lie and the truth, and thus uncover even the subtlest of differences. The findings are fascinating. Honestly.

Take a look at the questionnaire at the start of this section. How many ticks did you put into the 'True' column? All the behaviours listed in the questionnaire are things people do when they become nervous: they avoid eye contact, squirm in their seats, sweat and start to gabble their words. According to the researchers who have spent hours coding the behaviour of liars and truth tellers, not one of the items in the table is reliably associated with lying. In fact, liars are just as likely to look you in the eye as truth tellers, they don't move their hands nervously and they don't shift about in their seats.

However, because most people hold these mind myths in their heads, they are terrible at deciding whether someone is lying. Present them with videotapes of people lying and telling the truth and ask them to spot the liar, and they perform little better than chance. Show adults films of children describing a true event and a fictitious one and the adults are unable to tell which is which.[21] Ask someone to convince their long-term partner that they found a photograph of an attractive person unattractive, and they are surprisingly successful.[22] Even groups of lawyers, police officers, psychologists and social workers have been unable to reliably detect deception.[23]

So what really gives away a liar? Although lying does not always make people stressed, it usually taxes their minds. Lying involves having to think about what other people already know or could find out, what is plausible and what fits in with what you have said before. Because of this, liars tend to do the things that correspond with thinking hard about a problem or issue. They tend not to move their arms and legs so much, cut down on gesturing, repeat the same phrases, give shorter and less detailed answers, take longer before starting to answer, pause and hesitate more. In addition, there is also evidence that they distance themselves from the lie, causing their language to become more impersonal. As a result, liars often reduce the number of times that they say words like 'I', 'me' and 'mine', and tend to use 'his' and 'her' rather than people's names. Finally, there is increased evasiveness, wherein liars tend to avoid answering the question completely, perhaps by switching topics or asking a question of their own.

To detect deception, forget about looking for signs of tension, nervousness and anxiety. Instead, a liar is likely to look as though they are thinking hard for no good reason, converse in a strangely impersonal tone, and incorporate an evasiveness that would make even a politician or second-hand-car salesman blush.

IN 59 SECONDS OR LESS

Body Language. For successful lie detection, jettison the behavioural myths surrounding the Anxiety Hypothesis, and look for signs more commonly associated with having to think hard. Forget the idea that liars have sweaty palms, fidget and avoid eye contact. Instead, look for a person suddenly becoming more static and cutting down on their gestures. Also, learn to listen. Be on your guard for a sudden decrease in detail, an increase in pauses and hesitations and a sudden avoidance of the words 'me', 'mine' and 'I', but an increase in 'her' and 'him'. If someone suddenly becomes very evasive, press for a straight answer.[24]

To help spot possible shifts, try establishing what researchers have referred to as an 'honest baseline'. Before asking questions that are likely to elicit deceptive answers, start with those that are far more likely to make the person respond in an honest way. During these initial answers, develop an understanding of how they behave when they are telling the truth by looking at their body language and listening to the words they say. Then, during the answers to the trickier questions, watch out for the behavioural shifts outlined above.

Also, remember that even if you do see these signals, they are not an absolute guarantee of a lie. Unlike taxes and death, nothing is that certain when it comes to lying. Instead, they are simply an indication that all is perhaps not as it should be, and a good reason to dig deeper.

DECISION MAKING

Email Me. Communication expert Jeff Hancock and his colleagues at Cornell University asked students to spend a week making a note of all of their significant face-to-face conversations, telephone chats, texts and emails, and then work through the list indicating which contained lies.[25] The results revealed that people lied in 14 per cent of emails, 21 per cent of texts, 27 per cent of face-to-face conversations and 37 per cent of telephone calls. According to Hancock, people are reluctant to lie in emails because they are recorded, and so their words could come back to haunt them. So, if you want to help minimize the risk of a lie, ask them to email you.

Deciding How Long Something Will Take

In an insightful study into time management, Roger Buehler from Wilfrid Laurier University asked students to indicate when they expected to finish an important term essay.[26] The students believed they would hand in their work, on average, 10 days before the deadline. They were, however, being far too optimistic and, in reality, tended to finish the essays just one day before the deadline. This effect, known as the Planning Fallacy, is not limited to students trying to finish their essays on time. Research shows that people have a strong tendency to underestimate how long a project will take, and that people working in groups are especially likely to have unrealistic expectations.[27] Even when they are trying to be realistic, people tend to imagine that everything will go to plan, and do not consider the inevitable unexpected delays and unforeseen problems.

However, Buehler's work has also suggested a quick and effective way of overcoming the problem. When his students were told to think about when they had managed to finish similar tasks in the past, their answers for meeting future deadlines proved much more accurate. It seems that to get an accurate estimate of the time needed to complete a project, you need to look at how long it took to finish broadly similar projects in the past.

If that doesn't work, you could always try a technique investigated by Justin Kruger and Matt Evans at the

University of Illinois at Urbana-Champaign.[28] In their studies, participants estimated how long they would take to carry out a relatively complicated activity, such as getting ready for a date. One group were asked to make their estimates, while another group were encouraged to 'unpack' the activity into its constituent parts (showering, changing clothes, panicking) before deciding. Those who carried out the mental unpacking produced estimates that proved far more accurate than other participants. So, to find out how long it really will take you to do something, isolate all of the steps involved before making your time estimate.

9. PARENTING

The Mozart myth, how to choose the best name for a baby,
instantly divine a child's destiny using just three marshmallows,
and effectively praise young minds.

Wolfgang Amadeus Mozart was born in 1756, composed some of the world's greatest pieces of classical music and died, probably of acute rheumatic fever, in 1791. He was a genius. However, some people believe his music is able to reach parts of the brain other compositions can't, and can make you more intelligent. Moreover, they seem convinced that this effect is especially powerful with young impressionable minds, recommending that babies be exposed to a daily dose of Mozart for maximum impact. Their message has spread far and wide, but is it really possible to boost a youngster's brainpower using the magic of Mozart?

In 1993, researcher Frances Rauscher and her colleagues from the University of California published a scientific paper that changed the world.[1] They had taken a group of 36 college students, randomly placed them in one of three groups, and asked each group to carry out a different 10-minute exercise. One group was asked to listen to Mozart's Sonata for Two Pianos in D major, the second group was played a standard relaxation tape, and the third sat in complete silence. Following the exercise, everyone completed a standard test designed to measure one aspect of intelligence, namely the ability to manipulate spatial information mentally (see illustration opposite). The results revealed that those who had listened to Mozart scored significantly higher than those subjected to the relaxation tape or complete silence.

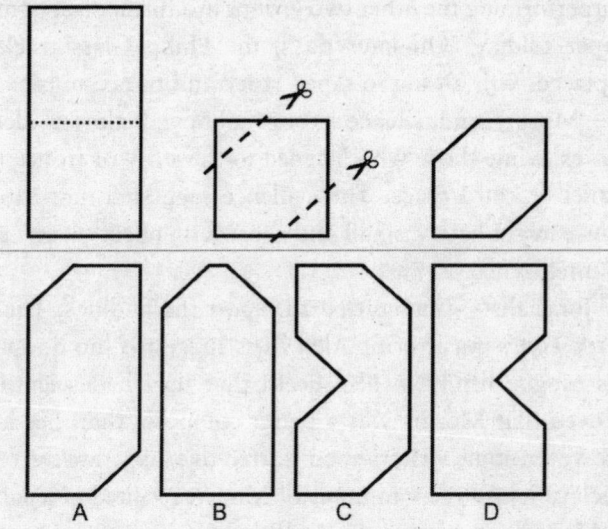

The type of item that might appear in a test to measure the ability to manipulate spatial information mentally. The top row shows a piece of paper being folded in half and then having two pieces cut away. Participants are asked to look at the four shapes along the bottom row and choose the shape you would see when you unfolded the cut paper.

The authors also noted that the effect was only temporary, lasting between 10 and 15 minutes.

Two years later, the same group followed up their initial study with a second experiment involving a larger group of students, which took place over the course of several days.[2] The students were again randomly placed into one of three groups. In the first part of the experiment, one group listened to Mozart, another group sat in silence and a third heard a Philip Glass track ('Music In Changing Parts'). Again, strong differences emerged, with those who listened to Mozart outperforming the other two groups in a further test of mental paper folding. On later days, the Philip Glass track was replaced with an audio-taped story and trance music. Now, the Mozart and silence groups obtained almost identical scores, while those who listened to the story or trance music trailed in third place. The evidence suggested that Mozart's music might have a small and short-term effect on one aspect of intelligence.

Journalists soon started to report the findings. The *New York Times* music critic Alex Ross suggested (no doubt with his tongue firmly in his cheek) that they had scientifically proved that Mozart was a better composer than Beethoven. However, some writers soon started to exaggerate the results, declaring just a few minutes of Mozart resulted in a substantial long-term increase in intelligence.

The idea spread like wildfire, and during the latter half of the 1990s the story mutated even further away from the original research. Up to that point, not a single study had examined the effect of Mozart's music on the intelligence of babies. However, unwilling to let the facts get in the way of a good headline, some journalists reported that babies became brighter after listening to Mozart. These articles were not isolated examples of sloppy journalism. About 40 per cent of the media reports published towards the end of the 1990s mentioned this alleged benefit to babies.[3] The continued popular media's coverage of what was now being labelled the 'Mozart effect' even impacted upon social policy. In 1998, the state of Georgia supported the distribution of free CDs containing classical music to mothers with new-borns, and the state of Florida passed a bill requiring state-funded day-centres to play classical music on a daily basis.

The alleged Mozart effect had become transformed into an urban legend, and a significant slice of the population incorrectly believed that listening to Mozart's music could help boost all aspects of intelligence, that the effects were long-lasting, and that even babies could benefit. However, as the 1990s turned into the twenty-first century, the situation went from bad to worse. First, Christopher Chabris from Harvard University collected together the findings from all the studies that had attempted to replicate Rauscher's original results, and concluded that the effect, if it existed at all, was much smaller than had originally been thought.[4] Then, other work suggested that even if it did exist, the effect may have nothing to do with the special properties of Mozart's Sonata for Two Pianos in D major, and could in fact be associated with the general feelings of happiness produced by this type of classical music. For example, in one study, researchers compared the effects of Mozart's music with a much sadder piece (Albinoni's Adagio in G minor for Organ and Strings), and found evidence that, once again, Mozart had more of an effect than the alternative.[5] However, when the research team conducted a control experiment about how happy and excited the music made participants feel, the alleged Mozart effect suddenly vanished. In another study, psychologists compared the effect of listening to Mozart with that of hearing an audiotape of Stephen King's short story 'The Last Rung on the Ladder'.[6] When participants preferred Mozart to King, their performance on the mental-manipulation task was better than when listening to the piano music. However, when they preferred King to Mozart, they performed better after they had heard his story.

The public's belief about the alleged Mozart effect is a

mind myth. There is almost no convincing scientific evidence to suggest that playing his piano music to babies will have any long-term or meaningful impact on their intelligence. Would it be fair to conclude that there is no way of using music to boost children's intelligence? Actually, no. In fact, evidence for the benefits of music exists, but it involves throwing away the Mozart CDs and adopting a more hands-on attitude.

Some research has shown that children attending music lessons tend to be brighter than their classmates. However, it is difficult to sift correlation from causation. It could be that having music lessons makes you brighter, or that brighter or more privileged children are more likely to take music lessons. A few years ago, psychologist Glenn Schellenberg decided to carry out a study to help settle the matter.[7]

Schellenberg started by placing an advertisement in a local newspaper offering free weekly arts lessons to six-year-old children. The parents of over 140 children replied, and each was randomly assigned to one of four groups. Three of the groups were given lessons over several months at the Royal Conservatory of Music in Toronto, while the fourth group acted as a control and didn't receive their lessons until after the study had finished. Of those who attended the lessons, one third were taught keyboard skills, another third were given voice training, the final third went to drama classes. Before and after their lessons, all the children completed a standard intelligence test.

The results showed clear IQ improvements in children who had been taught keyboard skills and given voice lessons, whereas those given drama lessons were no different to the control group. Why should this be the case? Well, Schellenberg believes that learning music involves several key skills that help children's self-discipline and thinking, including long periods of focused attention, practising and memorization.

Whatever the explanation, when it comes to boosting the brainpower of your offspring, perhaps it is time to take that Mozart CD out of the player and get the kids to start tinkling the ivories.

Playing the Name Game

Parents often find it surprisingly difficult to decide what to call their baby, in the knowledge that their child is going to spend his or her entire life living with the consequences of their choice. Research suggests that they are right to give the issue careful thought because of the large body of work showing that people's names can have a strange, and sometimes powerful, effect.

For example, in my previous book, *Quirkology*, I described work suggesting that when it comes to where people choose to live, there is an over-representation of people called Florence living in Florida, George in Georgia, Kenneth in Kentucky and Virgil in Virginia.[8] Also, in terms of marriage partners, research has revealed that more couples share the same letter of their family name than is predicted by chance. It is even possible that people's political views are, to some extent, shaped by their names. Research into the 2000 presidential campaign indicated that people whose surnames began with the letter 'B' were especially likely to make contributions to the Bush campaign, whereas those whose surnames began with the letter 'G' were more likely to contribute to the Gore campaign.

Since then, I have conducted additional work that has uncovered other ways in which your surname might influence your life. I recently teamed up Roger Highfield, then science editor of the *Daily Telegraph*, to discover whether people who had surnames that began with a letter towards the start of the alphabet were more successful in life than those with names towards the end. In other words, are the Abbots and Adams of the world are more likely to do better than the Youngs and the Yorks?

There was good reason to think there may indeed be a link. In 2006, American economists Liran Einav and Leeat Yariv analysed the surnames of academics working in economics departments at American universities, and found that those whose initials came early in the alphabet were more likely to be in the best-rated departments, become fellows of the Econometric Society, and win a Nobel Prize.[9] Publishing their remarkable findings in the *Journal of Economic Perspectives*, they argued that 'alphabetical discrimination' was probably due to the list of authors on academic journal papers often being placed in alphabetic order, resulting in academics with initials towards the start of the alphabet appearing more prominent than their alphabetically challenged peers.

I wondered whether the same type of effect might apply outside the world of economics. After all, whether it's on a school register, at a job interview or in the exam hall, people with surnames towards the start of the alphabet are accustomed to being put first. We often associate the top of a list with winners and the bottom with losers, so could all these small experiences accumulate and make a long-term impact?

Everyone participating in the experiment stated their sex, age, surname and rated how successful they had been in various aspects of their life. The results revealed that those with surnames beginning with letters towards the start of the alphabet rated themselves more successful than those with later letters. The effect was especially pronounced in career success, suggesting that alphabetical discrimination is alive and well in the workplace.

What could account for this strange effect? One pattern in the data provided an important clue. The surname effect increased with age, giving the impression that the effect was not due to childhood experiences, but gradually increased over the years. It seems that the constant exposure to being at the top or bottom of the alphabet league slowly makes a difference to the way in which people see themselves. So should these results give those whose surname initial falls towards the end of the alphabet cause for concern? As a Wiseman, and therefore someone with a lifetime's experience of coming towards the end of alphabetical lists, I take some comfort from the fact that the effect is theoretically fascinating, but, in practical terms, very small.

Even after drawing up a shortlist of possible names for their offspring, and asking friends and family for advice, some people still struggle. Is it better to go with a traditional or a modern name? Is naming a child after a celebrity a good idea? Is it more important to have a name that rolls off the tongue or stands out from the crowd? Psychology can lend a helping hand.

Previous work has shown that people with names with positive associations do especially well in life. For example, teachers tend to award higher essay grades to children with names that are seen as more likeable (Rose, for example),[10] whereas college students whose names have undesirable associations experience high levels of social isolation, and those whose surnames happen to have negative connotations (such as 'Short', 'Little' or 'Bent') are especially likely to suffer feelings of inferiority.[11]

I teamed up with the Edinburgh International Science Festival to help discover which first names were seen as especially successful and attractive in the twenty-first century. This study involved more than 6,000 people going online and indicating whether they thought some of the most popular first names in the UK appeared successful and attractive. Strong trends emerged. Traditional names with royal associations (such as James and Elizabeth) were viewed as highly successful and intelligent. In contrast, the most attractive female names tended to be soft-sounding and end with the 'ee' sound (such as Lucy and Sophie), whereas the sexiest male names were short and often more rugged-sounding (such as Jack and Ryan). At the other end of the spectrum, Lisa and Brian were seen as the least successful, and Ann and George as the most unattractive.

There is also the issue of initials. As noted in *Quirkology*, research by Nicholas Christenfeld and his co-workers from the University of California suggests that a person's initials may become an issue of life or death.[12] After analysing a huge computerized database containing millions of Californian death certificates, they discovered that men with positive initials (such as ACE, HUG and JOY) lived around four-and-a-half years longer than average, whereas those with negative initials (such as PIG, BUM and DIE) died about three years earlier. Women with positive initials lived an extra three years, although there was no detrimental effect for those with negative initials.

New research conducted in 2007 by Leif Nelson and Joseph Simmons indicates that these effects are not just limited to the relatively small number of people whose initials happen to make especially positive or negative words.[13] According to their work, even the hint of initial-based positivity or nega-tivity is enough to exert a major influence over people's lives.

In certain situations, single letters are associated with suc-cess or failure. Perhaps the best known, and, in many ways, most important example of this occurs during the grading of many exams. In most forms of testing, those who have done well are awarded As and Bs, whereas those towards the bottom of the class tend to receive Cs and Ds. Nelson and Simmons wondered whether people whose first or last initials matched one of the two top grades might be unconsciously motivated to perform well in exams, whereas those whose names start with either C or D might not try to achieve such high marks. To find out if this bold hypothesis was true, the duo analysed 15 years of students' grade-point averages from a large American university. Remarkable as it may seem, the results revealed that students with first or last names start-ing with an A or B obtained significantly higher grade-point averages than those beginning with the letters C or D.

Excited by their initial success, Nelson and Simmons turned their attention to the impact that this effect might have on peoples' lives. They thought that if students whose names began with an A or B obtained higher exam marks than those beginning with C or D, the former group might find it easier to get into better graduate schools and so have more successful careers. However, to test their hypothesis, they needed to find a large, searchable database containing students' initials and the graduate school they had attended. After much searching, they eventually found the perfect resource – the online database of the American Bar Associa-tion. The research team created a computer program capable of scanning the online information for the number of people

PARENTING

with the key initials in each of the 170 law schools listed. After designating the quality of the schools using information from the *U.S. News and World Report*, and comparing this with the data from almost 400,000 lawyers, Nelson and Simmons had their result. As the quality of law schools declined, so too did the proportion of lawyers with the initials A or B. As they note at the end of their report, 'It seems that people with names like Adlai and Bill tend to go to better law schools than do those with names like Chester and Dwight.'

IN 59 SECONDS OR LESS

Research shows that people with surnames beginning with a letter towards the start of the alphabet are more successful in life than those with names towards the end. Obviously, the potential for choosing a successful surname is limited, unless you are prepared to change your name by deed poll, or, if you are female, marry a man with a surname towards the start of the alphabet. However, when choosing a child's first name, other research can provide a helping hand. For example, traditional names with royal associations are seen as particularly successful and intelligent. Finally, do not underestimate the power of initials. Avoid creating a set of initials that make a word with negative associations, and help ensure exam success by going for names starting with the letter A or B, and avoiding those beginning with the letters C or D.

Praise Be!

Almost every manual on good parenting promotes the power of praise, with some self-help gurus suggesting that the single best thing you can do for your child is to build up their self-esteem by constantly giving compliments. Tell your children how intelligent they are when they pass an exam. Congratulate them on their artistic streak when they produce a nice drawing. Celebrate their athletic abilities when they score a goal or win a race. According to this approach, negativity should be banished when the focus is firmly placed on even the smallest of successes.

The idea has enormous intuitive appeal. Always tell the little ones they are wonderful, and surely they will grow up into confident and happy people. So far, so good. There is, however, just one small problem with this rather utopian view of the human psyche. Research suggests that telling a child that they are bright and talented is a terrible thing to do.

In the late 1990s, Claudia Mueller and Carol Dweck from Columbia University conducted a large-scale programme of research into the psychology of praise.[14] Their experiments involved more than 400 children, aged between ten and twelve, who were drawn from a variety of ethnic and socio-economic backgrounds. In a typical study, the children were presented with an intelligence test in which they were asked to look at rows of shapes and, based on logic alone, work out which shape should come next in each series. After they had worked through the problems, the experimenters took away their workbooks, calculated the scores but provided each child with false feedback. They explained that each child had done really well and solved 80 per cent of the problems correctly.

In addition to this feedback, one group of the children were told they must be really bright to have solved so many puzzles, while another group were greeted with stony silence. According to the self-help gurus who promote the positive power of praise, just spending a few seconds compliment-ing a child's ability can have a dramatic effect. The results revealed that they are right, but perhaps not quite in the way they had anticipated.

In the next stage of the experiment, the researchers told the children that they could choose one of two tasks. They were told one of the tasks was quite difficult and so they might not succeed, but they would be challenged and learn even if they failed. In contrast, the other task was much easier, so they were likely to do well but learn little. Around 65 per cent of the children who had been told they were intelligent opted for the easy task, compared to just 45 per cent of those who had not been praised. The children who had been told they were intelligent were far more likely to avoid challeng-ing situations, and instead stick to the easy stuff. This is not exactly good news for the 'praise be' approach to parenting. However, worse was still to come.

In the next phase of the experiment, the researchers gave the children some more puzzles. This time, the puzzles were much harder than the first set and so, as a result, most of the children did not perform especially well. Afterwards, all the children were asked how much they had enjoyed the puzzles and whether they would continue working on them at home. Dramatic differences between the groups emerged. The children who had received just a single sentence praising their intelligence found the difficult puzzles far less enjoyable than their classmates, and were far less likely to work on them in their own time.

Even more bad news for the advocates of praise emerged in the third and final part of the study. After struggling with the difficult puzzles, the experimenters asked the children to try one final test. This last set of puzzles was just as easy as the one the children had encountered at the start of the study. Even though the two groups of children had obtained roughly the same scores at the beginning of the experiment, their performance on the final test was very different. The pattern of results was exactly the opposite of that predicted by many self-help gurus. The children who had been told they were intelligent obtained far lower scores than the others.

Why should praise have counter-intuitive and counter-productive effects? According to Mueller and Dweck, there are several factors at work. Telling a child they are intelligent might make them feel good, but can also induce a fear of failure, causing the child to avoid challenging situations because they might look bad if they are not successful. In addition, telling a child they are intelligent suggests they do not need to work hard to perform well. Because of this, children may be less motivated to make the required effort and be more likely to fail. Unfortunately, if they subsequently obtain a low mark, it is also more likely that their motivation will collapse, and a sense of helplessness will set in. After all, low marks suggest they are not as bright as they were told and that there is nothing they can do about it. The psychological impact of poor results should not be underestimated. At one point in the Mueller and Dweck study, all the children were asked to tell their classmates how well they had performed on the test involving the difficult puzzles. Almost 40 per cent of the children who had been praised lied about their grade, compared to around 10 per cent of those who had not been praised.

Does this mean that all praise is bad praise? So far, I have only described the results from two of the three groups of children involved in the Mueller and Dweck experiment. After getting their initial 'well done, you obtained 80 per cent' feedback, a third group also received a single sentence of praise. However, this time the experimenters praised effort not ability, noting that they must have tried really hard to have achieved such a high mark. These children behaved very differently from those in the two other groups. When it came to choosing between a challenging or easy task, only about 10 per cent of them opted for the easy option. Compared to the children who had been told that they were intelligent, or received no praise at all, those in the 'you must have tried very hard' group found the hard problems more enjoyable and were more likely to try to solve them in their own time. Finally, when given another set of easy problems at the end of the experiment, those in this third group solved significantly more than they did first time round.

The results clearly show that being praised for effort is very different to being praised for ability. According to Mueller and Dweck, the children praised for effort were encouraged to try regardless of the consequences, therefore sidestepping any fear of failure. As a result, the possibility of learning outweighs the fear of obtaining a low mark, and they prefer taking the challenging task to the easy option. Also, by definition, these children are more motivated to try hard in future tests and are more likely to succeed. And, even if they do fail in the future, they can easily attribute their low marks to not trying hard enough, which avoids the sense of helplessness that can set in when poor results are seen as an indication of an innate inability to think.

Although the Mueller and Dweck study was conducted in secondary schools, other research has obtained the same type of findings among younger children and adolescents.[15] They agree that all praise is not created equal. Some praise can have devastating effects on a child's motivation, while other praise can help them achieve their very best. Telling a child they possess a certain trait, such as being bright or talented, is not good for their psychological health because it encourages them to avoid challenging situations, not try so hard and quickly become demotivated when the going gets tough. In contrast, praising effort encourages people to stretch themselves, work hard and persist in the face of difficulties.

IN 59 SECONDS OR LESS

It is easy to fall into the trap of trying to make children feel good by praising their abilities and talents. However, research shows that such compliments can have a detrimental effect, and that it is far better to focus on their effort, concentration and organizational skills. So, for example, when your daughter gets a good exam grade, recognize how hard she must have studied, how well she organized her revision time and how good she must have been at performing under pressure. Similarly, when your son wins a place on the school football team, praise his ability to train hard and work well with others. This praise encourages effort, resilience and persistence in the face of failure. To help focusing further, consider asking reflective questions about the techniques and strategies that they used ('What parts of that did you enjoy the most?' or 'How did you deal with any problems that came up?'), and try to make any praise as specific as possible ('You played well at football today' rather than 'You are good at football').[16]

The Secret Science of Self-Discipline

Let's start with a quick thought experiment. Imagine you have decided to spend an hour or so in an upmarket coffee shop. You walk in and are presented with a long and tempting list of cakes and pastries. The portions are very small, but the quality is incredible. In your mind's eye, look down the list and choose your favourite item – perhaps a wonderful cheesecake, an amazing gateau or a tasty tart. Next, imagine giving your order and the waiter bringing a tiny but perfectly formed portion of your dream dessert. Visualize the dessert sitting in front of you right now, looking irresistibly mouth-watering. Then, just as you are about to tuck in, the waiter explains that today the coffee shop is running a special scheme. You can eat a single portion of the dessert right now, or you can wait 30 minutes and have a double-sized portion for the same price. What would you do? Could you wait and get more, or would you have demolished the dessert before the waiter had even finished describing the offer?

In the late 1960s, Stanford University psychologist Walter Mischel carried out an amazing experiment involving a real-life version of the scenario described above.[17] Mischel and his team armed themselves with a large bag of marshmallows and a bell, went to a local school and presented four-year-old children with a dilemma. An experimenter invited the children into a room one at a time, and showed them to a table on which were a single marshmallow, a bell and then two more marshmallows. It was explained to each child that the experimenter had to go out of the room for a few minutes, but that if the child could keep their hands off all the goodies on the table until the experimenter came back, he or she could eat the two marshmallows. The experimenter also explained that the child could ring the bell at any point and the experimenter would return, but that if this happened the child would only be allowed to eat the single marshmallow.

Each child was presented with a slightly less glamorous version of the dessert-based dilemma that you faced a few moments ago. Ring the bell early and get a single marshmallow or wait awhile and get twice the prize. This deceptively simple test provided an accurate measure of each child's level of self-discipline, with about a third of the children grabbing the single marshmallow right away, another third taking a little longer before hitting the bell and a final third waiting for the experimenter to return and therefore enjoying their two marshmallows.

However, Mischel was not just interested in discovering the percentage of children who were able to resist temptation. Instead, just like the children who obtained the two marshmallows by waiting, he was eager to carry out a truly impressive piece of work by thinking long-term. Ten years later, Mischel contacted the parents of as many of the children as possible. He asked after their children, who by then were adolescents. How well were they coping with life? Did they tend to plan ahead? Was there a tendency for them to give up when the going got tough? The few moments spent in the company of three marshmallows and a bell many years before proved to be amazingly predictive. The children who had waited for the experimenter to return before getting their two marshmallows tended to have developed into self-motivating and organized adults who were good at coping with difficulties and persisted in the face of failure. In contrast, those who immediately grabbed the single marshmallow were easily distracted, less motivated and highly disorganized.

The ability to delay instant gratification and focus more on long-term success is vital for achieving important aims and ambitions. For example, research shows that school pupils' level of self-discipline provides a better predictor of their future academic success than their scores on intelligence tests.[18] Outside the classroom, dieters who are able to resist that mouth-watering slice of cake quickly lose weight, students who endure the hardship of revision achieve better exam grades and sportspeople who are prepared to spend hours training win more medals. Mischel's results suggest that this ability is formed early in life, and continues unchanged into adulthood. His work also suggests that a very large percentage of children prefer to gobble down one marshmallow right now, rather than two in a few minutes' time, and struggle to get what they want out of life.

If you happen to find yourself in the company of a marshmallow-grabbing child, what is the best way of helping them control their impulses and behave themselves? Is it better, for example, to play good cop ('Would you be a little darling and please only spend 30 minutes on the computer'), or adopt a more threatening approach ('If you don't get off the computer now, that optical mouse is going right up your USB port'). In the mid-1960s, Jonathan Freedman from Stanford University conducted an experiment into this issue with surprising results.[19] His study involved a group of about forty boys, aged between seven and ten, who were attending one of two local schools in California. One at a time, the boys were invited into a room and asked to rate the degree to which they liked five toys by assigning each a number between 0 ('very, very bad toy') and 100 ('very, very good toy'). Four of the toys were fairly mundane: a cheap plastic submarine; a child's baseball glove; a toy tractor; and a Dick Tracy toy rifle. In contrast, the fifth toy was far more expensive and exciting. This was a toy among toys, a battery-controlled robot that represented the very height of 1960s technological wonder.

After completing the ratings, the researcher explained that he had an errand to run, and would have to leave the room for a few minutes. He told the boy that he was free to play with four toys but was not to touch the robot. Half the boys were clearly told that bad things would happen if they disobeyed the experimenter ('If you play with the robot I'll be very angry and will have to do something about it'), while the other half were subjected to a more 'softly softly' approach ('Do not play with the robot. It is wrong to play with the robot'). The experimenter then left, leaving the boy staring longingly at the robot and its 'come and play with me' flashing eyes. About 5 minutes later, the experimenter returned, thanked the boy for taking part and allowed him to leave.

Did the boys succumb to temptation? To find out, the researchers had fitted the robot with a secret device that measured whether the toy had been turned on. The data revealed that only two of the boys had the self-control to leave the robot alone. One of the boys came from the group that had been given stern instructions not to play with the robot, while the other was from the group that had been subjected to the 'softly softly' approach. When the experimenter was not present to enforce the instruction not to play with the robot, both approaches proved equally ineffective.

However, Freedman hadn't expected any real difference in the short term, and was instead far more interested in any differences that might emerge over a long period. About six weeks later, he sent a female experimenter back to the schools, apparently to conduct a different study with the same boys. Each boy was invited into the room and asked to make a drawing. Exactly the same collection of toys had been placed in the corner of the room and, when the children had finished their drawings, the experimenter explained that they could now spend a few minutes playing with any of the toys. This time, none of the toys were designated out of bounds, and so all of them were up for grabs. A big difference emerged between the two groups. Of the earlier 'I'll be really angry and will have to do something about it' group, 77 per cent played with the robot, compared to just 33 per cent of those in the 'softly softly' group. Remarkably, just a slight change in the experimenter's instructions several weeks before had had a significant impact on the boys' subsequent behaviour, with the softer wording producing far more compliance.

Why the big difference? There are several possible explanations. According to some researchers, it is the way in which people think about threats. Normally, people only need to be threatened when someone does not want them to do something that they want to do. And the more they want to do something, the bigger the threat needed to prevent them from doing it. According to this approach, the children who heard the stronger threats would have unconsciously thought, 'Wow, people only give out big threats like that when I really want to do something they don't want me to do, so I must really want to play with the robot.' Using the same logic, quietly asking the other boys not to play with the robot resulted in them convincing themselves that they didn't really want to play with the toy.

Other researchers argue that the threat instantly elevated the robot to the status of forbidden fruit and elicited the age-old tendency to want to do something because it is not permitted. Although academic arguments rage about whether this tendency is driven by a sense of curiosity, bloody-mindedness or rebellion, everyone agrees that the effect is powerful and reliable, and explains why attempts to ban teenage smoking, drinking and fast driving frequently back-fire.[20]

In the secret science of self-discipline, the truth is that some children have an almost innate ability to control their impulses, whereas others find it difficult to resist instant gratification. And to instil self-discipline into those who grab the single marshmallow rather than wait for two later, it's clear that the smaller the threat you make, the bigger the impact.

IN 59 SECONDS OR LESS

The Marshmallow Test. It is easy to carry out the marshmallow test with your own children and friends. Find a food that they like, and offer them the option of a small portion now, or a larger portion if they will sit and wait for about 10 minutes. If you are going to carry out this quick and fun assessment, make sure your guinea pigs can see the small and large portions of food throughout the test. Mischel's research suggests that the experiment is most effective when people are continuously tempted by the sight of their favourite food!

Heads and Toes. Whereas the Marshmallow Test measures impulsiveness, other researchers have focused on the kind of self-discipline children need to listen to instructions, pay attention and do what is required of them rather than the first thing that comes into their minds. Some of this work, conducted by Megan McClelland and her colleagues at Oregon State University, has involved asking hundreds of children, aged between four and five, to play a game called 'Head to Toes'.[21] During the game, the experimenter says the phrase 'Touch your head' or 'Touch your toes'. The children have to touch their toes when they hear the phrase 'Touch your head' and touch their head when they hear the phrase 'Touch your toes'. Research suggests that young children's scores on the game predict their reading and mathematical abilities. To play the game, explain the rules to your child, and give them a couple of practice sessions. Then, randomly say the phrases 'Touch your head' or 'Touch your toes', and award 2 points if your child makes the correct response without hesitation, 1 point when they start to make the incorrect response and then correct themselves, and 0 for an incorrect response. Try a list of ten commands and see how they score. On average, three-year-old children tend to obtain 3 points, four-year-olds score about 10 and five-year-olds get about 14. If your child does not score within this range, don't panic! It is perfectly normal for children to get a range of scores, but a low score may indicate he or she could benefit from some of the games described below.

Focusing on Focus. Research suggests that playing certain types of games can help children learn to pay attention, follow directions and develop self-control.[22] In the Freeze Game, tell your child to dance to music and then freeze when the music stops. In the first part of the game, your child has to dance slowly to slow songs and quickly to fast songs. However, once they have mastered this stage, ask them to do the opposite. In a similar exercise, called 'Conducting the Orchestra', give your child any musical instrument and conduct their music using a makeshift baton. In the first part of the game, ask them to play when you wave the baton but stop when you put it down. Next, ask them to play quickly when you move the baton quickly, and slowly when you move the baton slowly. Finally, ask your child to do the opposite. In addition, there are several other techniques that can help children understand, value and develop the power of self-discipline. Try asking them to write their name with their non-dominant hand, repeat the months of the year or days of the week in reverse order, or name as many objects in a certain category (e.g. vegetables, pets, countries) as they can in 30 seconds. Also, when you see your child concentrating very hard on something, encourage them to reflect on their behaviour by, for example, asking them how long they thought they were concentrating (point out that time flies when you are focused), or how it felt when someone interrupted them (point out the value of being able to get back into a task when someone interrupts you).

Avoiding threats. Threats work well in the short term, but can actually prove counter-productive over longer periods of time. By pointing out all the terrible things that will happen if your child follows a course of action, you may be making that activity more attractive in their minds. Instead, try the 'softly softly' approach used in the toy robot experiment. State that you do not want them to do something and leave it there. If they really do insist on knowing why you are stopping them, try to get them to identify some possible reasons.

10. PERSONALITY

Why not to trust graphology, how to gain an apparently
magical insight into other people's personality from their fingers
and thumbs, their pets and the time they go to bed.

In 2005, world leaders gathered together at a major economic forum in Switzerland to discuss some of the biggest problems facing planet earth. From poverty to privatization, capitalism to climate change, nothing escaped their eagle eyes and influential minds. However, despite the enormity of the issues, much of the media coverage focused on one single sheet of paper that had been carelessly left by one of the attendees at a press conference.

The newspapers had managed to get hold of a page of scribbled notes and doodles apparently made by Tony Blair during the event. They asked various graphologists to make a psychological assessment of the then British prime minister on the basis of his handwriting and drawings. The graphologists quickly rose to the challenge, noting how, for example, his disconnected letters, right-sloping writing and strange way of writing Ds showed the 'Blair Flair at work', and revealed that he was struggling to keep control of a confusing world, was a daydreamer hoping for the best, was unable to complete tasks and possessed an unconscious death wish towards his political career.

At the time, Blair was trying to deal with various political problems and scandals, including facing a forthcoming election with the smallest of majorities, so the observations seemed to present an accurate insight into his personality. However, a few days later things did not look so rosy, with

Downing Street pointing out that the page did not belong to Blair, but had instead been produced by fellow attendee Bill Gates, founder of Microsoft and one of the world's most successful businessmen.

According to the proponents of graphology, the Blair–Gates mix-up is just a small blot on their copybook and, in general, a person's handwriting can reveal an amazingly accurate insight into their personality, intelligence, health and even criminal intent.[1] These claims are taken seriously by many personnel departments, with surveys revealing that between 5 and 10 per cent of UK and US businesses regularly use graphology to eliminate unsuitable candidates in their recruitment procedures.

But is there really anything to it, or is graphology just another mind myth? Researcher Geoffrey Dean has devoted a great deal of time to examining the topic, gathering hundreds of scientific studies into graphology and using them to examine the claims made by the proponents of this ancient art form. The results make for chilling reading.

In one analysis, Dean collated the findings from sixteen academic papers that had examined graphology in the workplace. He compared graphologists' predictions of employee performance with supervisors' ratings of success during job training. The results revealed that there was little relationship between graphologists' predictions and measures of job success. In fact, the graphologists were about as accurate as a control group of untrained laypeople who had no experience in graphology at all.

In another analysis, Dean examined studies in which researchers had compared graphologists' attempts to determine a person's character with that person's scores on scientifically validated personality tests. Dean collected the journal articles (this time, fifty-three of them) and analysed the results. Not only was graphologists' accuracy poor, but control groups of people with absolutely no training or background in assessing personality from handwriting scored just as well as the so-called experts.

When it comes to obtaining a graphology-based insight into the personality of others, the writing is on the wall. The Blair–Gates mix-up does not represent a momentary slip of the pen, but is symbolic of the findings of scientific studies that have investigated graphology. Contrary to the claims made by proponents, research suggests that graphology does not provide an amazingly accurate and reliable insight into personality, and should not be seen as a useful way of predicting employee performance.

So if you cannot tell someone's personality on the basis of their handwriting, how can you gain an insight into their real character? The answer involves a concept known as the Big Five, the eighteenth-century womanizer Giacomo Casanova and the stickers that people place on their cars.

The Big Five

Some of the world's greatest thinkers have attempted to understand the complexities of human personality. Freud believed that people were best categorized on the basis of the bodily orifice from which they derived greatest pleasure, maverick Victorian scientist Sir Francis Galton examined bumps on the skull and Jung was convinced that personalities were determined by the position of the stars at the moment of birth.

While Freud, Galton and Jung were busy wasting their time exploring dreams, the shape of skulls or looking to the heavens for inspiration, other scientists pursued a more level-headed and ultimately productive approach.[2] These researchers believed that the secret structure of the human psyche was buried deep within language. They speculated that the words people use to describe themselves and others were created because they accurately reflect fundamental dimensions of personality. They thought that if this were the case, it should be possible to discover this fundamental structure by carefully collecting and collating all the words that could be used to describe a person.

The enterprise began in the 1930s, with a group of dedicated researchers carefully poring over each page of an unabridged dictionary. They selected each and every word that could be used to describe personality. From 'amusing' to 'abhorrent', 'benign' to 'belligerent', the team eventually compiled a list of over 18,000 words. They then worked through the list and identified 4,000 words that described relatively stable and central traits. In the 1940s, another group of researchers continued the effort and subjected this shortened list to an early form of computerized analysis that reduced it to a set of about 200 words. Over the next forty years or so, thousands of people were asked to rate themselves and others on various sub-sets of these adjectives, and researchers employed increasingly sophisticated statistical techniques to analyse the data in an attempt to identify the key dimensions on which people differed. Consensus finally emerged in the early 1990s, when several large-scale studies from many different countries and cultures confirmed the presence of five fundamental dimensions of personality.[3]

Together these factors represent the holy grail of personality research, and are collectively referred to as the Big Five. The five dimensions have received different labels over the years, but are commonly referred to as 'Openness', 'Conscientiousness', 'Extraversion', 'Agreeableness' and 'Neuroticism' (easily remembered using the acronym OCEAN or CANOE). Each dimension is seen as a continuous scale running from high to low, and everyone can be described by five scores that indicate where they sit on each scale. Additional work has shown that the dimensions are determined by a combination of genes and childhood experiences, that they tend to remain unchanged throughout a person's life and influence almost every aspect of their behaviour including relationships, performance in the workplace, leisure activities, consumer choice, religious and political beliefs, creativity, sense of humour and health.

So what lies at the heart of these five dimensions, and

what does it mean to obtain a high or low score on each of them?

'Openness' represents the degree to which a person seeks and appreciates new, interesting and unusual experiences. High scorers are curious and broad-minded. They get bored easily, but are particularly good at tolerating ambiguity and are skilled at seeing situations and problems from many different perspectives. They are creative, original, wise, funny, imaginative and unconventional. They have a rich inner life, like new ideas, tend to remember their dreams and make good hypnotic subjects. In contrast, low scorers tend to be more conventional, down to earth and better able to focus on the practical side of things. They are more comfortable with familiar places and food and tend to work through problems on a step-by-step basis.

'Conscientiousness' reflects the degree of organization, persistence and self-discipline employed to achieve goals. High scorers are very organized, reliable, hard-working, persevering and can forego short-term rewards for long-term success. They tend to do well in the workplace, keep their New Year's resolutions and are highly punctual. They also generally live significantly longer than others because they don't tend to engage in high-risk behaviours, such as reckless driving, and are far more likely to exercise, eat a balanced diet and have regular medical check-ups. Low scorers tend to be less reliable, more easy-going and hedonistic. They are harder to motivate and more easily distracted, but can show greater flexibility in the face of changing circumstances.

'Extraversion' reflects the need for stimulation from the outside world and other people. Those who obtain high scores on this dimension are fun to be with, impulsive, optimistic, happy, enjoy the company of others, and have a wide circle of friends and acquaintances. They prefer to lead rather than follow, enjoy aggressive and sexually explicit humour, drink more, are skilled at multi-tasking, strive for instant gratification, have more sexual partners than others and are more likely to cheat on their partner. Low scorers tend to be far more considered, controlled and reserved. Their social life revolves round a relatively small number of very close friends and they prefer reading a good book to a night out on the town. They are more sensitive to pain, good at focusing on a single task, prefer more intellectual forms of humour such as puns and prefer to work in closed offices with few distractions.

'Agreeableness' is the degree to which a person cares about others. High scorers are trustworthy, altruistic, kind, affectionate and, perhaps most important of all, likeable. They are less likely to divorce, are perceived much more favourably in job interviews and are more likely to be promoted at work. Low scorers tend to be far more aggressive, hostile and uncooperative. They tend to see things from their own point of view, value being right over caring about other people's thoughts and feelings, perform better in situations that require tough-mindedness and are less likely to be taken advantage of by others.

The fifth and final dimension, 'neuroticism', reflects the degree to which a person is emotionally stable and able to cope with potentially stressful situations. High scorers are far more prone to worry, have low self-esteem, set themselves unrealistic aspirations and frequently experience a range of negative emotions including distress, hostility and envy. Their strong need to be loved, coupled with low self-esteem, can lead to them forming overly possessive and dependent relationships. Low scorers tend to be calm, relaxed, resilient in the face of failure and emotionally secure. They are unfazed by negative life events, skilled at using humour to reduce anxiety in themselves and others, cope well with misfortune and sometimes even thrive on stress.

Most psychologists now believe that the apparent complexity of human personality is an illusion. In reality, people vary on just five fundamental dimensions. Understand these dimensions and you gain an important insight into your behaviour and thinking. Likewise, being able to quickly understand the personality of people around you will help you understand their actions and how best to communicate with them. Modern-day research suggests that Freud, Galton and Jung were wrong, and that the secret to understanding personality lies in the five fundamental factors are embedded deep within our language and lives.

IN 59 SECONDS OR LESS

Psychologists have created several questionnaires to measure carefully people's responses on each of the Big Five dimensions. Unfortunately, they tend to contain a large number of questions, and take a considerable amount of time to complete. However, some researchers have created a quick and easy version that will help you discover your position on each of the five main dimensions.[4] It does not provide a perfect description, but is a useful guide to the fundamental forces that make up your personality.

To complete the questionnaire, please use the rating scale below to describe how accurately each statement describes you. Describe yourself as you generally are now, not as you wish to be in the future. Describe yourself as you honestly see yourself, in relation to other people you know of the same sex as you are and roughly the same age. At this point, ignore the numbers in the top right-hand corner of each box.

Scoring

Look at the numbers in the top right-hand corner of the boxes you have ticked in statements 5 ('having excellent ideas') and 10 ('having difficulty understanding abstract ideas'). Add these two numbers to find your score on the Openness dimension. If your score is 10 or less then you should see yourself as a low scorer, whereas if your score is above 10 then you should see yourself as a high scorer. Record your scores on p. 308: write your total on the line and then tick either the Low or High score box.

I see myself as . . .	Disagree strongly	Disagree moderately	Disagree a little	Neither agree nor disagree	Agree a little	Agree moderately	Agree strongly
1 the life of the party	1	2	3	4	5	6	7
2 feeling little concern for others	7	6	5	4	3	2	1
3 always prepared	1	2	3	4	5	6	7
4 getting stressed out easily	1	2	3	4	5	6	7
5 having excellent ideas	1	2	3	4	5	6	7
6 not talking a lot	7	6	5	4	3	2	1
7 interested in people	1	2	3	4	5	6	7
8 often forgetting to put things back in their proper place	7	6	5	4	3	2	1
9 relaxed most of the time	7	6	5	4	3	2	1
10 having difficulty understanding abstract ideas	7	6	5	4	3	2	1

Openness

Total of statements 5 and 10: ___

☐ Low (10 and below)   ☐ High (above 10)

Now repeat this process for the remaining four dimensions:

Conscientiousness

Total of statements 3 and 8: ___

☐ Low (11 and below)   ☐ High (above 11)

Extroversion

Total of statements 1 and 6: ___

☐ Low (9 and below)   ☐ High (above 9)

Agreeableness

Total of statements 2 and 7: ___

☐ Low (10 and below)   ☐ High (above 10)

Neuroticism

Total of statements 4 and 9: ___

☐ Low (9 and below)   ☐ High (above 9)

A Quick Analysis and a Few Handy Hints, Based on Your Scores

Openness. High scorers tend to be imaginative and creative, but are also prone to boredom and strive to feed their mind continually with new ideas and experiences. Low scorers are more down-to-earth and tend to seek out situations in which they have to turn an existing idea into reality, take small steps rather than initiate radical change and follow well-established patterns and rules.

Conscientiousness. High scorers are methodical, well organized and dutiful. They perform best in highly structured and pre-dictable environments where there is a place for everything and everything is in its place. Low scorers are far more laid back, find it easy to enjoy life, but may well need a helping hand when it comes to self-discipline.

Extroversion. High scorers are energized by the company of others, evening types and motivated more by carrots than the stick. In contrast, low scorers tend to be happiest working alone and in quiet surroundings, are most alert in the morning and are motivated more by the fear of punishment than the promise of rewards.

Agreeableness. High scorers tend to be trusting, friendly and cooperative, but have to be careful to avoid situations in which others might take advantage of their overly giving nature. Low scorers tend to be more aggressive and competitive, and bloom in situations that require tough thinking and straight talking.

Neuroticism. High scorers are prone to insecurity and emotional distress, avoiding situations they find upsetting because those negative feelings take some time to fade away. Low scorers tend to be more relaxed, less emotional, less prone to distress and operate well in situations others find stressful.

Behind the Big Five

Research suggests that differences in brain function and upbringing may account for differences on the fundamental dimensions of personality.

For example, a relationship exists between extroversion and brain activation. If you open the top of someone's skull and look in, you will see the wrinkled mass of tissue that is their cortex. This large lump of meat makes up about 80 per cent of the weight of a brain and contains an amazing 100 billion neurons. Every cortex has a different pre-set level of arousal, much like a TV has a pre-set volume when you turn it on. Brain scans have revealed that people scoring low on extroversion have a high pre-set level of arousal. As a result, they avoid situations that further arouse their stimulated brains, so are most comfortable when they are engaged in quiet, predictable activities. The exact opposite is true of high extroversion. Their brains have a much lower pre-set level of arousal, so they have a need for continuous stimulation. Because of this, they enjoy the constant stimulation that results from being with other people, risk-taking and impulsive behaviour.

Other work has focused more on the relationship between personality and upbringing. For example, University of California psychologist Frank Sulloway believes that levels of openness are determined, at least to some extent, by whether people are the oldest or youngest child.[5] According to Sulloway's theory, because younger children haven't developed their older siblings' abilities and skills, they explore novel ways to get their parents' love and attention, and this, in turn, causes them to develop into more open, creative, unconventional, adventurous and rebellious people. To test his theory, Sulloway analysed the biographies of more than 6,000 well-known people from many different walks of life, and claims that the evidence is overwhelming. He notes that the vast majority of American presidents (including Jimmy Carter, George W. Bush and Bill Clinton) were first-borns, whereas leaders of revolutions, such as Jefferson, Marx and Castro, were later borns. Likewise, when it comes to science, first-borns tend to be members of the scientific establishment, whereas later-borns, such as Darwin and Copernicus, are the ones proposing radically new ideas. If correct, it is a striking example of how subtle differences in childhood experience can have a surprisingly dramatic effect on personality.

The Casanova Effect

Imagine deciding to quit your job and embark on a new career as a professional palmist. You invest in the requisite purple kaftan, set up a small booth on the busy promenade of the nearest seaside town, and nervously wait for your first customer. A few moments later, a man walks in, sits down and crosses your palm with silver. You look carefully at the stranger's hand, and try to spot any telltale clues that might give you a magical insight into his life. Is his soft skin a sign of office work? Do his chewed nails signal a recent job loss? Is his calloused palm suggestive of too much time at the gym, or does it reflect a strong need to find a girlfriend? According to some psychologists, you would be much better off ignoring his soft skin, chewed nails and calloused palms, and instead shift your attention to the length of his index and ring fingers. Their argument is a curious one and links the famous eighteenth-century womanizer Giacomo Casanova with some of Britain's most famous football players.

According to his colourful autobiography, Casanova enjoyed the company of many famous European kings, cardinals, poets and artists.[6] At one point he describes how he spent time with the eminent German painter Anton Raphael Mengs. After a while, they started to argue, with Mengs berating Casanova for not observing his religious duties, and Casanova accusing Mengs of being a child-beating alcoholic. As the situation moved from bad to worse, Casanova took it upon himself to criticize one of Mengs' paintings. He pointed out that the index finger of a principal male character was longer than the ring finger, and was therefore anatomically incorrect, as men's ring fingers were longer than their index fingers. Mengs defended his work by showing that his own index finger was longer than his ring finger. Casanova stuck to his argument, showing that *his* ring finger was longer than his index finger, claiming that this was true of most men, and arguing that his hands were thus 'like that of all the children descended from Adam'. Affronted, Mengs asked Casanova, 'Then from whom do you suppose I am descended?' to which Casanova replied, 'I have no idea; but it is certain that you are not of my species.' As the argument escalated, they raised a bet of 100 pistoles on the issue, and promptly rounded up the painter's servants to discover who was right. A quick perusal of the servants' hands revealed that Casanova was correct, with Mengs saving face by rejoicing in the fact that he could now boast of being unique in something.

Evolutionary psychologist Professor John Manning from the University of Central Lancashire has dedicated much of his professional life to studying the difference in finger lengths described by Casanova, and argues that they reveal a fascinating, and important, insight into the human psyche.[7] Manning and his colleagues measure the length of people's index and ring fingers, and then divide the first length by the second to obtain what is commonly referred to as the '2D:4D' (second digit: fourth digit) ratio. If the ring and index fingers are exactly the same length, then the 2D:4D ratio will be 1.00. If, however, the ring finger is longer than the index finger, then the ratio will be less than 1.00, and conversely, if the index finger is longer than the ring finger, it will be greater than 1.00.

The research has conclusively revealed that the finger-length pattern described by Casanova tends to be associated far more with men than women, with the average 2D:4D ratio for men being about 0.98, while the corresponding figure for women hovers around 1.00. In short, men's ring fingers tend to be longer than their index fingers, whereas women's fingers tend to be about the same length.

Why should this be the case? According to Manning, the explanation dates back to the very start of a person's life, and is closely linked to testosterone levels in the womb. After about six weeks or so, the level of testosterone in the womb changes, and those foetuses that are exposed to large amounts of the hormone develop more male characteristics, whilst those exposed to much smaller levels develop more female attributes. Manning argues that testosterone also plays a key role in determining the length of a person's index and ring fingers, with high levels resulting in a relatively long ring finger. If Manning's theory is right, a person's 2D:4D ratio is related to the amount of testosterone they were exposed to in the womb, and should provide a good indication of the degree to which they possess psychological and physical traits commonly associated with either masculinity or femininity. According to this theory, people with low 2D:4D ratios will be more likely than others to exhibit masculine characteristics, while those with high 2D:4D ratios will be significantly more likely to be in touch with their feminine side.

It is a controversial idea, and one that has attracted its fair share of criticism.[8] However, proponents argue that a large body of research now supports the theory, including work examining physical strength and sporting success. In one study, a group of men had their finger lengths measured, and were then asked to complete various strength tests, including shoulder, overhead and bench presses.[9] The results revealed the expected relationships. Men who had lower 2D:4D ratios were able to lift heavier weights than those with higher ratios. Often the differences were far from trivial. For example, for overhead presses, those with 2D:4D ratios of 0.91 lifted 11 kilos more than those with ratios of over 1.00. In another study, researchers turned their attention to student sprinters, and found that the time taken to complete 100-metre, 800-metre and 1,500-metre races were all related to 2D:4D ratios, with the faster runners having lower ratios.[10] In another remarkable experiment, Manning and his team managed to measure the finger lengths of some of the best-known and most highly skilled football players in Britain.[11] Attending a centenary celebration designed to mark the end of the 100th English League Championship, the researchers persuaded more than 300 players to have their hands photocopied, and then compared their finger lengths to a control group of more than 500 men who had never ventured onto a football pitch. The 2D:4D ratio of the players was significantly lower than the controls. Strong differences also emerged among the different groups of players, with high-performing 'League legends' (including Kenny Dalglish, Trevor Francis and Paul Gascoigne) and those having played at an international level having especially low ratios.

Other work suggests that the 2D:4D effect may also extend to certain psychological traits. A large amount of research has shown that men tend to outperform women in tests involving the mental manipulation of spatial information (perhaps explaining the alleged fondness of women for turning maps round when navigating). In line with this finding,

Manning believes that his research suggests that men with low 2D:4D ratios (and therefore, according to his theory, possessing more 'masculine' brains) tend to outperform others on these tasks.[12] Similarly, he cites other work suggesting that when it comes to personality, women with lower 2D:4D ratios tend to exhibit traits that the researchers believe to be more male-oriented, including being more assertive and risk-taking.[13]

According to Manning, the effect even extends to making music. Noting that there are about ten times as many professional male musicians as females, Manning argues that musical ability is associated more with a masculine than feminine brain, and therefore highly skilled performers should have an especially low 2D:4D ratio. To test this idea, he measured the ratio of fifty-four male members of a well-known British symphony orchestra. Several sections of the orchestra were organized in a hierarchical way, with more highly skilled musicians taking key positions. Manning discovered that performers in these key positions did indeed have significantly lower 2D:4D ratios than their fellows.[14]

In order to obtain a mysterious insight into yourself and others, it may well be better to forget traditional palmistry and instead focus your attention on the apparently important relative length of the index and ring finger.

IN 59 SECONDS OR LESS

Some researchers believe that the relative length of your first and third fingers provides a considerable insight into your psychological and physical abilities. To quickly assess yourself, hold your right hand palm up in front of you and look at the length of your first (index) and third (ring) fingers. Look at where your first finger joins the palm of your hand. There will be several creases there. Place the zero mark of a ruler on the middle of the bottom crease and measure to the tip of your finger (not your nail) in millimetres. Now repeat exactly the same procedure for your right third finger. To find the 2D:4D ratio, divide the length of your first finger by the length of your third finger.

Research shows that the average male ratio is about .98, and a ratio of around .94 would be seen as especially masculine, while a ratio of 1.00 would be viewed as more feminine. For women, the average ratio is about 1.0, and a score of around .98 would be seen as more masculine while a ratio of 1.02 would be seen as more feminine.

Celebrity Fingers

When I first came across research suggesting that 2D:4D ratio predicted sporting and musical excellence, I wondered whether the same effect might emerge among people who had made a name for themselves in other occupations. However, as measuring the finger lengths of the rich and famous seemed rather problematic, I filed the idea in the somewhat cramped mental box marked 'probably never going to happen'. Then, about a year ago, I was watching a television programme documenting a road-trip across America and suddenly had an idea. One of the scenes was filmed in Los Angeles, and involved chatting to people walking along Hollywood Boulevard. In the background I could see the world-famous Grauman's Chinese Theatre, and suddenly the penny dropped.

Since the 1920s, many of the world's most famous celebrities have had their signatures, footprints and handprints set in concrete blocks on the forecourt of the theatre. Was it possible, I wondered, to accurately measure finger lengths from the casts and thus discover the 2D:4D ratios of some of the best-known figures in show business? My mind started to race. Would leading men have especially high levels of testosterone and therefore especially low 2D:4D ratios? What about comedians? Their success often rests on being verbally skilled and creative rather than having rugged good looks – would that be reflected in a high 2D:4D ratio?

There was just one small problem – I was in London and the casts were in Los Angeles. Never one to let a few thousand miles get in the way of research, I contacted a colleague of mine named Jim Underdown. Jim is an ex- stand-up comedian from Chicago who now works for the Centre for Inquiry – an American organization that promotes the sceptical and scientific investigation of alleged paranormal phenomena. He heads a branch of the organization based in Los Angeles and has been involved in all sorts of strange projects, including examining sightings of alleged UFOs and testing people claiming to have psychic powers.

I emailed Jim and asked whether he might be able to help out. More specifically, could he obtain some digital callipers, and arrange for a colleague (who was unaware of the 2D:4D theory) to measure as many of the concrete handprints as possible? Jim accepted the challenge. A few weeks later, he emailed me explaining that callipers had been purchased, and that he had teamed up with another researcher named Spencer Marks and spent several days avoiding puddles and security guards, eventually collecting initial data from thirty-seven of the best-known leading men and nine comedians.

The list of leading men read like a *Who's Who* of the film industry, and included Paul Newman, Bruce Willis, Johnny Depp, John Travolta, Warren Beatty and Jack Nicholson. Previous work suggests that the average male 2D:4D ratio tends to be about 0.98. The average ratios for the leading men's left and right hands were 0.96, suggesting that they are an especially testosterone-fuelled bunch. The comedians involved formed an equally impressive group, and contained some of the funniest people of all time such as George Burns, Peter Sellers, Bob Hope and Robin Williams. The average right-hand 2D:4D ratio came in at a surprisingly high 1.01.

The work is still in its infancy, but the initial results look as intriguing as they are promising. If the phenomenon is genuine, it might really be possible to discover whether someone has that magic X-factor by simply looking at their hands.

Quick Tips for Gaining Insight into Someone's Personality in 60 Seconds or Less

Ask People About Their Pets. A few years ago, I conducted a large-scale online study examining the possible relationship between the personality of owners and their pets. Over 2,000 owners rated their personality and the personality of their pets on several factors (e.g. sociability, emotional stability and sense of humour). In addition, they indicated how long they had owned their pet. Fish owners turned out to be the happiest, dog owners the most fun to be with, cat owners the most dependable and emotionally sensitive and reptile owners the most independent. Weirdly, the results also revealed telling differences in rating pets' sense of humour. According to their owners, 62 per cent of dogs have a good sense of humour, compared to just 57 per cent of fish, 48 per cent of cats, 42 per cent of horses, 38 per cent of birds and 0 per cent of reptiles.

The findings also revealed significant similarities between the personality of owners and their pets. Interestingly, this similarity increased over time, suggesting that pets may slowly come to adopt their owner's personality or vice versa. For years, owners have insisted that their pets have a unique personality – not only do my results suggest they might be right, but also reveal that people's pets are a reflection of themselves.

So, if you meet someone who has a dog and want to gain a genuine insight into their personality within seconds, ask them to describe the personality of their canine pal.

Bumper Stickers. William Szlemko and colleagues speculated that many people who personalize their car by adding bumper or window stickers may be sending out powerful signals of territoriality, and they were curious to discover if having to share public roads with others could increase the chances of these drivers experiencing road rage.[15] To investigate, hundreds of participants were asked to report how many bumper and window stickers they had, and also rate their level of aggressive driving. The results revealed that drivers with more stickers admitted to driving more aggressively, including a greater frequency of tailgating and ramming. So, if you find yourself driving behind a car covered in bumper and window stickers, probably best to give them that extra inch or two.

All Thumbs. The brain can be seen as working in two general modes. In one mode (often called 'right-brained'), it is more intuitive, visual and creative. In the other (often called 'left-brained'), it is more logical, sequential and language-based. In many ways, it is like having an artist and accountant arguing in your head, and flipping between the two. All of us work in both modes, but everyone naturally tends towards one or the other. Right-handers can try this quick test to discover if they tend to be more right- than left-brained, or vice versa. Interlock the fingers of your hands and place one thumb on top of the other. People who place their right thumb on top of their left thumb tend to be left-brain dominant, and are thus more verbal and analytical.[16] Those placing their left thumb on top of their right thumbs tend to be right-brain dominant, and excel in visual, creative and intuitive tasks.

Morning or Evening? If you wanted to feel at your best, and were free to get up at any time of the day, when would you choose to climb out of bed? At 7 a.m., 8 a.m., 9 a.m. or even 10 a.m.? And how about the opposite end of the day: if you had your way, and were free from all other demands, when would choose to go to bed? 10 p.m., midnight, 1 a.m.? The way in which you have just answered those two questions helps reveal whether you are a morning type (going to bed and getting up early), or an evening type (late to bed and late to rise). Recent research also suggests that your answer reveals a great deal about your personality and style of thinking.[17] Questionnaire results from more than 350 people showed that morning types are attracted to concrete information rather than abstract thinking, and like to rely on logic rather than intuition. They tend to be introverts, self-controlled and eager to make a good impression on others. In contrast, evening types have a far more creative outlook on life, are more prepared to take risks, are more independent and nonconforming and a little impulsive.

Conclusion

Sophie's answer: Ten techniques in 59 seconds.

At the start of this book I described going to lunch with my friend Sophie a few years ago. As we chatted, Sophie said that she had bought a book on increasing happiness, and I had expressed considerable skepticism about the self-help industry. When I launched into a lengthy account of academic work into happiness, Sophie politely interrupted me, and essentially posed the question that acted as a catalyst for this book: are there any scientifically-supported techniques that could help improve people's lives in less than a minute? I didn't know the answer, but Sophie's question piqued my curiosity. After surveying thousands of studies in countless journals, I realized that behavioural researchers working in many different areas had indeed developed such techniques.

Sophie, here are ten of the most interesting studies that I wish I had known about when you asked. On a good day, I think I could describe all ten in just under a minute.

Develop the gratitude attitude

Having people list three things that they are grateful for in life, or three events that have gone especially well over the past week, can significantly increase their level of happiness for about a month. This, in turn, can cause them to be more optimistic about the future and improve their physical health.

CONCLUSION

Place a picture of a baby in your wallet

Putting a photograph of a smiling baby in a wallet increases the chances of the wallet being returned if lost by 30 per cent. The baby's big eyes and button nose initiates a deep-seated evolutionary mechanism that causes people to become more caring, and thus increases the likelihood of them returning it.

Hang a mirror in your kitchen

Placing a mirror in front of people when they are presented with different food options results in a remarkable 32 per cent reduction in their consumption of unhealthy food. Seeing their own reflection makes them more aware of their body and more likely to eat food that is good for them.

Buy a pot plant for the office

Adding plants to an office results in a 15 per cent boost in the number of creative ideas reported by male employees, and helps their female counterparts produce more original solutions to problems. The plants help reduce stress and induce good moods which, in turn, promote creativity.

Touch people lightly on the upper arm

Lightly touching someone on their upper arm makes them far more likely to agree to a request because the touch is unconsciously perceived as a sign of high status. In one dating study, the touch produced a 20 per cent increase in the number of people accepting the offer of a dance in a nightclub and a 10 per cent increase in people giving their telephone number to a stranger on the street.

Write about your relationship

Partners spending a few moments each week committing their deepest thoughts and feelings about their relationship to paper boosts the chances of them sticking together by over 20 per cent. Such 'expressive writing' results in partners using more positive language when they speak to one another, leading to a healthier and happier relationship.

Deal with potential liars by closing your eyes and asking for an email

The most reliable clues to lying are in the words that people use, with liars tending to lack detail, use more 'ums' and 'ahs', and avoid self-references ('me', 'mine, 'I'). In addition, people are about 20 per cent less likely to lie in an email than telephone call, because their words are on record and so more likely to come back and haunt them.

Praise children's effort over ability

Praising a child's effort rather than their ability ('well done, you must have tried very hard') encourages them to try regardless of the consequences, therefore side-stepping any fear of failure. This, in turn, makes them especially likely to attempt challenging problems, find these problems more enjoyable, and try to solve them in their own time.

Visualize yourself doing, not achieving

People who visualize themselves taking the practical steps needed to achieve their goals are far more likely to succeed than those who simply fantasize about their dreams becoming a reality. One especially effective technique involves adopting a third-person perspective: those who visualize themselves as others see them are about 20 per cent more successful than those adopting a first-person view.

Consider your legacy

Asking people to spend just a minute imagining a close friend standing up at their funeral and reflecting on their personal and professional legacy helps them to identify their long-term goals, and assess the degree to which they are progressing towards making those goals a reality.

Notes

Introduction

1 This work is described in the Motivation chapter of this book, page 83.
2 L. Tabuk (2007). 'If Your Goal is Success, Don't Consult the Gurus'. *Fast Company*, 18 December.
3 J. Rodin and J. E. Langer (1997). 'Long-term Effects of a Control-Relevant Intervention with the Institutionalized Aged'. *Journal of Personality and Social Psychology*, 35 (12), pages 897–902.

HAPPINESS

1 S. Lyubomirsky, L. A. King and E. Diener (2005). 'The Benefits of Frequent Positive Affect: Does Happiness Lead to Success?' *Psychological Bulletin*, 131, pages 803–55.
2 See, for example, D. G. Myers (2000). 'The Funds, Friends, and Faith of Happy People'. *American Psychologist*, 55, pages 56–67.
3 P. Brickman, D. Coates and R. Janoff-Bulman (1978). 'Lottery Winners and Accident Victims: Is Happiness Relative?' *Journal of Personality and Social Psychology*, 36, pages 917–27.
4 Cited in D. G. Myers (2007). The work relating to the relationship between GNP and happiness involved examining data from the World Bank and the 'happiness' and 'life satisfaction' scales of the 1990–1991 World Values Survey.

6 S. Lyubomirsky, K. M. Sheldon and D. Schkade (2005).
    'Pursuing Happiness: The Architecture of Sustainable Change'.
    Review of General Psychology, 9, pages 111–31. Figuring out
    the genetic component of happiness has involved asking identical
    and non-identical twins to rate how happy they are. Identical
    twins have the same genetic make-up while fraternal twins do
    not, so it is possible to calculate the genetic basis for happiness
    by carefully comparing the results from the two groups.

7 J. L. S. Borton and E. C. Casey (2006). 'Suppression of Negative
    Self-Referential Thoughts: A Field Study'. *Self and Identity*, 5,
    pages 230–46.

8 For an overview of this work, see D. M. Wegner (1989). *White
    Bears and Other Unwanted Thoughts: Suppression, Obsession,
    and the Psychology of Mental Control*. New York: Viking.

The chocolate study is described in J. A. K. Erskine (2007).
    'Resistance Can Be Futile: Investigating Behavioural Rebound'.
    Appetite, 50, pages 415–21.

I made up the finding about George Bush.

9 E. Zech (1999). 'Is it Really Helpful to Verbalize One's
    Emotions?'. *Gedraf en Gezondheid*, 27, pages 42–7.

10 E. Zech and B. Rimé (2005). 'Is Talking About an Emotional
     Experience Helpful? Effects on Emotional Recovery and
     Perceived Benefits'. *Clinical Psychology and Psychotherapy*, 12,
     pages 270–87.

11 S. Lyubomirsky and C. Tkach (2003). 'The Consequences of
     Dysphoric Rumination'. C. Papageorgiou and A. Wells (eds),
     *Rumination: Nature, Theory, and Treatment of Negative
     Thinking in Depression*, pages 21–41. Chichester, England: John
     Wiley & Sons.

12 For a review of this work, see S. J. Lepore and J. M. Smyth
     (eds). *The Writing Cure: How Expressive Writing Promotes
     Health and Emotional Well-Being*. Washington, DC: American
     Psychological Association.

13 S. Spera, E. Buhrfeind and J. W. Pennebaker (1994). 'Expressive Writing and Coping with Job Loss'. *Academy of Management Journal*, 3, pages 722–33.

14 R. A. Emmons and M. E. McCullough (2003). 'Counting Blessings Versus Burdens: An Experimental Investigation of Gratitude and Subjective Well-Being in Daily Life'. *Journal of Personality and Social Psychology*, 84, pages 377–89.

15 L. A. King (2001). 'The Health Benefits of Writing About Life Goals'. *Personality and Social Psychology Bulletin*, 27, pages 798–807.

16 C. M. Burton and L. A. King (2004). 'The Health Benefits of Writing About Intensely Positive Experiences'. *Journal of Research in Personality*, 38, pages 150–63.

17 K. Floyd, A. C. Mikkelson, C. Hesse and P. M. Pauley (2007). 'Affectionate Writing Reduces Total Cholesterol: Two Randomized, Controlled Trials'. *Human Communication Research*, 33, pages 119–42.

18 M. E. P. Seligman, T. Steen, N. Park and C. Peterson (2005). 'Positive Psychology Progress: Empirical Validation of Interventions'. *American Psychologist*, 60, pages 410–21.

19 L. Van Boven and T. Gilovich (2003). 'To Do or to Have: That Is the Question'. *Journal of Personality and Social Psychology*, 85, pages 1193–202.

20 This questionnaire is based on work described in M. L. Richins, and S. Dawson (1992). 'A Consumer Values Orientation for Materialism and Its Measurement: Scale Development and Validation'. *Journal of Consumer Research*, 19 (3), pages 303–16.

21 Ibid.

22 E. W. Dunn, L. Aknin and M. I. Norton (2008). 'Spending Money on Others Promotes Happiness'. *Science*, 319, pages 1687–88.

23 B. T. Harbaugh, U. Mayr and D. Burghart (2007). 'Neural

Responses to Taxation and Voluntary Giving Reveal Motives for Charitable Donations'. *Science*, 316 (5831), pages 1622–5.

24 S. Lyubomirsky, K. M. Sheldon and D. Schkade (2005). 'Pursuing Happiness: The Architecture of Sustainable Change'. *Review of General Psychology*, 9, pages 111–31.

25 L. N. Chaplin and D. R. John (2007). 'Growing up in a Material World: Age Differences in Materialism in Children and Adolescents'. *Journal of Consumer Research*, 34 (4), pages 480–94.

26 For a review of this work, see J. D. Laird (2007). *Feelings: The Perception of Self*. New York: Oxford University Press.

27 J. Förster (2004). 'How Body Feedback Influences Consumer's Evaluation of Products'. *Journal of Consumer Psychology*, 14, pages 415–25.

28 F. Strack, L. L. Martin and S. Stepper (1988). 'Inhibiting and Facilitating Conditions of the Human Smile: A Nonobstrusive Test of the Facial Feedback Hypothesis'. *Journal of Personality and Social Psychology*, 54, pages 768–77.

29 S. Schnall and J. D. Laird (2003). 'Keep Smiling: Enduring Effects of Facial Expressions and Postures on Emotional Experience'. *Cognition and Emotion*, 17, pages 787–97.

30 T. A. Roberts and Y. Arefi-Afsha (2007). 'Not All Who Stand Tall Are Proud: Gender Differences in the Propioceptive Effects of Upright Posture'. *Cognition and Emotion*, 21, pages 714–27.

31 For a fascinating review of this work, see S. Gosling (2008). *Snoop: What Your Stuff Says About You*. London: Profile Books. The findings presented in this section are based on the types of movements, attributes and traits that tend to be displayed by extroverts, with other research showing a strong link between extroversion and happiness.

32 K. M. Sheldon and S. Lyubomirsky (2007). 'Is it Possible to Become Happier? (And if so, How?)'. *Social and Personality Psychology Compass*, 1, pages 129–45.

And also K. M. Sheldon and S. Lyubomirsky (2006). 'Achieving Sustainable Happiness: Change Your Actions, Not Your Circumstances'. *Journal of Happiness Studies*, 7, pages 55–86.

PERSUASION

1 M. R. Lepper, D. Greene and R. E. Nisbett (1973). 'Undermining Children's Intrinsic Interest With Extrinsic Reward: A Test of the "Overjustification" Hypothesis'. *Journal of Personality and Social Psychology*, 28, pages 129–37.

2 This experiment was carried out as part of the BBC television programme *The People Watchers*. It is based on similar studies into 'cognitive dissonance', a term which refers to that uncomfortable feeling that people get when they hold two contradictoy ideas simultaneously.

3 For a review of this work, see A. Kohn (1993). *Punished by Rewards: The Trouble With Gold Stars, Incentive Plans, A's, Praise and Other Bribes*. Boston: Houghton Mifflin Company.

4 C. A. Higgins and T. A. Judge (2004). 'The Effect of Applicant Influence Tactics on Recruiter Perceptions of Fit and Hiring Recommendations: A Field Study'. *Journal of Applied Psychology*, 89, pages 622–32.

5 E. Jones and E. Gordon (1972). 'Timing of Self-Disclosure and its Effects on Personal Attraction'. *Journal of Personality and Social Psychology*, 24, pages 358–65.

6 K. D. Williams, M. J. Bourgeois and R. T. Croyle (1993). 'The Effects of Stealing Thunder in Criminal and Civil Trials'. *Law and Human Behavior*, 17, pages 597–609.

7 T. Gilovich, V. H. Medvec and K. Savitsky (2000). 'The Spotlight Effect in Social Judgment: An Egocentric Bias in Estimates of the Salience of One's Own Actions and Appearance'. *Journal of Personality and Social Psychology*, 78, pages 211–22.

NOTES

8 P. Raghubi: and A. Valenzuela (2006). 'Centre-of-Inattention:
   Position Biases in Decision-Making'. *Organisational Behaviour
   and Human Decision Processes*, 99, pages 66–80.

9 A. Alter and D. M. Oppenheimer (2006). 'Predicting Short-Term
   Stock Fluctuations by Using Processing Fluency'. *Proceedings of
   the National Academy of Sciences, USA*, 103, pages 9369–72.

10 D. M. Oppenheimer (2005). 'Consequences of Erudite
   Vernacular Utilized Irrespective of Necessity: Problems With
   Using Long Words Needlessly'. *Journal of Applied Cognitive
   Psychology*, 20, pages 139–56.

11 For a review of the research examining the impact of likeability
   on politics, relationships, health and the workplace, see
   T. Sanders (2005). *The Likeability Factor*, New York: Crown
   Publishers.

12 J. Jecker and D. Landy (1969). 'Liking a Person as Function of
   Doing Him a Favor'. *Human Relations*, 22, pages 371–78.

13 E. Aronson, B. Willerman and J. Floyd (1966). 'The Effect of a
   Pratfall on Increasing Interpersonal Attractiveness'. *Psychonomic
   Science*, 4, pages 227–8.

14 This study was conducted as part of the BBC series *The People
   Watchers*.

15 J. J. Skowronski, D. E. Carlston, L. Mae and M. T. Crawford
   (1998). 'Spontaneous Trait Transference: Communicators Take
   on the Qualities they Describe in Others'. *Journal of Personality
   and Social Psychology*, 74, pages 837–48.

16 D. A. Small, G. Loewenstein and P. Slovic (2007). 'Sympathy
   and Callousness: The Impact of Deliberative Thought on
   Donations to Identifiable and Statistical Victims'. *Organisational
   Behaviour and Human Decision Processes*, 102, pages 143–53.

17 D. J. Howard (1990). 'The Influence of Verbal Responses to
   Common Greetings on Compliance Behavior: The Foot-in-the-
   Mouth Effect'. *Journal of Applied Social Psychology*, 20, pages
   1185–96.

18 See, for example, G. H. S. Razran (1940). 'Conditional Response

Changes in Rating and Appraising Sociopolitical Slogans'.
Psychological Bulletin, 37, page 481.

19 G. V. Bodenhausen (1993). 'Emotions, Arousal, and Stereotypic
Judgments: A Heuristic Model of Affect and Stereotyping', in
D. M. Mackie and D. L. Hamilton (eds), *Affect, Cognition, and
Stereotyping*, pages 13–37. San Diego, CA: Academic Press.

20 P. Y. Martin, J. Laing, R. Martin and M. Mitchell (2005).
'Caffeine, Cognition, and Persuasion: Evidence for Caffeine
Increasing the Systematic Processing of Persuasive Messages'.
Journal of Applied Social Psychology, 35, pages 160–182.

21 M. S. McGlone and J. Tofighbakhsh (2000). 'Birds of a Feather
Flock Conjointly: Rhyme as Reason in Aphorisms'.
Psychological Science, 11, pages 424–8.

22 Described in R. Garner (2005). 'Post-It Note Persuasion:
A Sticky Influence'. *Journal of Consumer Psychology*, 15,
pages 230–7.

23 G. V. Caprara, M. Vecchione, C. Barbaranelli and R. C. Fraley
(2007). 'When Likeness Goes With Liking: The Case of Political
Preference'. *Political Psychology*, 28, pages 609–32.

24 K. O'Quin and J. Aronoff (1981). 'Humor As a Technique of
Social Influence'. *Social Psychology Quarterly*, 44, pages
349–57.

25 A thorough discussion of the exact circumstances surrounding
the attack, and the unreliability of many media and textbook
descriptions of the incident, can be found at
www.kewgardenshistory.com/kitty_genovese-001.html.

26 For a review of this work, see B. Latané and S. Nida (1981).
'Ten Years of Research on Group Size and Helping'.
Psychological Bulletin, 89 (2), pages 308–24.

27 B. Latané and J. M. Darley (1968). 'Group Inhibition of
Bystander Intervention in Emergencies'. *Journal of Personality
and Social Psychology*, 10, pages 215–21.

28 B. Latané and J. M. Dabbs (1975). 'Sex, Group Size and Helping
in Three Cities'. *Sociometry*, 38, pages 180–94.

29 R. Manning, M. Levine and A. Collins (2007). 'The Kitty
    Genovese Murder and the Social Psychology of Helping: the
    Parable of the 38 Witnesses'. *American Psychologist*, 62 (6),
    pages 555–62.

30 N. J. Goldstein, S. J. Martin and R. B. Cialdini (2007). *Yes! 50
    Secrets From the Science of Persuasion.* London: Profile Books.

31 R. B. Cialdini and D. A. Schroeder (1976). 'Increasing
    Compliance by Legitimizing Paltry Contributions: When Even a
    Penny Helps'. *Journal of Personality and Social Psychology*, 34,
    pages 599–604.

32 P. R. Kunz and M. Woolcott (1976). 'Season's Greetings: From
    My Status to Yours'. *Social Science Research*, 5, pages 269–78.

33 D. T. Regan (1971). 'Effects of a Favor and Liking on
    Compliance'. *Journal of Experimental Social Psychology*, 7,
    pages 627–39.

34 D. B. Strohmetz, B. Rind, R. Fisher and M. Lynn (2002).
    'Sweetening the Till: The Use of Candy to Increase Restaurant
    Tipping'. *Journal of Applied Social Psychology*, 32, pages 300–9.

35 M. E. Schneider, B. Major, R. Luhtanen and J. Crocker (1996).
    'When Help Hurts: Social Stigma and the Costs of Assumptive
    Help'. *Personality and Social Psychology Bulletin*, 22, pages
    201–9.

36 R. Goei, A. J. Roberto, G. Meyer and K. E. Carlyle (2007). 'The
    Effects of Favor and Apology on Compliance'. *Communication
    Research*, 34, pages 575–95.

37 M. W. Morris, J. Podolny and S. Ariel (2001). 'Culture, Norms,
    and Obligations: Cross-National Differences in Patterns of
    Interpersonal Norms and Felt Obligations Toward Co-Workers'
    in W. Wosinska, R. B. Cialdini, D. W. Barrett and J. Reykowski
    (eds), *The Practice of Social Influence in Multiple Cultures*,
    Mahwah, New Jersey: Lawrence Erlbaum Associates, pages
    97–123.

38 F. J. Flynn (2003). 'What Have You Done For Me Lately?

Temporal Changes in Subjective Favor Evaluations'.
Organizational Behavior and Human Decision Processes, 91 (1),
pages 38–50.

39 H. A. Hornstein, E. Fisch and M. Holmes (1968). 'Influence of a
Model's Feeling About His Behavior and His Relevance As a
Comparison on Other Observers' Helping Behavior'. *Journal of
Personality and Social Psychology,* 10, 3, pages 222–6.

40 M. L. Kringelbach, A. Lehtonen, S. Squire, A. G. Harvey, M. G.
Craske *et al.* (2008). 'A Specific and Rapid Neural Signature for
Parental Instinct'. PLoS ONE, 3(2): e1664
doi:10.1371/journal.pone.0001664.

MOTIVATION

1 L. B. Pham and S. E. Taylor (1999). 'From Thought to Action:
Effects of Process- Versus Outcome-Based Mental Simulations on
Performance'. *Personality and Social Psychology Bulletin,* 25,
pages 250–60.

2 G. Oettingen and T. A. Wadden (1991). 'Expectation, Fantasy,
and Weight Loss: Is the Impact of Positive Thinking Always
Positive?'. *Cognitive Therapy and Research,* 15, pages 167–75.

3 G. Oettingen and D. Mayer, D. (2002). 'The Motivating
Function of Thinking About the Future: Expectations Versus
Fantasies'. *Journal of Personality and Social Psychology,* 83,
pages 1198–212.

4 M. Deutsch and H. B. Gerard (1955). 'A Study of Normative
and Information Social Influences Upon Individual Judgement'.
Journal of Abnormal and Social Psychology, 51, pages 629–36.

5 S. C. Hayes, I. Rosenfarb, E. Wolfert, E. Munt, Z. Korn and
R. D. Zettle (1985). 'Self-Reinforcement Effects: An Artifact of
Social Setting?' *Journal of Applied Behavior Analysis,* 18 (3),
pages 201–14.

6 S. Schnall, K. D. Harber, J. K. Stefanucci and D. R. Proffitt
   (2008). 'Social Support and the Perception of Geographical
   Slant'. *Journal of Experimental Social Psychology*, in press.

7 B. V. Zeigarnik (1927). 'Über das Behalten von erledigten und
   unerledigten Handlungen' ('The Retention of Completed and
   Uncompleted Activities'). *Psychologische Forschung*, 9, pages
   1–85.

8 B. A. Fritzsche, B. R. Young and K. C. Hickson (2003).
   'Individual Differences in Academic Procrastination Tendency
   and Writing Success'. *Personality and Individuality Differences*,
   35 (7), pages 1549–57.

9 A. V. Zeigarnik (2007). 'Bluma Zeigarnik: A Memoir'. *Gestalt
   Theory*, 29 (3), pages 256–68.

10 G. Oettingen, H. Pak and K. Schnetter (2001). 'Self-Regulation
   of Goal Setting: Turning Free Fantasies About the Future into
   Binding Goals'. *Journal of Personality and Social Psychology*,
   80, pages 736–53.

11 G. Oettingen (2000). 'Expectancy Effects on Behavior Depend
   on Self-Regulatory Thought'. *Social Cognition*, 18, pages
   101–29.

12 G. Oettingen and P. M. Gollwitzer (2002). 'Self-Regulation of
   Goal Pursuit: Turning Hope Thoughts into Behavior'.
   Psychological Inquiry, 13, pages 304–7.

13 B. Wansink, J. E. Painter and J. North (2005). 'Bottomless
   Bowls: Why Visual Cues of Portion Size May Influence Intake'.
   Obesity Research, 13 (1), pages 93–100.

14 See, for example, R. B. Stuart (1967). 'Behavioral Control of
   Overeating'. *Behavior Research and Therapy*, 5, pages 357–65.

15 C. K. Martin, S. D. Anton, H. Walden, C. Arnett, F. L.
   Greenway and D. A. Williamson (2007). 'Slower Eating Rate
   Reduces the Food Intake of Men, but Not Women: Implications
   for Behavioural Weight Control'. *Behaviour Research and
   Therapy*, 45, pages 2349–59.

16 B. Wansink and K. van Ittersum (2005). 'Shape of Glass and Amount of Alcohol Poured: Comparative Study of the Effect of Practice and Concentration'. *British Medical Journal*, 331, pages 1512–14.

17 J. E. Painter, B. Wansink and J. B. Hieggelke (2002). 'How Visibility and Convenience Influence Candy Consumption'. *Appetite*, 38 (3) pages 237–8.

   B. Wansink, J. E. Painter and Y. K. Lee (2006). 'The Office Candy Dish: Proximity's Influence on Estimated and Actual Candy Consumption'. *International Journal of Obesity*, 30 (5), pages 871–5.

18 P. Chandon and B. Wansink (2002). 'When are Stockpiled Products Consumed Faster? A Convenience-Salience Framework of Post-purchase Consumption Incidence and Quantity'. *Journal of Marketing Research*, 39 (3), pages 321–35.

19 B. Wansink and S. Park (2001). 'At the Movies: How External Cues and Perceived Taste Impact Consumption Volume'. *Food Quality and Preference*, 12 (1), pages 69–74.

20 F. Bellisle and A. M. Dalix (2001). 'Cognitive Restraint Can Be Offset by Distraction, Leading to Increased Meal Intake in Women'. *American Journal of Clinical Nutrition*, 74, pages 197–200.

21 B. Wansink, K. van Ittersum and J. E. Painter (2006). 'Ice Cream Illusions: Bowl Size, Spoon Size, and Self-Served Portion Sizes'. *American Journal of Preventive Medicine*, 31 (3), pages 240–3.

22 A. B. Geier, P. Rozin and G. Doros (2006). 'Unit Bias. A New Heuristic that Helps Explain the Effect of Portion Size on Food Intake'. *Psychological Science*, 17, pages 521–5.

23 J. F. Hollis, C. M. Gullion, V. J. Stevens *et al.* (2008). 'Weight Loss During the Intensive Intervention Phase of the Weight-Loss Maintenance Trial'. *American Journal of Preventative Medicine*, 35, pages 118–26.

24 C. Abraham and P. Sheeran (2004). 'Deciding to Exercise: The

Role of Anticipated Regret'. *British Journal of Health Psychology*, 9, pages 269–78.

25 K. A. Martin Ginis, S. M. Burke and L. Gauvin (2007). 'Exercising With Others Exacerbates the Negative Effects of Mirrored Environments on Sedentary Women's Feeling States'. *Psychology and Health*, 22, pages 945–62.

26 S. M. Sentyrz and B. J. Bushman (1998). 'Mirror, Mirror on the Wall, Who's the Thinnest One of All? Effects of Self-Awareness on Consumption of Fatty, Reduced-Fat, and Fat-Free Products'. *Journal of Applied Psychology*, 83, pages 944–9.

27 R. Coelho do Vale, R. Pieters and M. Zeelenberg (2008). 'Flying Under the Radar: Perverse Package Size Effects on Consumption Self-Regulation'. *Journal of Consumer Research*, 35, 3, pages 380–90.

28 E. Jonas, J. Schimel and J. Greenberg (2002). 'The Scrooge Effect: Evidence that Mortality Salience Increases Prosocial Attitudes and Behavior'. *Personality and Social Psychology Bulletin*, 28, pages 1342–53.

29 C. Peterson (2006). *A Primer in Positive Psychology*, Oxford: Oxford University Press.

CREATIVITY

1 A. F. Osborn (1957). *Applied Imagination*, New York: Scribner.

2 B. Mullen, C. Johnson and E. Salas (1991). 'Productivity Loss in Brainstorming Groups: A Meta-Analytic Integration'. *Basic and Applied Social Psychology*, 12, pages 3–23.

3 M. Ringelmann (1913). 'Recherches sur les moteurs animés: Travail de l'homme'. *Annales de l'Institut National Argonomique*, 12, pages 1–40.

4 S. J. Karau and K. D. Williams (1993). 'Social Loafing: A Meta-Analytic Review and Theoretical Integration'. *Journal of Personality and Social Psychology*, 65, pages 681–706.

5 S. M. Smith (2002). 'Getting Into and Out of Mental Ruts: A Theory of Fixation, Incubation and Insight' in R. J. Sternberg and J. E. Davidson (eds), *The Nature of Insight*, Cambridge, Massachusetts: MIT Press, pages 229–51.

6 A. Dijksterhuis and T. Meurs (2006). 'Where Creativity Resides: The Generative Power of Unconscious Thought'. *Consciousness and Cognition*, 15, pages 135–46.

7 R. S. Ulrich (1984). 'View Through a Window May Influence Recovery From Surgery'. *Science*, 224, pages 420–1.

8 E. O. Moore (1982). 'A Prison Environment's Effect on Health Care Service Demands'. *Journal of Environmental Systems*, 11 (1), pages 17–34.

9 F. E. Kuo and W. C. Sullivan (2001). 'Environment and Crime in the Inner City: Does Vegetation Reduce Crime?' *Environment and Behavior*, 33, pages 343–65.

10 A. F. Taylor, A.Wiley, F. E. Kuo and W. C. Sullivan (1998). 'Growing Up in the Inner City: Green Spaces As Places to Grow'. *Environment and Behavior*, 30, pages 3–27.

11 A. J. Elliot, M. A. Maier, A. C. Moller, R. Friedman and J. Meinhardt (2007). 'Color and Psychological Functioning: The Effect of Red on Performance in Achievement Contexts'. *Journal of Experimental Psychology: General*, 136, pages 154–68.

12 P. Kahnjr, B. Friedman, B. Gill, J. Hagman, R. Severson, N. Freier, E. Feldman, S. Carrere and A. Stolyar (2008). 'A Plasma Display Window: The Shifting Baseline Problem in a Technologically Mediated Natural World'. *Journal of Environmental Psychology*, 28, pages 192–9.

13 C. J. Nemeth and M. Ormiston (2007). 'Creative Idea Generation: Harmony Versus Stimulation'. *European Journal of Social Psychology*, 37 (3), pages 524–35.

14 H. K. Choi and L. Thompson (2005). 'Old Wine in a New Bottle: Impact of Membership Change on Group Creativity'. *Organisational Behaviour and Human Decision Processes*, 98, pages 121–32.

15 A. Dijksterhuis and A. van Knippenberg (1998). 'The Relation Between Perception and Behavior, or How to Win a Game of Trivial Pursuit'. *Journal of Personality and Social Psychology*, 74 (4), pages 865–77.

16 K. D. Vohs, N. L. Mead and M. R. Goode (2006). 'The Psychological Consequences of Money'. *Science*, 314, pages 1154–6.

17 Cited in B. Carey (2007). 'Who's Minding the Mind?' *New York Times*, 31 July.

18 R. W. Holland, M. Hendriks and H. Aarts (2006). 'Smells Like Clean Spirit: Nonconscious Effects of Scent on Cognition and Behavior'. *Psychological Science*, 16 (9), 689–93.

19 A. C. Kay, S. C. Wheeler, J. A. Bargh and L. Ross (2004). 'Material Priming: The Influence of Mundane Physical Objects on Situational Construal and Competitive Behavioral Choice'. *Organizational Behavior and Human Decision Processes*, 95, pages 83–96.

20 J. Förster, R. Friedman, E. M. Butterbach and K. Sassenberg (2005). 'Automatic Effects of Deviancy Cues on Creative Cognition'. *European Journal of Social Psychology*, 35, pages 345–59.

21 A. Dijksterhuis, R. Spears, T. Postmes, D. A. Stapel, W. Koomen, A. van Knippenberg and D. Scheepers (1998). 'Seeing One Thing and Doing Another: Contrast Effects in Automatic Behavior'. *Journal of Personality and Social Psychology*, 75, pages 862–71.

22 R. Friedman and J. Förster (2002). 'The Influence of Approach and Avoidance Motor Actions on Creative Cognition'. *Journal of Experimental Social Psychology*, 38, pages 41–55.

23 R. Friedman and A. J. Elliot (2008). 'The Effect of Arm Crossing on Persistence and Performance'. *European Journal of Social Psychology*, 38, pages 449–61.

24 D. M. Lipnicki and D. G. Byrne (2005). 'Thinking on Your Back: Solving Anagrams Faster When Supine Than When Standing'. *Cognitive Brain Research*, 24, pages 719–22.

ATTRACTION

1 S. Worchel, J. Lee and A. Adewole (1975). 'Effects of Supply and Demand on Ratings of Object Value'. *Journal of Personality and Social Psychology*, 32, pages 906–14.

2 E. Hatfield, G. W. Walster, J. Piliavin and L. Schmidt (1973). 'Playing Hard to Get: Understanding an Elusive Phenomenon', *Journal of Personality and Social Psychology*, 26, pages 113–21.

3 N. Guéguen (2007). 'Woman's Bust Size and Men's Courtship Solicitation'. *Body Image*, 4, pages 386–90.

4 N. Guéguen (2007). 'Bust Size and Hitchhiking: A Field Study'. *Perceptual and Motor Skills*, 105, pages 1294–8.

5 N. Guéguen (2007). 'The Effect of a Man's Touch on Woman's Compliance to a Request in a Courtship Context'. *Social Influence*, 2, pages 81–97.

6 Ibid.

7 B. Major and R. Heslin (1982). 'Perceptions of Cross-Sex and Same-Sex Nonreciprocal Touch: It Is Better to Give Than Receive'. *Journal of Nonverbal Behavior*, 6, pages 148–62.

   D. L. Summerhayes and R. W. Suchner (1978). 'Power Implications of Touch in Male–Female Relationships'. *Sex Roles*, 4, pages 103–10.

8 Based upon work described in C. Hendrick and S. S. Hendrick (1986). 'A Theory and Method of Love'. *Journal of Personality and Social Psychology*, 30, pages 392–402.

9 R. van Baaren, R. Holland, B. Steenaert and A. van Knippenberg (2003). 'Mimicry for Money: Behavioral Consequences of Imitation'. *Journal of Experimental Social Psychology*, 39, pages 393–98.

10 Reported in A. Dijksterhuis, P. K. Smith, R. B. van Baaren and D. H. Wigboldus (2005). 'The Unconscious Consumer: Effects of Environment on Consumer Behavior'. *Journal of Consumer Psychology*, 15, pages 193–202.

11 P. W. Eastwick, E. J. Finkel, D. Mochon and D. Ariely (2007). 'Selective Versus Unselective Romantic Desire: Not All Reciprocity Is Created Equal'. *Psychological Science*, 18, pages 317–19.

12 S. Chu, R. Hardaker and J. E. Lycett (2007). 'Too Good to Be "True"? The Handicap of High Socio-Economic Status in Attractive Males'. *Personality and Individual Differences*, 42, pages 1291–1300.

13 S. Kelly and R. Dunbar (2001). 'Who Dares Wins: Heroism Versus Altruism in Female Mate Choice'. *Human Nature*, 12, pages 89–105.

14 D. G. Dutton and A. P. Aron (1974). 'Some Evidence for Heightened Sexual Attraction Under Conditions of High Anxiety'. *Journal of Personality and Social Psychology*, 30, pages 510–17.

15 C. M. Meston and P. F. Frohlich (2003). 'Love at First Fright: Partner Salience Moderates Roller-Coaster-Induced Excitation Transfer'. *Archives of Sexual Behavior*, 32, pages 537–44.

16 B. Cohen, G. Waugh and K. Place (1989). 'At the Movies: An Unobtrusive Study of Arousal-Attraction'. *Journal of Social Psychology*, 129, pages 691–3.

17 A. Aron, E. Melinat, E. N. Aron, R. Vallone and R. Bator (1997). 'The Experimental Generation of Interpersonal Closeness: A Procedure and Some Preliminary Findings'. *Personality and Social Psychology Bulletin*, 23, pages 363–77.

18 B. C. Jones, L. M. DeBruine, A. C. Little, R. P. Burriss and D. R. Feinburg (2007). 'Social Transmission of Face Preferences Among Humans'. *Proceedings of the Royal Society of London B*, 274 (1611), pages 899–903.

19 V. Swami and M. J. Tovee (2005). 'Does Hunger Influence Judgments of Female Physical Attractiveness'. *British Journal of Psychology,* 97 (3), pages 353–63.

20 E. Aronson (1999). *The Social Animal* (8th edn.), New York: Worth Publishers.

E. Aronson and D. Linder (1965). 'Gain and Loss of Esteem as Determinants of Interpersonal Attractiveness'. *Journal of Experimental Social Psychology*, 1, pages 156–71.

21 J. K. Bosson, A. B. Johnson, K. Niederhoffer and W. B. Swann Jr (2006). 'Interpersonal Chemistry Through Negativity: Bonding by Sharing Negative Attitudes About Others'. *Personal Relationships*, 13, pages 135–50.

22 E. Krumhuber, A. S. R. Manstead and A. Kappas (2007). 'Temporal Aspects of Facial Displays in Person and Expression Perception. The Effects of Smile Dynamics, Head-Tilt and Gender'. *Journal of Nonverbal Behavior*, 31, pages 39–56.

23 G. C. Gonzaga, R. A. Turner, D. Keltner, B. C. Campos and M. Altemus (2006). 'Romantic Love and Sexual Desire in Close Bonds'. *Emotion*, 6, pages 163–79.

24 D. T. Kenrick, J. M. Sundie, L. D. Nicastle and G. O. Stone (2001). 'Can One Ever Be Too Wealthy or Too Chaste? Searching for Nonlinearities in Mate Judgment'. *Journal of Personality and Social Psychology*, 80, pages 462–71.

STRESS

1 B. J. Bushman (2002). 'Does Venting Anger Feed or Extinguish the Flame? Catharsis, Rumination, Distraction, Anger, and Aggressive Responding'. *Personality and Social Psychology Bulletin*, 28, pages 724–31.

2 H. Tennen and G. Affleck (2001). 'Benefit-Finding and Benefit-Reminding' in C. R. Snyder and S. J. Lopez (eds), *Handbook of Positive Psychology*, Oxford: Oxford University Press, pages 584–97.

3 M. E. McCullough, L. M. Root and A. D. Cohen (2006). 'Writing About the Benefits of an Interpersonal Transgression Facilitates Forgiveness'. *Journal of Consulting and Clinical Psychology*, 74, pages 887–97.

4 C. Peterson and M. E. P. Seligman (2003). 'Character Strengths Before and After September 11'. *Psychological Science*, 14, pages 381–4.

5 C. Peterson, N. Park, and M. E. P. Seligman (2006). 'Greater Strengths of Character and Recovery from Illness'. *Journal of Positive Psychology*, 1, pages 17–26.

6 N. Krause (2003). 'Praying for Others, Financial Strain, and Physical Health Status in Late Life'. *Journal for the Scientific Study of Religion*, 42, pages 377–91.

7 S. Chafin, M. Roy, W. Gerin and N. Christenfeld (2004). 'Music Can Facilitate Blood Pressure Recovery from Stress'. *British Journal of Health Psychology*, 9, pages 393–403.

8 M. C. Keller, B. L. Fredrickson, O. Ybarra, S. Cote, K. Johnson, J. Mikels, A. Conway and T. Wager (2005). 'A Warm Heart and a Clear Head. The Contingent Effects of Weather on Mood and Cognition'. *Psychological Science*, 16, pages 724–31.

9 H. M. Lefcourt (2005). 'Humor' in C. R. Snyder and S. J. Lopez (eds), *Handbook of Positive Psychology*, Oxford: Oxford University Press, pages 619–31.

10 E. Friedmann and S. A. Thomas (1995). 'Pet Ownership, Social Support, and One-Year Survival After Acute Myocardial Infarction in the Cardiac Arrhythmia Suppression Trial (CAST)'. *American Journal of Cardiology*, 76, pages 1213–17.

11 D. L. Wells (2007). 'Domestic Dogs and Human Health: An Overview'. *British Journal of Health Psychology*, 12, pages 145–56.

12 K. Allen, J. Blascovich and W. B. Mendes (2002). 'Cardiovascular Reactivity and the Presence of Pets, Friends, and Spouses: The Truth About Cats and Dogs'. *Psychosomatic Medicine*, 64 (5), pages 727–39.

13 See, for example, D. C. Turner, G. Rieger and I. Gygax (2003). 'Spouses and Cats and Their Effects on Human Mood'. *Anthrozoös*, 16, pages 213–28.

14 E. Friedmann and S. A. Thomas, op. cit.

15 K. Allen, B. Shykoff and J. Izzo (2001). 'Pet Ownership, but not ACE Inhibitor Therapy, Blunts Home Blood Pressure Responses to Mental Stress'. *Hypertension*, 38, pages 815–20.

16 See, for example, J. J. Lynch, S. A. Thomas, M. E. Mills *et al.* (1974). 'The Effects of Human Contact on Cardiac Arrhythmia in Coronary Care Patients'. *Journal of Nervous and Mental Disease*, 158, pages 88–98.

17 D. L. Wells (2004). 'The Facilitation of Social Interactions by Domestic Dogs'. *Anthrozöös*, 17 (4), pages 340–352.

18 S. J. Hunt, L. A. Hart and R. Gomulkiewicz (1992). 'Role of Small Animals in Social Interactions Between Strangers'. *Journal of Social Psychology*, 132, pages 245–56.

19 M. R. Banks, L. M. Willoughby and W. A. Banks (2008). 'Animal-Assisted Therapy and Loneliness in Nursing Homes: Use of Robotic Versus Living Dogs'. *Journal of the American Medical Directors Association*, 9, pages 173–7.

20 D. Wells (2005). 'The Effect of Videotapes of Animals on Cardiovascular Responses to Stress'. *Stress and Health*, 21, pages 209–13.

21 Cited in A. J. Crum and E. J. Langer (2007). 'Mind-Set Matters. Exercise and the Placebo Effect'. *Psychological Science*, 18, pages 165–71.

22 Ibid.

RELATIONSHIPS

1 J. M. Gottman, J. A. Coan, S. Carrere and C. Swanson (1998). 'Predicting Marital Happiness and Stability from Newlywed Interactions'. *Journal of Marriage and the Family*, 60, pages 5–22.

2 See, for example, K. Hahlweg, L. Schindler, D. Revensdorf and J. C. Brengelmann (1984). 'The Munich Marital Therapy Study'

in K. Hahlweg and N. S. Jacobson (eds), *Marital Interaction: Analysis and Modification*, New York: The Guilford Press.

N. S. Jacobson, K. B. Schmaling and A. Holtzworth-Monroe (1987). 'Component Analysis of Behavioral Marital Therapy: 2-Year Follow-up and Prediction of Relapse'. *Journal of Marital and Family Therapy,* 13, pages 187–195.

3 J. Kellerman, J. Lewis and J. D. Laird (1989). 'Looking and Loving: The Effects of Mutual Gaze on Feelings of Romantic Love'. *Journal of Research in Personality*, 23, pages 145–61.

4 A. Aron, C. C. Norman, E. N. Aron, C. McKenna and R. Heyman (2000). 'Couples' Shared Participation in Novel and Arousing Activities and Experienced Relationship Quality'. *Journal of Personality and Social Psychology*, 78, pages 273–83.

5 R. F. Baumeister, E. Bratslavsky, C. Finkenauer and K. D. Vohs (2001). 'Bad Is Stronger Than Good'. *Review of General Psychology*, 5, pages 323–70.

6 J. Gottman (1984). *Why Marriages Succeed or Fail*, New York: Simon and Schuster.

7 R. B. Slatcher and J. W. Pennebaker (2006). 'How Do I Love Thee? Let Me Count the Words. The Social Effects of Expressive Writing'. *Psychological Science*, 17, pages 660–4.

8 B. P. Buunk, F. L. Oldersma and C. K. W. de Dreu (2001). 'Enhancing Satisfaction Through Downward Comparison: The Role of Relational Discontent and Individual Differences in Social Comparison Orientation'. *Journal of Experimental Social Psychology*, 37, pages 452–67.

9 S. L. Murray and J. G. Holmes (1999). 'The (Mental) Ties that Bind: Cognitive Structures that Predict Relationship Resilience'. *Journal of Personality and Social Psychology*, 77, pages 1228–44.

10 S. D. Gosling, S. J. Ko, T. Mannarelli and M. E. Morris (2002). 'A Room with a Cue: Judgments of Personality Based on Offices and Bedrooms'. *Journal of Personality and Social Psychology*, 82, pages 379–98.

11 A. Lohmann, B. Ximena, X. B. Arriga and W. Goodfriend (2003). 'Close Relationships and Placemaking. Do Objects in a Couple's Home Reflect Couplehood?' *Personal Relationships*, 10, pages 437–49.

12 J. K. Maner, D. A. Rouby and G. Gonzaga (2008). 'Automatic Inattention to Attractive Alternatives: The Evolved Pscychology of Relationship Maintenance'. *Evolution and Human Behavior*, 29, pages 343–349.

DECISION MAKING

1 J. A. F. Stoner (1961). 'A Comparison of Individual and Group Decisions Involving Risk'. Unpublished master's thesis, Massachusetts Institute of Technology.

2 D. G. Myers and G. D. Bishop (1971). 'Enhancement of Dominant Attitudes in Group Discussion'. *Journal of Personality and Social Psychology*, 20, pages 386–91.

3 G. Whyte (1993). 'Escalating Commitment in Individual and Group Decision-Making: A Prospect Theory Approach'. *Organizational Behavior and Human Decision Processes*, 54, pages 430–55.

4 Much of the work discussed in this paragraph is outlined in I. Janis (1982). *Groupthink*, 2nd edn, Boston: Houghton-Mifflin.

5 S. J. Solnick and D. Hemenway (1998). 'Is More Always Better? A Survey on Positional Concerns'. *Journal of Economic Behavior and Organization*, 37, pages 373–83.

6 J. M. Burger (1986). 'Increasing Compliance by Improving the Deal: The That's Not All Technique'. *Journal of Personality and Social Psychology*, 51, pages 277–83.

7 M. Santos, C. Leve and A. Pratkanis (1994). 'Hey, Buddy, Can You Spare Seventeen Cents? Mindful Persuasion and the Pique Technique'. *Journal of Applied Social Psychology*, 29, pages 755–64.

8 B. P. Davis and E. S. Knowles (1999). 'A Disrupt-Then-Reframe Technique of Social Influence'. *Journal of Personality and Social Psychology*, 76 (2), pages 192–9.

9 J. Freedman and S. Fraser (1966). 'Compliance Without Pressure: The Foot-in-the-Door Technique'. *Journal of Personality and Social Psychology*, 4, pages 195–202.

10 A. L. Beaman, C. M. Cole, B. Klentz and N. M. Steblay (1983). 'Fifteen Years of the Foot-in-the-Door Research: A Meta-Analysis'. *Personality and Social Psychology Bulletin*, 9, pages 181–96.

11 R. Cialdini, J. Vincent, S. Lewis, J. Catalan, D. Wheeler and B. Darby (1975). 'Reciprocal Concessions Procedure for Inducing Compliance: The Door-in-the-Face Technique'. *Journal of Personality and Social Psychology*, 31, pages 206–15.

12 A. Pascual and N. Guéguen (2006). 'Door-in-the-Face Technique and Behavioral Compliance: An Evaluation in a Field Setting'. *Psychological Reports*, 103, pages 974–8.

13 A. Dijksterhuis and Z. van Olden (2006). 'On the Benefits of Thinking Unconsciously: Unconscious Thought Increases Post-Choice Satisfaction'. *Journal of Experimental Social Psychology*, 42, pages 627–31.

14 See, for example, T. Betsch, H. Plessner, C. Schwieren and R. Gütig (2001). 'I Like it but I Don't Know Why: A Value-Account Approach to Implicit Attitude Formation'. *Personality and Social Psychology Bulletin*, 27, pages 242–53 and A. Dijksterhuis, M. W. Bos, L. F. Nordgren and R. B. van Baaren (2006). 'On Making the Right Choice: The Deliberation-Without-Attention Effect'. *Science*, 311, pages 1005–7.

15 See, for example, T. Gilovich and V. H. Medvec (1995). 'The Experience of Regret: What, When, and Why'. *Psychological Review*, 102, pages 379–95 and T. Gilovich and V. H. Medvec (1994). 'The Temporal Pattern to the Experience of Regret'. *Journal of Personality and Social Psychology*, 67, pages 357–65.

16 Based on work described in B. Schwartz, A. Ward,

J. Monterosso, S. Lyubomirsky, K. White and D. R. Lehman (2002). 'Maximizing Versus Satisficing: Happiness is a Matter of Choice'. *Personality and Social Psychology*, 83 (5), pages 1178–97.

17 S. S. Iyengar, R. E. Wells and B. Schwartz (2006). 'Doing Better but Feeling Worse. Looking for the Best Job Undermines Satisfaction'. *Psychological Science*, 17, pages 143–9.

18 C. Peterson (2006). *A Primer In Positive Psychology*, Oxford: Oxford University Press, page 191.

19 Sources: R. Highfield (25 March 1994). 'How Age Affects the Way We Lie'. *Daily Telegraph*, 26; A. Vrij (2000). *Detecting Lies and Deceit*, Chichester: John Wiley and Sons; survey conducted by the Royal and Sun Alliance Insurance Company (2007).

20 R. H. Gramzow, G. Willard and W. B. Mendes (2008). 'Big Tales and Cool Heads: Academic Exaggeration Is Related to Cardiac Vagal Reactivity'. *Emotion*, 8, pages 138–44.

21 L. A. Stromwall, P. A. Granhag and S. Landstrom (2007). 'Children's Prepared and Unprepared Lies: Can Adults See Through Their Strategies?'. *Applied Cognitive Psychology*, 21, pages 457–71.

22 Cited in B. M. DePaulo and W. L. Morris (2004). 'Discerning Lies from Truths: Behavioural Cues to Deception and the Indirect Pathway of Intuition' in P. A. Granhag and L. A. Stromwall (eds), *The Detection of Deception in Forensic Contexts*, Cambridge: Cambridge University Press, pages 15–40.

23 P. Ekman and M. O'Sullivan (1991). 'Who Can Catch a Liar?'. *American Psychologist*, 46 (9), pages 913–20.

24 A. Vrij (2004). 'Why Professionals Fail to Catch Liars and How They Can Improve'. *Legal and Criminological Psychology*, 9, pages 159–83.

25 J. T. Hancock, J. Thom-Santelli and T. Ritchie (2004). 'Deception and Design: The Impact of Communication Technologies on Lying Behavior'. *Proceedings, Conference on Computer Human Interaction*, 6, pages 130–6.

26 R. Buehler, D. Griffin and M. Ross (2002). 'Inside the Planning
     Fallacy: The Causes and Consequences of Optimistic Time
     Predictions' in T. Gilovich, D. Griffin and D. Kahneman (eds),
     Heuristics and Biases: The Psychology of Intuitive Judgment.
     Cambridge: Cambridge University Press, pages 250–70.
27 R. Buehler, D. Messervey and D. Griffin (2005). 'Collaborative
     Planning and Prediction: Does Group Discussion Affect
     Optimistic Biases in Time Estimation'. *Organisational Behaviour
     and Human Decision Processes*, 97, pages 47–63.
28 J. Kruger and M. Evans (2004). 'If You Don't Want to Be Late,
     Enumerate: Unpacking Reduces the Planning Fallacy'. *Journal of
     Experimental Social Psychology*, 40, pages 586–98.

PARENTING

1 F. H. Rauscher, G. L. Shaw and K. N. Ky (1993). 'Music and
    Spatial Task Performance'. *Nature*, 365, page 611.
2 F. H. Rauscher, G. L. Shaw and K. N. Ky (1995). 'Listening to
    Mozart Enhances Spatial-Temporal Reasoning: Towards a
    Neurophysiological Basis'. *Neuroscience Letters*, 185, pages
    44–7.
3 A. Bangerter and C. Heath (2004). 'The Mozart Effect: Tracking
    the Evolution of a Scientific Legend'. *British Journal of Social
    Psychology*, 43, pages 605–23.
4 C. F. Chabris (1999). 'Prelude or Requiem for the "Mozart
    Effect"?' *Nature*, 400, page 827.
5 W. F. Thompson, E. G. Schellenberg and G. Husain (2001).
    'Arousal, Mood, and the Mozart Effect'. *Psychological Science*,
    12, pages 248–51.
6 K. M. Nantais and E. G. Schellenberg (1999). 'The Mozart
    Effect: An Artifact of Preference?' *Psychological Science*, 10,
    pages 370–3.

7 E. G. Schellenberg (2004). 'Music Lessons Enhance IQ'.
   Psychological Science, 15, pages 511–14.

8 B. W. Pelham, M. C. Mirenberg and J. K. Jones (2002). 'Why
   Susie Sells Seashells by the Seashore: Implicit Egotism and Major
   Life Decisions'. *Journal of Personality and Social Psychology*,
   82, pages 469–87.

9 L. Einav and L. Yariv (2006). 'What's in a Surname? The Effects
   of Surname Initials on Academic Success'. *Journal of Economic
   Perspectives*, 20 (1), pages 175–88.

10 H. Harari and J. W. McDavid (1973). 'Name Stereotypes and
   Teachers' Expectations'. *Journal of Educational Psychology*, 65,
   pages 222–5.

11 W. F. Murphy (1957). 'A Note on the Significance of Names.
   Psychoanalytical Quarterly, 26, pages 91–106.

12 N. Christenfeld, D. P. Phillips and L. M. Glynn (1999). 'What's
   in a Name: Mortality and the Power of Symbols'. *Journal of
   Psychosomatic Research*, 47 (3), pages 241–54.

13 L. D. Nelson and J. P. Simmons (2007). 'Moniker Maladies.
   When Names Sabotage Success'. *Psychological Science*, 18, pages
   1106–11.

14 C. M. Mueller and C. S. Dweck (1998). 'Praise for Intelligence
   Can Undermine Children's Motivation and Performance'.
   Journal of Personality and Social Psychology, 75, pages 33–52.

15 For a short summary of this work, see C. S. Dweck (1999).
   'Caution–Praise Can Be Dangerous'. *American Educator*, 23,
   pages 4–9.

16 A. Cimpian, H.-M. C. Arce, E. M. Markman and C. S. Dweck
   (2007). 'Subtle Linguistic Cues Affect Children's Motivation'.
   Psychological Science, 18, pages 314–16.

17 Y. Shoda, W. Mischel and P. K. Peake (1990). 'Predicting
   Adolescent Cognitive and Self-Regulatory Competencies from
   Preschool Delay of Gratification'. *Developmental Psychology*,
   26 (6), pages 978–86.

18 A. L. Duckworth and M. E. P. Seligman (2005). 'Self-Discipline Outdoes IQ in Predicting Academic Performance of Adolescents'. *Psychological Science*, 16, pages 939–44.

19 J. L. Freedman (1965). 'Long-Term Behavioral Effects of Cognitive Dissonance'. *Journal of Experimental Social Psychology*, 1, pages 145–55.

20 D. Filley (1999). 'Forbidden Fruit: When Prohibition Increases the Harm it Is Supposed to Reduce'. *Independent Review*, 3, pages 441–51.

21 See, for example, C. E. Cameron Ponitz, M. M. McClelland, C. M. Connor, A. M. Jewkes, C. L. Farris and F. J. Morrison (2008). 'Touch Your Toes! Developing a Direct Measure of Behavioral Regulation in Early Childhood'. *Early Childhood Research Quarterly*, 23, pages 141–58.

    M. M. McClelland, C. E. Cameron, C. M. Connor, C. L. Farris, A. M. Jewkes and F. J. Morrison (2007). 'Links Between Behavioral Regulation and Preschoolers' Literacy, Vocabulary, and Math Skills'. *Developmental Psychology*, 43, pages 947–59.

22 S. Tominey and M. M. McClelland (April 2008). '"And When They Woke Up, They Were Monkeys!" Using Classroom Games to Promote Preschoolers' Self-Regulation and School Readiness'. Poster presented at the biennial Conference on Human Development, Indianapolis, IN.

PERSONALITY

1 B. L. Beyerstein (2007). 'Graphology – A Total Write-Off' in S. D. Sala (ed.), *Tall Tales About the Mind and Brain: Separating Fact From Fiction*, Oxford: Oxford University Press, pages 233–270.

2 For a review of this approach to personality, see G. Matthews, I. J. Deary and M. C. Whiteman (2003). *Personality Traits*, 2nd edn. Cambridge: Cambridge University Press.

NOTES

3 L. R. Goldberg (1993). 'The Structure of Phenotypic Personality Traits'. *American Psychologist*, 48, pages 26–34.

4 For further information about this work, see http://ipip.ori.org/.

5 F. J. Sulloway (1996). *Born to Rebel: Birth Order, Family Dynamics, and Creative Lives*, New York: Pantheon.

   However, some of this work has been called into question. See, for example: T. Jefferson, J. H. Herbst and R. R. McCrae (1998). 'Associations between birth order and personality traits: Evidence from self-reports and observer ratings'. *Journal of Research in Personality*, 32, pages 498–509.

6 G. Casanova (1997). *History of My Life: Giacomo Casanova, Chevalier de Seingalt*, vol. 11, trans. Willard R. Trask. Baltimore, Maryland: The John Hopkins University Press.

7 For a fascinating summary of this work, see J. Manning (2008). *The Finger Book: Sex, Behaviour and Disease Revealed in the Fingers*, London: Faber and Faber.

8 See, for example, D. A. Putz, S. J. C. Gaulin, R. J. Sporter and D. H. McBurnley (2004). 'Sex Hormones and Finger Length: What Does 2D:4D Indicate?' *Evolution and Human Behavior*, 25, pages 182–99.

9 J. T. Manning and D. Sturt (2004). '2nd to 4th Digit Ratio and Strength in Men'. Unpublished study, cited in Manning's *The Finger Book,* op.cit.

10 J. T. Manning, P. Bundred and R. Taylor (2003). 'The Ratio of the 2nd to 4th Digit Length: A Prenatal Correlate of Ability at Sport'. *Kinanthropometry*, 8, pages 165–74.

11 J. T. Manning and R. P. Taylor (2001). '2nd to 4th Digit Ratio and Male Ability in Sport: Implications for Sexual Selection in Humans'. *Evolution and Human Behavior*, 22, pages 61–9.

12 Ibid.

13 B. Fink, J. T. Manning and N. Neave (2004). 'Second to Fourth Digit Ratio and the "Big Five" Personality Factors'. *Personality and Individual Differences*, 37, pages 495–503.

   E. J. Austin, J. T. Manning, K. McInroy and E. Mathews

(2002). 'A Preliminary Investigation of the Association Between Personality, Cognitive Ability and Digit Ratio'. *Personality and Individual Differences*, 33, pages 1115–24.

G. D. Wilson (1983). 'Finger-Length as an Index of Assertiveness in Women'. *Personality and Individual Differences*, 4, pages 111–12.

14 V. Sluming and J. Manning (2000). 'Second to Fourth Digit Ratio in Elite Musicians: Evidence for Musical Ability as an Honest Signal of Male Fitness'. *Evolution and Human Behaviour*, 21, pages 1–9.

15 W. J. Szlemko, J. A. Benfield, P. A. Bell, J. L. Deffenbacher and L. Troup (2008). 'Territorial Markings as a Predictor of Driver Aggression and Road Rage'. *Journal of Applied Social Psychology*, 38 (6), pages 1664–88.

16 Y. Ida (1987). 'The Manner of Hand Clasping and the Individual Differences in Hemispheric Asymmetries'. *Japanese Journal of Psychology*, 58, pages 318–21.

Y. Ida (1988). 'The Manner of Clasping the Hands and Individual Differences in Perceptual Asymmetries and Cognitive Modes'. *Psychologia*, 31, pages 128–35.

C. Mohr, G. Thut, T. Landis and P. Brugger (2003). 'Hands, Arms and Minds: Interactions between Posture and Thought'. *Journal of Clinical and Experimental Neuropsychology*, 25, pages 1000–1010.

17 J. F. Diaz-Morales (2007). 'Morning and Evening Types: Exploring Their Personality Styles'. *Personality and Individual Differences*, 43, pages 769–78.